THE THEORETICAL FRAMEWORK IN PHENOMENOLOGICAL RESEARCH

The Theoretical Framework in Phenomenological Research: Development and Application is an introduction to phenomenology in which the authors overview its origin, main ideas and core concepts. They show the application and relevancy of phenomenological tenets in practical qualitative research, as well as demonstrate how aligning theory and method enhances research credibility.

In this detailed but digestible explanation of phenomenological theories, the authors explore the ideas of the main founders pertaining to the meaning of perceived reality and the meaning of being, and how these founders articulated their methodologies. In doing so, *The Theoretical Framework in Phenomenological Research* fills the well-documented gap between theory and practice within phenomenology by providing a much-needed bridge between the foundational literature and applied research on the subject, focusing equally on theory and practice. The book includes practical demonstrations on how to create theoretical/conceptual frameworks in applied phenomenological research. It also features detailed, step-by-step illustrations and examples regarding how researchers can develop frameworks and use their concepts to inform the development of themes at the data analysis stage.

A reliable guide underpinned by foundational phenomenology literature, *The Theoretical Framework in Phenomenological Research* is an essential text for researchers, instructors, practitioners and students looking to design and conduct phenomenological studies in a manner that ensures credible outcomes.

Dr. Henrik Gert Larsen is Professor and phenomenology expert at Northcentral University (NCU). He is an alumnus from the University of Copenhagen and The Chicago School of Professional Psychology. Dr. Larsen's experience includes chairing dissertations, teaching qualitative methods and authoring several publications. He is a 2020 recipient of the NCU Teaching Excellence Award.

Dr. Philip Adu is a methodology expert at The Chicago School of Professional Psychology (TCSPP). He has spent over 8 years at TCSPP, providing methodology support to doctoral students. He has designed and taught numerous research method courses. He is the author of *A Step-by-Step Guide to Qualitative Data Coding* (2019).

THE THEORETICAL FRAMEWORK IN PHENOMENOLOGICAL RESEARCH

Development and Application

Henrik Gert Larsen and Philip Adu

Routledge
Taylor & Francis Group
LONDON AND NEW YORK

First published 2022
by Routledge
2 Park Square, Milton Park, Abingdon, Oxon OX14 4RN

and by Routledge
605 Third Avenue, New York, NY 10158

Routledge is an imprint of the Taylor & Francis Group, an informa business

British Library Cataloguing-in-Publication Data
A catalogue record for this book is available from the British Library

Library of Congress Cataloging-in-Publication Data
Names: Larsen, Henrik Gert, 1970– author. | Adu, Philip author.
Title: The theoretical framework in phenomenological research :
    development and application / Henrik Gert Larsen, Philip Adu.
Description: Abingdon, Oxon ; New York, NY : Routledge, 2021. |
    Includes bibliographical references.
Identifiers: LCCN 2021000660 (print) | LCCN 2021000661 (ebook) |
    ISBN 9780367540500 (hardback) | ISBN 9780367540524 (paperback) |
    ISBN 9781003084259 (ebook)
Subjects: LCSH: Phenomenology—Research—Methodology.
Classification: LCC B829.5 .L34 2021 (print) | LCC B829.5 (ebook) |
    DDC 142/.7—dc23
LC record available at https://lccn.loc.gov/2021000660
LC ebook record available at https://lccn.loc.gov/2021000661

ISBN: 978-0-367-54050-0 (hbk)
ISBN: 978-0-367-54052-4 (pbk)
ISBN: 978-1-003-08425-9 (ebk)

Typeset in Bembo
by Apex CoVantage, LLC

Vivat nostra societas, Vivant studiosi, Crescat una veritas . . .

I (Henrik Gert Larsen) dedicate this work to my grandmother, Vibe, and give special thanks to my family, near and far.

I (Philip Adu) dedicate this book to my lovely and supportive wife, Monique, and my wonderful children, Miriam, Olivia and Evan.

We also dedicate this book to all frontline health workers for their relentless effort and continuous commitment to help treat patients with COVID-19.

CONTENTS

FIGURES

EXHIBITS

TABLES

PREFACE

> Teaching is even more difficult than learning. We know that; but we rarely think about it. And why is teaching more difficult than learning? Not because the teacher must have a larger store of information and have it always ready. Teaching is more difficult than learning because what teaching calls for is: to learn. The teacher is ahead of his apprentices in this alone, that he has still far more to learn than they – he has to learn to let them learn. If the relation between the teacher and the taught is genuine, therefore, there is never a place in it for the authority of the know-it-all or the authoritative sway of the official.
>
> *(Heidegger, 1968, p. 15)*

We come to phenomenology from different paths. From the literature, we can see that some of us are philosophers, some are therapists, while others are researchers. Because there is no such thing as the perspective from nowhere, we interpret, understand and disseminate phenomenology by way of our professional roles. In other words, no one owns phenomenology, and each of us can find what we need within the dense body of phenomenological literature.

We, the authors of this book, are teachers. We teach doctoral students how to design and execute social research in a dissertation format. This is how we came to phenomenology. However, as the pile of phenomenological research proposals grew, it became clear that a clarification of terms, methods and theories was needed, not only for the sake of the credibility of our students' research projects, but also for the sake of the effectiveness of our instructions. The problem, quite frankly, presented itself in terms of what actually was the subject matter under investigation, how to justify the methods and consequently the credibility of applied phenomenological research outcomes.

This in turn led us to consider how applied phenomenological research has drifted away from its theoretical kin to the extent that very few of our students make much use of the philosophical perspectives when they frame their studies. Instead, students and novice researchers make use of all kinds of other theories. We realized that a different introduction and instruction was required in order to meet the needs of novice researchers and doctoral students. As teachers, we therefore had to learn how our students could better learn about phenomenology.

Consequently, we began to search for literature that could aid us in this purpose. Specifically, we looked for literature on how applied phenomenological approaches could be justified and defended by referring back to phenomenological theory and how ordinary psychosocial theories could be incorporated without undermining the descriptive nature of phenomenology. What we found in the secondary literature were largely reinterpretations with scattered clues as to how this could be done. Most of these clues pointed back to the foundational literature authored by Husserl, Heidegger, Merleau-Ponty and, from time to time, Ricoeur. Thus, we decided to return to the foundational literature with the perspective of a teacher: not a philosopher, not a professor, not a researcher, but a teacher. We quickly realized that we were only ahead of our students in the sense that we had far more to learn in order for our students to learn.

The result of this journey is this modest book, where two teachers joined forces and tried to merge their interests in phenomenology and research methodology, respectively, in the hope of bridging what we increasingly came to see as a comprehension gap that needed to be addressed. It is therefore our hope that this book will be useful for those who teach applied phenomenology and those who find themselves in the position of being taught and needing to develop credible phenomenological research designs.

In Chapter 1, we try to distill the essence of Husserl's, Heidegger's and Merleau-Ponty's ideas. We conceptualize two scholarly arches originating in Husserl's epistemological phenomenology of consciousness and Heidegger's ontological phenomenology of being. In the second chapter, we elaborate on how these two scholarly arches branch out into four distinct conceptualizations of the subject matter of phenomenological research (i.e., experiences). A conceptualization can assist novice researchers with framing their studies of experience in a manner that can help justify the application of specific analytical and interpretative procedures, hence providing alignment between theory and method. Therefore, the theme of our third chapter is the epoché and phenomenological reduction. Here, we also begin to address the possible role of ordinary psychosocial theories in aiding the descriptive endeavor of applied phenomenological research. This sets the stage for Chapter 4, where we turn our attention toward two schools of applied phenomenological research: psychological phenomenology and interpretative phenomenological analysis, as well as phenomenological research unaffiliated with any particular school. Here, we begin to consider the specific challenges of designing phenomenological research. This leads to Chapter 5, where we go into detail regarding how ordinary psychosocial theoretical/conceptual frameworks can be developed. In Chapter 6, we proceed with a practical illustration of how a theoretical/conceptual framework can be developed under the two phenomenological arches we identified in Chapter 1. In Chapter 7, we demonstrate how to apply theoretical/conceptual framework at the data analysis phase under the two phenomenological arches. We conclude with Chapter 8, where we lay out the decisions the researchers need to make regarding the main components of their research designs in order to maintain alignment with the two epistemological and ontological arches of pertaining to meaning of thought and meaning of being.

Throughout this book, we have quoted extensively from the foundational literature. For some readers, this may come across as an additional barrier due to the often-archaic writing styles of the "founding fathers." It, nevertheless, serves two purposes. On one hand, phenomenology is an idea-theory, which means that the "evidence" in support of our elaborations must come from salient quotes. Otherwise, readers could be forgiven for thinking we were pulling the content of this book out of a hat. On the other hand, the quotes serve the purpose of providing the novice researcher a glimpse of the voices of Husserl, Heidegger and Merleau-Ponty, voices they may never hear in the typical handbooks pertaining to qualitative research. It is therefore our hope that our approach will motivate readers to engage directly with the foundational literature and make phenomenology their own, as there is not, and never should be, a place for the know-it-all authority on phenomenology.

Henrik Gert Larsen, Ph.D.
Philip Adu, Ph.D.

ACKNOWLEDGMENTS

We want to thank Hannah Shakespeare, the Senior Commissioning Editor, Research Methods at Routledge, for her guidance and addressing all questions we had when working on the book. We also thank Dr. Kevin Schwandt, instructor at Hamline University, for his time and effort in editing our manuscript before submitting it to our publisher.

1

PRAGMATIC PERSPECTIVES ON PHENOMENOLOGY IN SOCIAL RESEARCH METHODS

Objectives

Readers will be able to

1 Describe the meaning of phenomenology.
2 Understand the history of phenomenology.
3 Identify the two main scholarly arches.
4 Distinguish between Husserl's and Heidegger's views on phenomenology.
5 Understand the overarching themes in the foundational literature.
6 Differentiate between phenomenology as a philosophy and as an empirical research paradigm.

Examining the meaning of phenomenology

Phenomenology emerged as an influential philosophical school in the later part of the nineteenth century and is credited to Edmund Husserl (1859–1938). Husserl (2017) stated in his seminal work *Ideas: General Introduction to Pure Phenomenology*, "the sole task and service of phenomenology is to clarify the meaning of this world" (p. 21). With this statement in mind, Husserl (2001) launched an ambitious project of redefining modern philosophy for the purpose of understanding what it means to think and what it means to know (see p. 98). To this end, Husserl envisioned a project with parallels to empirical research in the sense that it would be based on *observing* acts of thought absent any concrete content. In this manner, he hoped to elucidate how transcendental subjectivity plays a role in constituting what people normally find to be objective reality.

Husserl (2017) emphasized that phenomenology should not be confused with psychology because the object of research is not how cognitive functions establish meanings of real events, but how cognition is possible in the first place (i.e., the study of the essence of thought "and absolutely no facts" [p. 44]). Therefore, Husserl (2001) stated that the phenomenologist "is concerned with the essential structures of cognition and their essential correlation to things known" (p. xxvii). In other words, the phenomenologist attempts a "direct description of our experience as it is, without taking account of its psychological origin and the causal explanations, which the scientist, the historian or the sociologist may be able to provide" (Merleau-Ponty, 1978, p. vii).

In contrast, Martin Heidegger (1889–1976) argued that there is no consensus regarding the meaning of phenomenology and diverted from Husserl's focus on thinking acts and instead raised the more existential question of the *meaning of being* (Heidegger, 1988, pp. 2, 16). The essential difference between these two thinkers, who came to define the scope of phenomenology, can be reduced to the notion that the exploration of meaning of thought pertains to epistemology, while beings actually exist in the real world, and therefore Heidegger's phenomenology acquires a character of both existentialism and ontology. While a phenomenon can be understood as the appearance of something or what something encountered appears to be, then Heidegger argued that phenomenology is a method of uncovering the being of this phenomenon. Heidegger (2010) thereby clarified that a "phenomenon in the phenomenological understanding is always just what constitutes being . . . and phenomenology is the science of the being of beings – ontology" (p. 35).

While Husserl's transcendental phenomenology takes aim at the correlation between mind and world, Heidegger's phenomenology adds the perspective of the phenomenon of being. Zahavi (2019) therefore emphasized that "the proper focus on phenomenological analysis is not only the mind-world dyad, but the *self-other-world triad*" (p. 15). Consequently, the meaning of phenomenology in this book will be conceived as two scholarly arches: one based on Husserl's phenomenology that focuses on the epistemology of subjectivity (i.e., how we know things) and another that focuses on the ontology of how *being* is to be understood.

The problem with phenomenology in social research

Volumes have been written on the subject of phenomenology, and it is therefore with some hesitation we attempt to distill the essence of this significant but often difficult-to-access body of literature. It is, however, a necessary and timely endeavor because even a casual review of the research literature reveals an expanding application of phenomenology. For example, Gringeri et al. (2013) documented that 20% of qualitative dissertations within the field of social work applied phenomenology as the research methodology, and authors of a study of nursing dissertations between 2004 and 2018 documented a trend toward phenomenology, as 57% of the dissertations that applied a phenomenological research method were written in just the last 4 years of the review (de Sá et al.,

2019). In terms of peer-reviewed research, a study of select counseling publications between 2005 and 2010 documented that while only 9.87% of the published studies were qualitative, about 37% of these were phenomenological (Woo & Heo, 2013). Further, Flynn and Korcuska's (2018) meta-study of three counseling journals published between 2001 and 2015 documented that phenomenological studies comprised up to 48.8% of the published research.

In contrast to the increasing use of phenomenology in social research, phenomenological scholars point to a limited understanding of the basic tenets of phenomenology (see Moran, 2000, p. 3). The comprehension gap is partly a result of the often convoluted and complex presentations, which appear to be aimed at an audience of accomplished philosophers rather than the thousands of emerging researchers and students. An obvious consequence of the opaque writing styles, especially of the founders, is that emerging researchers rely on secondhand accounts of the phenomenological tenets, which may not always be adequate or accurate and therefore unintentionally contribute to expanding this comprehension gap (Zahavi, 2019).

For example, Creswell (2007) defined phenomenology as a study that "describes the meaning for several individuals of their lived experiences of a concept or a phenomenon" (p. 62). While this statement may seem straightforward, it does not clarify what is meant by a phenomenon or what function the lived experiences have in elucidating meanings. Further, van Manen (2017, p. 812) proposed that the founding fathers of phenomenology intended a method for recovering the lived meanings of past experiences, free from preconceptions and abstractions.

This is somewhat misconstrued, compared with the definition of phenomenology we provided at the beginning of this chapter. Nevertheless, Giorgi (2006) argued that due to the obvious absence of a scientific consensus within applied phenomenology, individual researchers are left to make their own decisions as to how to apply the ideas from the foundational literature. Scholars argue that without a clear and well-articulated alignment between the applied phenomenological research method and its corresponding philosophical underpinning, the research purpose and method become ambiguous and, consequently, the phenomenological credibility of the outcome may be compromised (Lopez & Willis, 2004). Flynn and Korcuska (2018) specifically identified an apparent trend to publish phenomenological research with "bare bones information" regarding the methodology, and they pointed to a gap in the understanding of basic phenomenological methodological concepts such as bracketing and epoché as well as the variations in terminology across different types of phenomenology.

Emerging scholars' embrace of phenomenology, combined with a lingering uncertainty pertaining to methodology and theoretical concepts, justifies our attempt to present a pragmatic and accessible account of phenomenology. We hope that going back to the foundational literature will provide the reader a better understanding of phenomenology's potential as a social research paradigm, as well as addressing Flynn and Korcuska's (2018) call for a more thorough induction of, for example, doctoral students into phenomenological philosophy prior to engaging in actual applied research.

It is of course true that nobody owns phenomenology. While there are scholars and researchers with firm ideas as to what phenomenology is and what it is not, in the following chapters we will show that the convictions by which the tenets of phenomenology are conveyed by individual scholars are equally matched by the diversity of ideas. While individual presentations of phenomenology may come across as doctrinaire or even dogmatic, the diversity of these doctrines points to a field that is far from monolithic in either thought or application. This, in turn, provides emerging scholars with a creative space and an opportunity to make phenomenology their own.

We will, in the following chapters, attempt to trace two phenomenological arches pertaining to the *phenomenology of experiencing* and the *phenomenology of being* from their theoretical and philosophical starting points through the challenges of translating these ideas into applied research. The hope is to convey a connection between ideas and applications that can assist emerging researchers in producing phenomenological research with a higher degree of theoretical credibility.

Emergence of phenomenology

The term *phenomenology* has been used by philosophers prior to what scholars consider the emergence of phenomenology as a distinct philosophy attributed to Husserl toward the end of the 1800s. While the origin of phenomenological philosophy can be debated, its emergence is part of a reaction against the perceived reductionism of the natural sciences concerning mind and consciousness. Thus, Husserl (1973) stated,

> In the same way in which sciences are built upon one another, and the conclusions of one of them can serve as premises for others. I am reminded of the favorite ploy of basing the theory of knowledge on the psychology of cognition and biology. In our day, reactions against these fatal prejudices are multiplying. And prejudices they are.
>
> *(p. 19)*

Accordingly, Merleau-Ponty (1978) argued that, as a result of the rise of the natural sciences, "the body became an exterior without interior, subjectivity became an interior without exterior, and impartial spectator" (p. 56).

Consequently, phenomenology came to draw on a wide range of philosophical ideas for the purpose of reorienting the scientific perspective back toward a more holistic view of the individual and the role of subjectivity in understanding the meaning of the world, hereunder the works of Kant, Brentano and Descartes.

Kant's rigorous philosophy

While some scholars have argued that Immanuel Kant (1724–1804) is part of the phenomenological tradition, considering his elaboration on phenomena and meaning (Rockmore, 2011), Kant's ideas are typically not considered part of the contemporary phenomenological tradition. This may be due to the fact that Kant's main objective was not to develop a distinct transcendental phenomenological philosophy and partly due to the fact that Husserl himself did not particularly credit Kant for his own insights. In his seminal work *Ideas: General Introduction to Pure Phenomenology*, first published in 1931, Husserl (2017) reflected on Kant's role in developing phenomenology into a distinct philosophy by stating that

> It becomes evident to us that Kant's mental gaze rested on this specific field, although he was not yet able to appropriate it and recognize it. . . . Thus, the transcendental deduction of the first edition of Critique of Pure Reason, for instance, already moves strictly on phenomenological ground; but Kant misinterprets the same as psychological, and therefore eventually abandons it of his own accord.
>
> *(p. 183)*

However, Luft (2018) credited Kant with inspiring Husserl's attempt at creating a scientifically based philosophy of knowledge and knowing. Thus, Kant's (2007) contribution lies in the notion that that knowledge is transcendental (see p. 52). This means that knowledge is not about objects but about how people know objects. Kant, however, assumed that establishing a rigorous philosophy of transcendental knowledge may not be feasible, and he therefore limited his efforts to a critique of what was considered the contemporary understanding of knowing and knowledge. It would, however, seem that Husserl's life project would become a quest to establish such transcendental philosophy. In *Ideas*, Husserl (2017), therefore stated that he aimed to "discover a radical beginning of a philosophy which, to repeat the Kantian Phrase, will be able to present itself as a science" (p. 27).

Brentano's discovery of intentionality

If some of our elaborations on consciousness and perception sound a bit like psychology, it is not by accident. Phenomenology is strongly influenced by psychology. It was Franz Brentano's (1838–1917) view that philosophy, in general, should be based on descriptive psychology (Moran, 2000). Therefore, in order to acquire a better understanding of the emergence of phenomenology, it is instructive to revisit his ideas and reflect on how these came to inform the fundamental tenets of Husserl's philosophical phenomenology.

Brentano distinguished between physical phenomena and mental phenomena, where the latter are to be understood as mental acts that contain objects of thought (King et al., 2009). Phenomenologists accept that objects that people encounter in their so-called lived experiences do exist independent of them on their own terms, but that they never just appear like they are in themselves and for themselves. Objects are given to people through perception. Therefore, perception is a mental act of consciousness that constitutes objects in people's minds and not just a passive transmission mechanism of actualities. Thus, consciousness is not a passive reflection of input from the external world, and consciousness can therefore only be understood in terms of being conscious of something (Heffernan, 2015). Accordingly, the defining feature of consciousness is its *intentionality*. Put in different and somewhat more operational terms, there is no thinking unless people are thinking of something; therefore, thinking requires some active directedness toward a phenomenon.

It was Brentano's essential insight that intentionality, as a mental act, imposes its own kind of constituting meaning that lies beyond the mere psychological meaning of the experience with a phenomenon. Thus, Brentano's discovery allowed Husserl to break from the metaphysical traditions of philosophy and embark on a project where he attempted to develop a scientific philosophy of the meaning of the world based on thinking acts rather than morality and what people think. Thus, in *Ideas*, Husserl (2017) explicitly stated that without Brentano's discovery of the intentionality of consciousness and the development of a descriptive psychological discipline, phenomenology would not have emerged (see p. 23).

Consequently, the phenomenological literature that draws from Husserl's ideas is somewhat obsessed with the notion of appearances of objects because the contemplation of relatively simple cases of perceptions, such as the perception of a musical note or even a blank piece of paper, typically is a starting point for Husserl's phenomenological methodical interrogation of experiences, which serves the purpose of uncovering the meaning embedded within intentionality.

Husserl's Cartesian doubt

Most academics, if not most people, would have encountered the famous phrase attributed to René Descartes (1596–1650): "I think therefore I am" (cogito ergo sum). In *Cartesian Meditations*, which is a range of published lectures Husserl conducted in the late 1920s, Husserl revealed the significant influence of Descartes' philosophy. Husserl went so far as to share that he considered his phenomenology to be a form of neo-Cartesian philosophy (see Husserl, 1960, p. 2). Fundamentally, Husserl (2017) accepted a Cartesian definition of consciousness as "I think," however, in the broadest possible form, including "every case of I perceive, I remember, I fancy, I judge, I feel, desire, will" and all similar manifestations of thought (p. 115).

An ongoing theme in Husserl's writing appears to be Descartes' logic and reasoning. Especially the Cartesian theme of "doubt" appears to serve as a starting point for Husserl's development of a transcendental phenomenological philosophy. Thus, Husserl rejected anything that can be brought into doubt as the basis of his philosophy and aimed to build only on what is immune to doubt, that which is self-evident and cannot be disputed (see Husserl, 1960, p. 3).

Husserl's (1973) conclusion was that because of the outcomes that the empirical sciences produce, hereunder psychology, all can be doubted; they therefore cannot serve as the foundation for establishing a new science of phenomenological philosophy (see p. 4). Consequently, Husserl (2017) formulated what he referred to as the "principle of all principles," which states that intuition is the authoritative set of data for knowledge and that whatever presents itself in intuition "is simple to be accepted as it gives itself out to be" (p. 92). In other words, while there can be much doubt about what, for example, it is that people perceive and the meaning of the phenomenon perceived, there can be no doubt that people are, in fact, perceiving. Because thinking and perceiving are self-evident, it therefore acquires a certain foundational sense of objectivity, which can serve as the starting point for phenomenological investigations of the meaning of the world. It is therefore the Cartesian principle of doubt with its exclusion of the ego and the ego's concrete thoughts that, in Husserl's (1960) view, makes it possible to philosophically move from "naïve objectivism to transcendental subjectivism" (p. 5).

Heidegger's existentialism

Similar to Husserl, Heidegger found inspiration in Descartes' notion of "Cogito ergo sum," but in contrast to Husserl, Heidegger argued that the problem is not the "cogito" (I think), but the "sum" (I am) because only when people are able to define what being means can the thinking acts and their meanings really be understood (Heidegger, 2010, p. 45).

Heidegger's insight was that people cannot see the individual as a separate entity from the objects in the world. The essence of being is not that people exist in this world, but that they inhabit it. Heidegger exemplified this in terms of what a phenomenological study of history would look like. Such inquiry would not aim at formulating a theory of how historical concepts are formed or a theory of history or of what can be known about history. His philosophy would aim at "the interpretation of genuinely historical beings within the context of their historical actuality" (Heidegger, 2010, p. 10). Consequently, Heidegger (2010) argued that "to describe the world phenomenologically means to show and conceptually and categorically determine the being of beings present in the world" (p. 63). Thus, Heidegger (2010) saw the separation between beings and their contexts as an artificial distinction because being should always be understood as being in relation to something, and it is in the engagement with the world (i.e., the lived experiences) that being acquires meaning (see p. 10).

Luft (2018) argued that Heidegger seems to reject the utility of subjectivity as the starting point for phenomenological analysis, which is what makes his phenomenology quite different from Husserl's (see p. 57). It also underscores the heterogeneous nature of the field, and some scholars may even argue that Heidegger was not a phenomenologist, as he diverges from Husserl's philosophical project (see Dahlstrom, 2018, p. 211). While Heidegger was certainly not interested in transcendental subjectivity, our position is that such discussions are pointless, as they only serve to elevate Husserl's transcendental phenomenology above other traditions, which is not a productive stance for applied researchers, who are not engaged in a philosophical project but in social research.

Delimitations

The foundational literature, some of it written over 100 years ago, can be difficult to read. Husserl's works published in English especially suffer from the translators' apparent struggles with German sentence structure, Husserl's linguistic idiosyncrasies and the scholarly style of the time. Moran (2000) captured the experience of reading Husserl's original work well, when he stated, "although Husserl was capable of writing clearly and incisively his published works tend to be abstract, technical discussions, stylistically dense and torturous, and notoriously lacking in concrete examples" (p. 63). It is clear that none of the seminal works on phenomenology were written with the emerging researcher or student in mind.

Consequently, most emerging scholars will rely on secondhand introductions to phenomenology, such as this book. Therefore, we have taken great pains to saturate our presentation of phenomenology with quotes from some of the seminal works of, especially, Husserl but also Merleau-Ponty and Heidegger. In this manner, our readers will have the chance not only to study our interpretations and perspectives, but also to glean meaning from salient quotes of the masters themselves. We find this to be an important approach because the various applied forms of phenomenology lay claim to validity partly from invoking one or more of the great philosophers. However, emerging scholars seldom have a chance to form their own ideas based the words of these thinkers, and we therefore hope our approach will contribute to this end.

Finally, Descartes' famous quote Cogito ergo Sum ("I think therefore I am") gives rise to two profound philosophical questions: What is the meaning of thinking and what is the meaning of being? (See Figure 1.1) Because no thinking acts would ever exist without somebody to think, these two arches of phenomenology will delimit our elaborations in this book.

The purpose of the following is to introduce the main philosophical tentpoles of phenomenology. While some of the terminology may sound familiar to researchers and students who have dabbled in phenomenological designs, it is important to bear in mind that the foundational literature and the ideas of these great scholars were not intended to inform the field of social research. Therefore, while it is important to understand the philosophical doctrines of phenomenology as it can assist scholars with aligning the components of research and provide theoretical credibility for the outcomes, researchers should not make the mistake of going to the foundational literature in search of guidance for the method section of, for example, a dissertation.

Edmund Husserl

Martin Heidegger

Phenomenology
of
Thought

Phenomenology
of
Being

"Transcendental subjectivity"

"Dasein"

COGITO   ergo   SUM

René Descertes: *"I think therefore I am"*

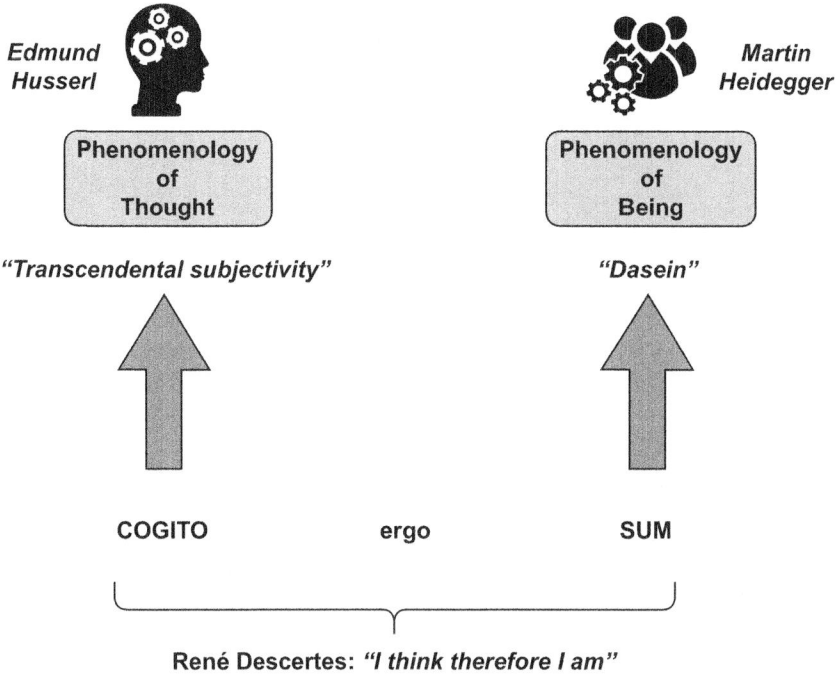

FIGURE 1.1 Two Philosophical Foci Under Phenomenology

Husserl's transcendental phenomenology

We have already introduced Husserl, and, as the founder of phenomenological philosophy, his importance cannot be understated. Husserl's thoughts are the point of reference for all noteworthy phenomenologists irrespective of their ultimate orientations within the field. The body of his literary work is extensive and broad in both thought and meaning. However, our purpose here is not to provide an all-encompassing account of Husserl's thoughts but to distill the parts of it which may be informative for students and emerging scholars contemplating engaging in phenomenological research. After all, Husserl's thoughts were, as is true of most thinkers, not ready-made, but demonstrate a process, in that he developed, modified, abandoned and restated ideas.

Transcendentalism

Husserl, in his later years, referred to his ideas as transcendental phenomenology. Many students and emerging researchers are sufficiently challenged by phenomenology, and the transcendental part adds yet another twist, which gives us ground to pause and ask, *what is transcendentalism about?* Husserl struggled to escape the notion that his ideas were nothing more than descriptive psychology, which he defined as an empirical investigation into individual apperceptions. Or, in other words, Husserl's ideas involved the study of how perceptions are psychologically connected with a body of preexisting knowledge and experiences pertaining to the object as perceived (Husserl, 1973, p. 34).

Obviously, such a frame of reference would not allow him to develop his ideas into an actual science of consciousness. He therefore argued that there is an empirical connection between a "psychological event" and some factual "object" that allows meanings to form in apperception (Husserl, 2017, p. 120), but this perspective does not really reveal the meaning in the mental act itself, as intentionality gives objects in certain ways to cognition. Husserl's epiphany was that by analyzing consciousness in the context of actual reality, phenomenology would still be situated in an empirical naturalist tradition with its notion of cause and effect. Consequently, he posited a distinction between the pure phenomenon of the mental cognitive act and the cognitive psychological phenomenon.

What Husserl aimed for was to understand how cognition is possible and how it is possible for cognition to reach an object, not how it does this in a scientific or descriptive sense. Husserl thus stated, "I want to come face to face with the essence of the possibility of that reaching" (Husserl, 1973, p. 4). Husserl (2017) therefore rejected the notion that there is a nexus between uncovering facts and uncovering the essence of consciousness (see p. 22). Husserl (2017) stated that "from facts follow always nothing but facts," and he thereby took critical aim at the naturalistic approach to psychology and philosophy by arguing for a focus on a subjectivity that transcends context and looks at the intentionality of consciousness on its own terms (p. 63).

From Husserl's perspective, consciousness needs to be understood as something that exists unaffected by the world, and therefore, this pure phenomenon of the mental act cannot be understood in the ordinary empirical psychological sense, but requires a totally different method of obtaining a descriptive knowledge of the essence of a phenomenon by placing the ego as the focus of description (Husserl, 2017).

Thus, Husserl's decisive turn away from descriptive psychology, or what he also called descriptive phenomenology, toward transcendentalism, manifested in his publications after 1900 and quite distinctively in his lectures on the idea of phenomenology around 1907 (Husserl, 1973). Husserl thus articulated a new science of consciousness preoccupied with grasping the essence of intentionality, which essentially makes his phenomenological analysis of experiences transcendental.

Method (in relation to epoché and phenomenological reduction)

Husserl took issue with what he perceived as the empirical tradition's dogma that "all knowledge must be grounded in immediate experience and in real world facts" and argued that the ordinary sciences confound facts with knowledge (Husserl, 2017, p. 82). He thus ridiculed what he called the "experience-proud psychology as rich with invented phenomena and with psychological analyses that are no analyses at all. Thus ideas of essence, they say, are 'concepts' and concepts are 'mental constructions'" (p. 89). Thus, Husserl rejected the psychological notion that an essence of an experience can be understood as merely a conceptual abstraction.

Husserl argued that the process of gaining insight into the essence, or as he called it the mental seeing of essence of intentionality, may take its starting point in cognition, but the essence is not found or articulated through abstractions or a result of inductive analytical approaches (Husserl, 2017, p. 57). He did not dispute that abstractions and inferences are the product of psychological analysis, but this is not where the essences he was looking for could be found. The essence Husserl tried to describe is not object- or even phenomenon-related but situated within the mental act of thinking itself.

Husserl tried to recast consciousness as an independent domain for scientific exploration, but at the same time, a domain that is not situated in the natural world. His ideas required a totally new methodology of what could be called scientific introspection that can transcend the empirical observable world. To this end, he introduced a range of hotly debated terms and steps that constitute the transcendental method of gaining access to the pure intentionality of consciousness, hereunder the two most important concepts: epoché and phenomenological reduction.

Epoché, in its own right, means "suspension of judgment." Husserl thus wanted people to suspend judgment, but what did he mean by this? Husserl was not particularly helpful in clearly explaining what epoché entails and referred to this process in several different ways over the years. However, Husserl made it clear that he did not mean the simple act of bracketing out the "preconceptions that normally would interfere with empirical research" (Husserl, 2017, p. 111). The point is, therefore, not that he was attempting simply to remove biases, but instead he intended to establish a nonempirical foundation for phenomenological investigations, and in order to do this, he had to suspend what he calls the natural attitude, which should be understood as the way people ordinarily make sense of the world as a system of causes and effects. Take, for example, the notion that people hear because something is making a sound. A person's natural attitude is to insert cause and effect, where, in fact, hearing is not caused by the sound, and the experience of hearing is not constituted by sound at all.

The next step is what Husserl referred to as reduction, stating, "the phenomenological reduction is simply a requirement to always "abide by the sense of the proper investigation, and not to confuse epistemology with a natural scientific (objectivistic) investigation" (as cited in Zahavi, 2008, p. 668). This could be understood in simple terms as to avoid psychoanalyzing the experience, which is well in line with his efforts to set phenomenology apart from psychology. Husserl's purpose was to examine the mental acts of cognitions by looking behind the psychological curtain that shields consciousness by bracketing out not only the object of experience but also its phenomenal representation in the mind.

Husserl rejects psychologism

For better or worse, Husserl "transcended" far beyond Brentano's descriptive psychology by focusing on consciousness on its own terms apart from empirical reality. Consequently, Husserl's moves toward a rejection start with Brentano's act psychology, and in his later years, Husserl argued that descriptive psychology can never be the basis of philosophy as "psychologism perverts the pure meaning of philosophy" (Husserl, 2017, p. 16). Transcendental phenomenology is, on the other hand, a "science of essential being that is aimed solely at establishing knowledge of essence" (p. 44). Husserl thus stated:

> In speaking about investigating the objects and modes of cognition, we always mean investigations into essences, which in the sphere of the absolute given exhibits in a general way, the ultimate meaning, the possibility, the essence of the objects of cognition and of the cognition of objects.
>
> *(Husserl, 1973, p. 11)*

Perhaps the above elaboration on Husserl's phenomenology has left more questions opened than answered. Husserl's contemporaries did not readily embrace transcendental phenomenology, and for the emerging researcher it is important to voice a few words of caution. Husserl's transcendentalism is an epistemological paradigm as opposed to the ontological orientation of the empirical sciences. Husserl's methods, as described earlier, are therefore fundamentally the antithesis of social research methods. So, while Creswell (2007) encouraged researchers to write about phenomenology in their theoretical framework, the nature of Husserl's transcendentalism may lead to a quite esoteric presentation that risks drawing the authors away from their purpose—research—and down the rabbit hole of phenomenological reduction.

Heidegger's existential phenomenology

Martin Heidegger (1889–1976) encountered phenomenology through Husserl's work and collaborated with him for years. The relationship between these thinkers was as complex and complicated as the contrasts between their respective versions of phenomenology. Husserl was initially skeptical of Heidegger's provenance as a philosopher due to his Catholic background and may initially have impeded Heidegger's career. Heidegger (1989) addressed this directly in his Marburger lectures, where he stated that the notion of a catholic phenomenology makes as much sense as protestant mathematics (see p. 28). Nevertheless, in 1926 Heidegger dedicated his seminal work *Being and Time* to "Edmund Husserl – in admiration and friendship," but less than 10 years later, Heidegger signed the official petition to remove non-Aryan professors from German universities and subsequently did not protest when the Nazi authorities ejected Husserl from his position at Freiburg University (Moran, 2000).

For the casual reader, it would indeed appear as if Heidegger threw out Husserl's concepts of epoché and phenomenological reduction because they do not appear to play a significant role in his elaborations. However, Heidegger did, in fact, address phenomenological reduction in his lectures during the late 1920s, where he explained that due to his focus on being, his approach was different from Husserl's. While the human being is situated in the natural world, the human being also has a way of being. In other words, Heidegger's (1989) phenomenological reduction is a shift of focus from the human being to the being of this human (see p. 29). Linguistically, this makes a lot more sense in German than in English. However, the main point is that while Husserl was interested in transcendental consciousness, Heidegger focused on the transcendental being or the ways of being. Heidegger therefore began his analysis of meaning with the phenomenon of the human being (i.e., the nature of beings' *thrownness* into the world), which he defined as Dasein or *being there* (Davidsen, 2013, p. 322).

"Dasein"—the phenomenon of human being

Heidegger's (2010) most famous contribution to the lexicon of phenomenology is likely *Dasein*. Heidegger (2010) stated, "This being, which we ourselves in each case are and which includes inquiry among the possibilities of its being, we formulate terminologically as "'Dasein'" (p. 7). However, Dasein is not the actual human being but can instead be understood as the phenomenon of a human being (Tan et al., 2009). Thus, Dasein is the central phenomenon under investigation in Heidegger's phenomenology, in which he posits that interrogating the structure of Dasein may uncover the meaning of being.

Dasein is different than transcendental subjectivity, as Dasein is aware of and relates to its own existence and ways of being. Dasein is therefore something we understand ourselves as. Thus, Heidegger (2010) argued that

> Dasein always understands itself in terms of its existence, in terms of its possibility to be itself or not to be itself. Dasein has either chosen these possibilities itself, stumbled upon them, or in each instance already grown up in them.
>
> *(p. 11)*

Consequently, Heidegger (2010) posited that the essence of Dasein is existence, and this existence is always a "who," "I am" and "you are."

In this manner, Heidegger's phenomenology acquires an existential character and departs from the epistemological orientation of transcendental phenomenology and Husserl's focus on intentionality and subjectivity. Instead, Heidegger approached phenomenology in an ontological manner. In other words, Heidegger's phenomenology becomes a descriptive method for investigating the ontological horizon of people's actual existence in the world (i.e., how Dasein is taking care of the "business of existence").

The being of Dasein—the hermeneutic turn

While the essence of Dasein is existence, the next question is what then is the being of Dasein? Heidegger appears to constitute Dasein in terms of: the "factual self," the "normative self" and "the authentic self." While the "factual self" perhaps does not need further elaboration, the "normative self" is what Heidegger referred to as "the they-self." By this, he meant that Dasein does not understand itself in its authentic mode, but rather in the mode of the they-self. Thus, Heidegger posited that "they-self" is the "dictatorships" of norms and conventions that people have internalized and that obscure the authentic self. In other words, the they-self "disburdens the Dasein in its everydayness. . . . Everyone is the other one and no one is himself. . . . The 'they' is the nobody whom the everyday Dasein has always surrendered itself" (Heidegger, 2010, p. 124).

Although we have clarified Dasein as an ontological structure of dealings and doings in the world in the mode of the they-self, the question of Dasein's being still remains unanswered. In this connection, Heidegger (2010, p. 297) argued that "The being that we ourselves in each case are is ontologically farthest from us" (p. 334). By this, he meant that Dasein primarily understands itself though taking care of things in the world and that this everydayness of Dasein is dominated by the "they-self." However, this everydayness of Dasein projects an inauthentic understanding of being, which covers up Dasein's own authentic being.

While the being of Dasein can be understood as "taking care of" (Heidegger, 2010, p. 347), then understanding the authentic being of the self requires interpretation. Consequently, Heidegger (2010, p. 298) stated that "the kind of being of Dasein requires of an ontological interpretation that has set as its goal . . . that it overcome the being of this being in spite of this being's own tendency to cover things over" (p. 298). This is not an easy project, as "the they-self" resists this uncovering. Heidegger even described this as an almost violent process of wrestling the authentic self out from underneath the inauthentic self. Nevertheless, this notion is what gives Heidegger's phenomenology a hermeneutic character alongside its existential character.

The understanding that Heidegger posited will emerge from this ontological interpretation of Dasein should not be construed as some form of cognitive act or a mental flight of fancy, but instead as a way of projecting. Heidegger (1988) therefore argued that understanding as an existential dimension of Dasein means "to project oneself upon a possibility" (p. 277) or "to be projecting toward a potentiality of being" (Heidegger, 2010, p. 321).

The meaning of being—temporality

The final question that remains to be contemplated is how people can understand this being or the meaning of being. Heidegger (2010, p. 321) argued that projecting is essentially futural and therefore proposed that "when one understands oneself projectively in an existentiell possibility, the future underlies this understanding." Consequently, Dasein is always leaning into the future and is ahead of itself. Thus, Heidegger (1988) asserted that "understanding is primarily futural, for it comes towards itself from its chosen possibility of itself" (p. 287)

However, Heidegger did not mean an ordinary future in terms of a now in the next moment. The phenomenological understanding of time and meaning is not limited to the psychological insight that past experiences convey meanings to the present and generate anticipations for the future. Instead, Heidegger saw the future not as the next now, but instead as a potential of becoming. Heidegger (2010) therefore argued that a person's entire ontology (i.e., what they can know) is anchored in temporality and stated that "time is the horizon of every under-standing and interpretation of being" (p. 17). In other words, the meaning of being of Dasein is temporality (Heidegger, 2010, p. 352), and temporality is the potential possibilities of being.

Merleau-Ponty's "phenomenology of perception"

The paradox of Maurice Merleau-Ponty (1908–1961) is his apparent ability to compartmentalize his political and philosophical positions to a degree where he, on one hand, defended the Stalinist labor camps and the political show trials as cogs in the wheel on the road toward socialism (Moran, 2000, p. 398), and on the other hand, railed against the empirical sciences' dehumanization of the individual.

Merleau-Ponty's phenomenology was inspired by Gestalt psychology and Husserl's phenomenology. Merleau-Ponty initially saw Heidegger's contribution to the field as merely elaborating on Husserl's ideas rather than any explicit break-through of thought (Merleau-Ponty, 1978, p. vii). While Heidegger departed from Husserl's philosophy in focusing on "being," Merleau-Ponty differed from Heidegger in his focus on the actual human being, but somewhat differed from Husserl by focusing on perception and psychological phenomena rather than intentionality and the transcendental ego.

Perceptions—gateway to consciousness

In his seminal work, *Phenomenology and Perception* (first published in 1945), Merleau-Ponty (1978) argued that "the real has to be described and not con-strued," and therefore perception occupies a unique place in his phenomeno-logical investigations (p. x). Thus, the universal meaning of experiences is not found in abstract reasoning or logical contemplation, but through the analysis of perceptions of real-life occurrences and objects in the world. It is, however, important to understand that Merleau-Ponty did not see perception as taking up a specific point of view. Instead, perception should be understood as the back-drop of all other mental acts, and Merleau-Ponty (1978) posited that there is no "inner man," where meanings reside, but that meanings are in the world, and perception is the foundational mode of being in the world (p. xi).

Merleau-Ponty (1978) thereby proposed a link between perception and consciousness in the mold of Gestalt psychology with sensitivity toward the context of subjects. Perception is then a proverbial switch that activates consciousness' ability to manifest Gestalts or representations of the perceived world. Consequently, there is a connection between these Gestalts and consciousness itself that provides a gateway to "a transcendental understanding of the world and consciousness" (Romdenh-Romluc, 2018, p. 344).

Embodied consciousness

Merleau-Ponty (1978, p. 53) allocated an extensive number of pages to bodily experiences and sensations and argues that sense experience is the central phenomenon of perceptual life. Thus, in contrast to Husserl, Merleau-Ponty did not consider consciousness as separate from our physical existence. Inspired by Gestalt psychology, Merleau-Ponty argued for a more holistic perspective in the sense that it is not consciousness that sees things, but the eyes. Thus, people's relations to things are always mitigated by the body's sensory capacities, and therefore people cannot conceive of anything that they cannot also somehow perceive. Consequently, Merleau-Ponty differed from Husserl by considering the body as a vessel of existence and therefore inseparable from consciousness. Consequently, Merleau-Ponty's phenomenology can best be described as a philosophy of the embodied consciousness (Moran, 2000, p. 408).

Merleau-Ponty's (1978) argument was that body and mind is "all inclusive" and that people therefore cannot delegate certain actions to physiology and others to consciousness (p. 124). In other words, the "phenomenon is not a state of consciousness, or a mental act and the experience of phenomena is not an act of introspection" (Merleau-Ponty, 1978, p. 57). If it were indeed the case that consciousness is separate from body, then one could conceivably argue that "insanity is only perversion of will" and that mental illness could be cured by thought alone (p. 125).

Method

Although Merleau-Ponty was an enthusiastic supporter of Husserl, his notion of embodiment of consciousness somewhat departs from the epistemological orientation of transcendental phenomenology. Consequently, methods such as phenomenological reduction are not widely discussed in his writings. In his revision of Husserl's ideas, he offered an insight similar to Heidegger's that the phenomenological reduction is not fully possible because people are not pure consciousness, but actually living in this world (p. xiv). Instead, Merleau-Ponty aimed at a limited phenomenological reduction that would not bracket individuals' entire world but take people to a "perceptual pre-conceptual" state as the starting point for phenomenological reflection (Moran, 2000, p. 402).

The purpose is, however, still the same as for Husserl (i.e., the elimination of causal presumptions that guide people's everyday lives). Nevertheless,

Merleau-Ponty questioned the feasibility of this because every reflection takes its starting point in something. Further, because people do not exist as pure consciousness, it is likely that they cannot cut the strings to the real world altogether (Merleau-Ponty, 1978, p. 63). In contrast to Husserl's phenomenological reduction and concurrent with his mind-body perspective on phenomenology, it is therefore in the analysis of "system breakdowns" that Merleau-Ponty gained insight into the phenomena of people's existence in the world (Moran, 2000, p. 419).

In *Phenomenology of Perception*, Merleau-Ponty (1978) engaged in a detailed analysis of mind-body phenomena, such as phantom limbs, which, in his view, neither physiology nor psychology can adequately explain. His phenomenology posited that the body is people's way of being in the world, and the phantom limb phenomenon is an example of a physical deficiency that reveals an "I," which, irrespective of whether the limb is there or missing, is committed to the sense of what this body part would be used for (Merleau-Ponty, 1978, p. 81). In other words, this example demonstrates that consciousness and body are not two separate entities, and it is reductionist of the natural sciences to delimitate between them.

It could be argued that, where Husserl's analysis ends in the idealization of consciousness, Merleau-Ponty ends up with an idealized body, and in this sense, both their versions of phenomenology are transcendental. In other words, the knowledge Husserl acquired is not derived from the phenomena or the actual object itself, and Merleau-Ponty's insights are not actually based on the body of anyone specific.

Exploring the main phenomenology-related tenets

In the previous review of Husserl, Heidegger and Merleau-Ponty, we have tried to distill their phenomenological philosophies, their key terminological apparatus and their methods. It is important to understand that such presentation is obviously an oversimplification and fails to capture the nuances and conceptual developments. The contrast we have demonstrated between these thinkers should also not be exaggerated. They mainly serve the purpose of illustrating the rich variation of ideas and concepts within the phenomenological field. Essentially, they are all phenomenologists, but each in their own way. From a bird's eye view, it can be argued that the key difference is whether we see phenomenology as a form of epistemological inquiry (i.e., how the world can be known and the meaning in that knowing) or if we see phenomenology as an ontological method (i.e., an inquiry into what there is to be known about the world). The following section is an attempt to illuminate the most significant themes that cut across the different orientations and subsequently may inform and inspire social researchers in articulating the frameworks for their applied phenomenological approaches.

Consciousness

Husserl (2017) stated that each of the sciences has its own specific object-domain, which constitutes its field of research, but what is the domain of phenomenology (see pp. 51–52)? The answer to this question typically ranges from the study of lived experiences to perceptions to meanings. In this respect, one may wonder what it is that phenomenology brings to the table that is not adequately covered in social psychology or psychoanalysis? In other words, how is phenomenology different from psychology? Essentially, phenomenology is the study of consciousness and psychology is the study of cognition. Thus, Zahavi (2008) argued that phenomenology is distinct from psychology because "phenomenology is not concerned with the psychological question of how a pre-existing reality is subjectively apprehended by physical beings; rather it is concerned with the question of what it means for something to be real" (p. 667).

While the relationship between cognitive functions and behaviors has been well researched, the notion of consciousness—"the interplay between experience and thinking," is still somewhat a mystery (Dennett, 1991, p. 26). It is important to note that no model of consciousness that can compare with the cognitive theories can be truly validated by empirical science.

Husserl (2017) argued that the fundamental problem with empirical science is that it assumes that facts can only be uncovered through direct observations (see p. 83). To him, this assertion about facts limits the scope of knowledge. Consequently, Merleau-Ponty (1978) argued that people's understanding of consciousness is hampered by empirical scientific thinking, which, in his words, "reduces all phenomena which bear witness to the union of subject and world . . . by severing the links which unite the thing and the embodied subject leaving only sensible qualities to make up our world" (p. 320).

Merleau-Ponty (1978) indicted behaviorism as being a rigid input-output dogma that fails to take into account that humans are more than the sum of their body parts. According to him, "we are not a collection of eyes, ears and organs of touch with their cerebral projections" (p. 59). Merleau-Ponty further claimed that it is a typical psychological fallacy to see consciousness as an inner world that reflects a somewhat distorted image of an outer world. To him, it is a misunderstanding to approach the study of this inner world with the same logical assumptions as an empirical researcher would when exploring the outer world. Merleau-Ponty (1967) stated, "consciousness cannot be treated as an effect since it is that which constitutes the relation of cause and effect" (p. 221).

Husserl's (2017) central thesis that provided his phenomenology with its transcendental character was that consciousness is walled-off from the natural world, and he therefore stated that it

> is essentially independent of all Being of the type of a world or nature, and it has no need for these for its existence. The existence of what is natural cannot condition the existence of consciousness since it arises as a correlate of consciousness.
>
> *(p. 157)*

Because consciousness is both part of reality and reality-constituting, the normal assumptions of cause and effect that underpin natural science are not applicable. Thus, Merleau-Ponty (1978) stated that "active meaning giving defines consciousness" (p. xi). Therefore, consciousness is not an object that scholars can study in the same manner as all other objects.

Husserl did not deny cognition and the existence of causal psychological processes and phenomena. Nevertheless, he assumed that each cognitive phenomenon requires an underlying or a priori knowledge in order to be possible. In other words, the act of thinking has its own meaning, constituted by the intentionality of consciousness, which is different from what is actually thought. This means that while people can think about any object (real or imagined in different ways), the object has to first be presented to cognition in a manner that makes this possible. For instance, if a person judges something, then that something has to be given to cognition in a way that makes it judgeable. In other words, consciousness and intentionality can be understood as giving objects to cognition in certain ways as to make the cognitive act possible and meaningful. To illustrate, we can imagine the mind as consisting of a baseball pitcher representing intentionality and a batter representing cognition, where the ball is the object. In order for the batter to hit the ball, the pitcher has to throw it first. However, the pitcher can throw this ball in many different ways, and each way of pitching is suitable for certain ways of batting. In their natural states, people see themselves just as the batter and objectify the pitcher. Thus, people do not realize that batter and pitcher are not on opposing teams, but on the same mental team and that, in fact, *their Consciousness* is pitching to their *Cognitive* batter. Thus, cognition and consciousness are two sides of the same coin. One cannot do without the other.

In contrast, Heidegger's (2010) phenomenology tried to break free of this epistemological perspective and posited that consciousness is a phenomenon of Dasein (see p. 259). Heidegger likened consciousness to an inner silent call to Dasein that answers back with self-interpretation. Rhetorically, Heidegger (2010) asked, "What is talked about in the call of consciousness, what is summoned . . . and to what is one summoned?" (p. 262). Heidegger answered this by stating that the call of consciousness summons Dasein to "one's own self" or rather to the many possibilities of being in this world. Ricoeur (1994) expressed this notion somewhat more poetically by stating that "consciousness is in truth, that place par excellence in which illusions about oneself is intimately bound up with the veracity of attestation" (p. 341).

The above considerations reveal different notions of consciousness that reflect the differences between Husserl's, Merleau-Ponty's and Heidegger's phenomenological philosophies. The illustration below is an attempt at demonstrating consciousness and Dasein as a continuum (see Figure 1.2). Husserl's "walled-off" transcendental consciousness delimits the study of consciousness to the meaning-giving structures of intentionality such as perceiving, judging and appreciating. In contrast, Heidegger conceptualizes consciousness as a phenomenon of Dasein which discloses the various ways of being in this world. All these notions are

Consciousness   *Dasein*

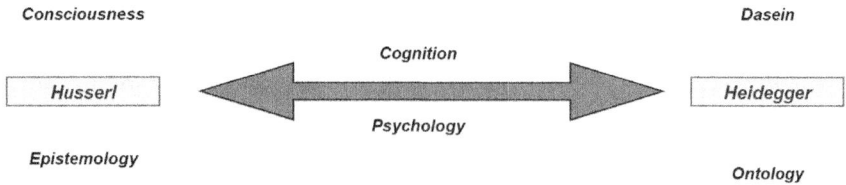

Cognition

Husserl ⟵⟶ *Heidegger*

Psychology

Epistemology

Ontology

FIGURE 1.2 Demonstration of Consciousness and Dasein as a Continuum

meaningful for the applied phenomenological researcher, as it informs an attitude toward research as either epistemological or ontological.

Perception and circumspection

In applied phenomenological research, scholars often encounter the term perception. The notion of perception is often built into the research question itself and
presents the main focus of the study as well as an implicit validation of the study's
phenomenological credentials. However, it is often far from clear what is meant
by perception. Heidegger (1988) argued that the lack of a clear definition means
that psychology "gropes about blindly in its investigations," which of course
is something that the social researcher should avoid, and, thus, the researcher
should be able to clearly state what is being studied and for what reason (p. 55).

The main difference between Husserl's and Heidegger's phenomenological
philosophies is the significance they bestow on perception as a starting point for
investigating the meaning of the world. This is a difference that is congruent
with these philosophers' guiding stars for finding meaning as either entombed in
consciousness or out there in the world with Dasein. Heidegger (1988) defined
perception simply as "directing oneself toward what is perceived" (p. 57). Similarly, for Husserl (2017), perception is simply the mode in which objects are
given and the starting point for a scientific inquiry into experiences (see p. 52).
Perception is therefore not to be understood as a particular point of view, opinion or meaning, nor is it to be understood as experience. Perception is simply
becoming aware of something, and, for Husserl and his followers, this awareness
in perception constitutes the descriptive data from which both psychologists and
phenomenologists extract meaning, although each discipline does so in its own
particular way.

Phenomenology and phenomenological psychology share the same data, but
consider these data differently. The phenomenologist approaches perception with
the aim of studying intentionality, while the psychologist does so with the aim of
studying apperception (i.e., psychological subjectivity). Husserl (1973) addressed
this point on multiple occasions and stated that the phenomenologist is confronted with two sets of intertwined but still distinct sets of data: (a) data pertaining to the way objects appear and (b) that which appears (see p. 8). For Husserl,

the purpose of phenomenology is to investigate the mode of appearing, or rather the meaning-constituting thinking acts absent any real-world references.

Husserl's (2017) *principle of all principles* explained the role of perception as giving the objects of the world to people in experience in a certain manner. Moreover, a mental act such as perception contains its own kind of knowledge. He therefore emphasized that

> every primordial dator intuition is a source of authority for knowledge, that whatever presents itself in intuition in primordial form is simply to be accepted as it gives itself out to be, though only within the limits in which it then presents itself.
>
> *(p. 92)*

Merleau-Ponty (1978) articulated this a bit more comprehensibly as he argued that the overarching mode of being in the world is perception and that "the perception of the world by Peter is not Peter's doing anymore that the perception of Paul is Paul's doing; in each case it is the doing of pre-personal forms of consciousness" (p. xi).

Figure 1.3 serves to demonstrate the interconnectedness between the active meaning-giving components of consciousness and how, in transcendental and psychological phenomenology, perception serves as a gateway to the meaning-giving structures of consciousness and therefore becomes the center of attention of many phenomenologists.

We have now established how perception is defined and its role within the foundational literature, but what we have described here is strictly from a first-person point of view. In other words, the "primordial dator" Husserl spoke of is his own perception. Therefore, the problem for social researchers is that they, in fact, do not have access to other people's perceptional data, which suggests the question: What data are we actually collecting in phenomenological research and on what grounds can we claim any phenomenological credibility of our findings?

Husserl (2017) was quite specific in this matter as he stated:

> We have primordial experience of ourselves and our states of consciousness in the so-called inner or self-perception, but not of others. . . . We behold the living experiences of others through the perception of their bodily

FIGURE 1.3 Demonstration of the Connecting Components of Consciousness

behavior. This beholding in the case of empathy is indeed intuitional dator but no longer a primordial dators act. . . . The other man and his physical life is indeed apprehended but . . . it is not given to our consciousness as primordial.

(p. 51)

Merleau-Ponty (1967) seconded this by stating that "The perception I have of him is never in the case of suffering or mourning, for example, the equivalent of the perception which he has of himself" (p. 222).

The data that the social researchers have to work with is typically interviews, which contain their subjects' disclosures and attestations with regard to their experiences. However, these data are not perceptions in the way perceptions are defined in the foundational literature. Consequently, social researchers need to adapt their methodologies and their phenomenological theoretical/conceptual frameworks to a situation where the data is not primordial.

In this connection, Heidegger (1988) argued that the role of perception is overstated and posited that perception is simply a "release of extant things, which lets them be encountered" (p. 70). However, in this process, the encountered is also uncovered by Dasein as something other than merely what was perceived. This uncovering is, however, not the function of perception, and Heidegger therefore introduced *circumspection* as an alternative to perception. His argument was that most of people's interaction with the world is not psychological, but quite practical. Circumspection is therefore different from perception, as this concept emphasizes people's active dealings with objects in the world that bring their beings into understanding through interpretation and decoding of references. Consequently, circumspection is distinctively ontological in nature in contrast to the more epistemological function of perception. The illustration below is an attempt at demonstrating a person's circumspective engagement with paint (see Figure 1.4). It also shows how the contextual and usefulness references point to the structure of the being of this paint as useful in a particular way through its references of canvas, paintbrush, etc. Further, Dasein's engagement with these paint tools reveals something about its being as well: not its existential and authentic being, but the possibility and potential of being (e.g., as an artist)./

Subjectivity, meaning and being

Congruent with the different views regarding the role and importance of perception, we have similar philosophical demarcations when it comes to meaning. Essentially, the difference is that transcendental and psychology-oriented phenomenologists connect epistemology and meaning, while Heidegger was oriented toward the ontological act of understanding. Consequently, subjectivity becomes the focus of attention within transcendental and phenomenological psychology, whereas uncovering and understanding Dasein's ways of being in the world remain the interest of existential and hermeneutic phenomenologists.

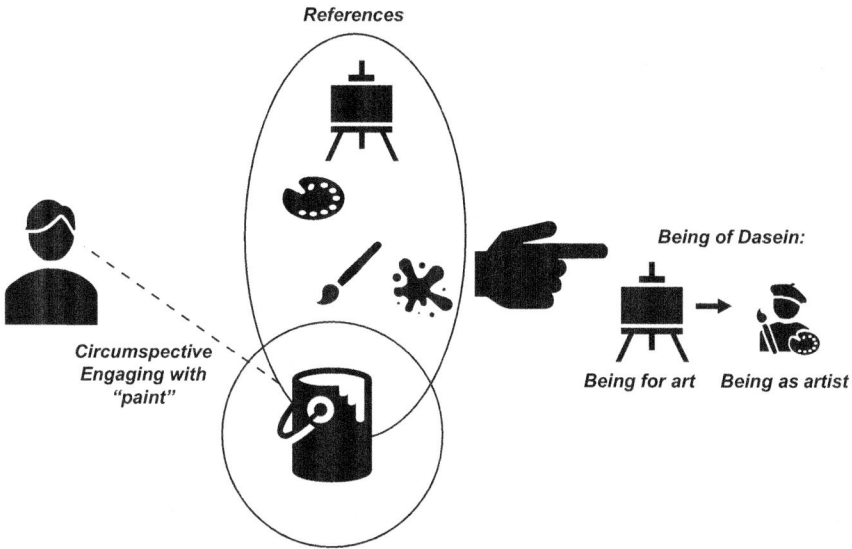

FIGURE 1.4   Demonstration of a Person's Circumspective Engagement

While subjectivity is much talked about in qualitative research, there is little consensus as to what it actually is. However, at least we can say that we understand subjectivity as the antithesis of objectivity, or can we? In the ordinary psychological and semantic sense, perhaps yes, but from a phenomenological perspective, subjectivity and objectivity are two sides of the same coin in the sense that only a subject can define what is objective. Thus, without subjectivity, objectivity cannot be. Therefore, Giorgi (2004) found it more illuminating to contrast subjectivity with subjectivism. Subjectivism refers to the notion that reality and truth are contingent on a personal perspective, which is an important difference because phenomenology does not prescribe to, for example, Berger and Luckmann's (1966) notion that reality is socially constructed at all. Therefore, the meaning of subjectivity is not to be understood as moral or social relativity.

It can be difficult to accept that there is a difference between transcendental subjectivity and psychological subjectivity. Transcendental subjectivity can be understood as the meaning-giving perspective of consciousness, whereas psychological subjectivity can be understood as the meaning-giving perspective of the individual (i.e., apperception). This is a distinction that demarcates phenomenology from psychology, but the distinction is more analytical than real because any phenomenological investigation would necessarily take its starting point in the very same perceptions that concern psychology.

Thus, psychological meaning can be understood as what manifests when the content of perception correlates with subjectivity. While this is the destination of descriptive psychology, it is just the starting point for the phenomenologist, who, through epoché and phenomenological reduction, attempts to strip away content in order to study in what ways perception gives objects to cognition, making psychological meaning making possible. The study of transcendental subjectivity is, however, the prerogative of philosophy and not social research as it "precludes a complete treatment of it in naturalistic terms" (Husserl, 2017, p. 341).

It is a valid question whether Husserl's transcendental turn makes his project what Dennett (2003) dubs a *"lone-wolf auto-phenomenology."* Husserl (1970), however, realized that people are not alone and that the meaning of the world is not solely constituted on the transcendental subjective (see p. 163). Therefore, Merleau-Ponty (1978) argued that "the world is an indivisible unity of value shared by Peter and Paul in which their perspectives blend" (p. xi). In other words, when individuals come into contact, the communalization of experiences gives rise to a new reality contingent on intersubjectivity. However, this new validity is not directly constituted in intentionality, and phenomenologists therefore do not consider intersubjectivity as a source of primordial data. Thus, the analysis of intersubjectivity cannot produce universal truths about the meaning of the world. Whereas transcendental subjectivity contains universal meanings constituted by consciousness and psychological subjectivity contains truths derived from cognition, then intersubjectivity simply contains social truths that are relative in time and context.

In contrast to transcendental and psychological phenomenology's emphasis on an analysis of the correlation between perception and subjectivity, Heidegger posited that the meaning is already part of Dasein's ontological structure. In this connection, Heidegger (1988) distinguished between "Perceiving, the perceived and the perceivedness of the perceived" (p. 55). Where the first two constructs are easily defined, then perceivedness of the perceived is the meaning of the object, which cannot be empirically observed in the object itself, nor does it belong to subjectivity. Heidegger (1988) argued that perceivedness is a mode of uncovering what is encountered that releases its being to our understanding (see p. 70). Thus, "perceivedness is grounded in understanding of extantness" (p. 71) and therefore already belongs to the ontological structure of Dasein.

Heidegger (1968) therefore found that by insistently focusing on how "actuality strikes man," scholars are prevented from uncovering the meaning of being (p. 9), which is what Dasein in its everydayness covers up. Therefore, Heidegger proposed that instead of focusing on what constitutes reality, scholars should be focused on what in reality eludes people and stated that "what withdraws may even concern and claim man more essentially than anything present" (p. 9).

Thus, the attempt to uncover the meaning of being draws Dasein toward what eludes it and, in turn, this drawing toward becomes the comportment of Dasein. Heidegger argued that this comportment of Dasein as being drawn toward means that the essential nature of the human being is that of pointing toward something and that the essential nature of something that points is that of being a sign. Heidegger (1968) therefore posited that "we are a sign that is not read" (p. 18).

The notion that pointing toward something in a certain way and thus humanity being an unread sign provides a hermeneutic perspective of the being as something that can be interpreted like a text. Consequently, in social research, subjects' disclosures should be conceived as attestations of this comportment of pointing toward something (i.e., intentions toward and dealings with things), and from a hermeneutic point of view, it can therefore be argued that the insights gained from these disclosures lead to the meaning of being rather than what it means for something to be real.

Objectivity constituted by subjectivity

Husserl (1970) stated that the purpose of phenomenology is not "to secure objectivity but to understand it" (p. 189). The first step is to accept that the dual world notion of objectivity being the antithesis of subjectivity is false. Subjectivity and objectivity should rather be understood as two poles at the same experience horizon. Second, if it is the subject that objectifies, then meaning does not belong with the object, but instead it belongs to subjectivity. Therefore, when Husserl aimed to understand the meaning of the world, he was not studying the world but instead focusing his attention on how subjectivity intends the world.

The illustration below is an attempt to capture the relationships between the transcendental subjectivity and the empirical objectivity poles. The illustration further shows the different regions of subjectivity as a continuum, where meanings are given in either intentionality or apperception (see Figure 1.5). The illustration further includes deductive meanings, which is what we often define as scientific objectivity. The notion here is that what people ordinarily refer to as science and believe to be scientifically objective truths are in fact just a certain way of describing what consciousness objectifies. Therefore, deductive meanings have no truth value, but are merely technical descriptions of a generalized

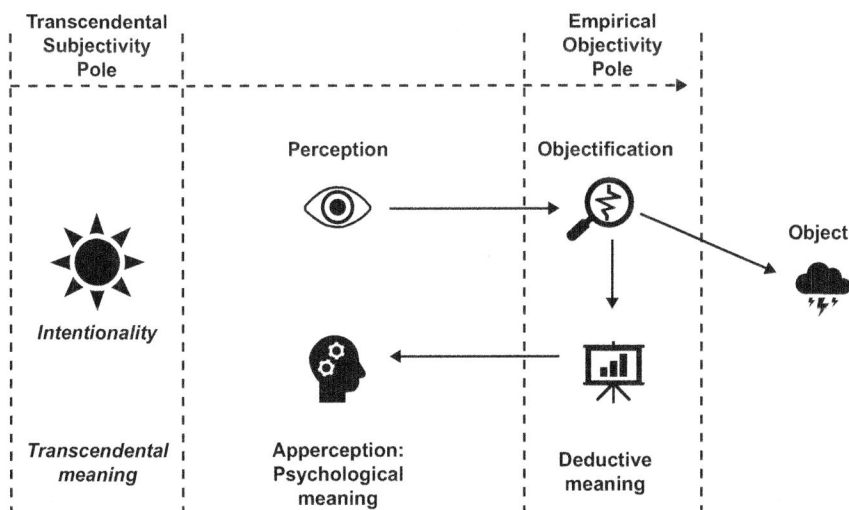

FIGURE 1.5 Demonstration of Different Regions of Subjectivity as a Continuum

phenomenon. Thus, Merleau-Ponty (1978) stated, "All my knowledge of the world, even my scientific knowledge, is gained form my own particular point of view, or from some experience of the world without which the symbols of science would be meaningless" (p. viii).

It would be misguided to conclude, as some social constructivists do, that reality is constructed, and that truth is socially negotiated. That is never the case from the phenomenological perspective because the structures of intentionality are the same for Peter and for Paul. Thus, when Berger and Luckmann (1966), from the perspective of social relativity, posited that "the knowledge of the criminal differs from the knowledge of the criminologist. It follows that specific agglomerations of reality and knowledge pertains to specific social contexts," they are, in fact, not addressing knowledge and truth in a phenomenological understanding (p. 3). However, they are merely identifying a form of know-how, which is essentially just an example of deductive meanings. Thus, Zahavi (2008) argued that phenomenologists' preoccupation with perception and subjectivity is precisely because only by investigating intentionality (i.e., the givenness of objects from consciousness) can scholars come to an understanding of how "physical objects, mathematical models, chemical processes, social relations, cultural products" appear as they do with the meanings they have (p. 674).

Scholars may be able to grasp the implication of phenomenology for scientific inquiry by considering the scientific procedure of hypothesis testing. Correlation studies aim at making statistically sound predictions about human behaviors through regression analysis. The first step is to formulate hypotheses, with the null hypothesis (H_0) stating, there is no statistically significant predictive relationship between two variables (i.e., one predictive and the other outcome variable). The alternative hypothesis (H_a) would be, there is a statistically significant predictive relationship between two variables. Inferential statistical analysis, which is simple regression, would result in the rejection of H_0 and acceptance of H_a or vice versa. Rejecting H_0 means that the predictor can statistically explain the variability (or changes) in the outcome variable and that this can be generalized if participants were randomly sampled from the targeted population.

It would appear that we were trying to evaluate a hypothetical statement by submitting it to logic; however, in the moment of applying logic, scholars suspend it and instead of looking for the "truth," search for "likelihood." The null hypothesis (H_0) can only be rejected with some degree of confidence, which is defined by alpha. By convention, alpha is set at 0.5, which means that there is only a 5% chance that the outcome is a result of chance (see Goodwin, 2010, pp. 153–154). Cohen (1994) called the conventional alpha a "permanent illusion" within inferential statistical analysis. He argued that an arbitrary variable such as the conventional alpha distorts the logical deductive process of investigation and that there is no qualitative difference between an alpha of 0.5 and an alpha of 0.6. Therefore, this example illustrates Husserl's principle of principles that perception in the final analysis is the basis of all scientific assumptions. Thus, conventional alpha is a phenomenon that assists scholars in objectifying inferential statistical measures; it is a way of describing what is already intuitively known about chance.

While the earlier example addresses perceptional subjectivity's role in objectifying deductive meanings, a better understanding of the corresponding role of transcendental subjectivity can emerge by moving into a realm yet more alien to the social researcher, quantum mechanics, where the constituting role of subjectivity is hotly debated. The problem is whether the observer is truly independent of what is being observed. The conundrum lies in the notion of superposition, where particles are known to be in different places and states at the same time, unless they are being observed. Thus, in mere passive observation, the state of superposition dissolves and the particles appear in one place only. Although this is referred to as the observer effect, it does not mean that subjectivity has a causal effect on the particles, but it raises the question of the role of subjectivity in giving objects to cognition in ways that make cognition possible. Accordingly, a recent study of the observer effect did not lend support to the hypothesis of observer independence in measuring the positions of photons. The experiment instead supported the hypothesis that the subjectivity constitutes the measured state of reality at quantum levels (Proietti et al., 2019).

Husserl (1970) emphasized that the ability to deductively predict or describe objects, although valuable, explains very little and that everything "objectively demands to be understood" (p. 189). Consequently, this can only be achieved through a better understanding of the role of subjectivity in constituting what would appear to be objective reality. However, for the social researcher, the explorations remain within psychological subjectivity. Nevertheless, a broader understanding of transcendental subjectivity enriches the phenomenological articulation of the meaning of experiences and can provide a theoretical counterweight to the natural attitude embedded in quantitative research methods in the sense that deductive meanings should be understood as just descriptions and not truths because truth belongs exclusively to subjectivity.

Lived experiences

Besides perception, **lived experiences** is likely one of the most recognizable catchphrases in applied phenomenological research. Readers often see the phenomenological research questions expressed as "what are the lived experiences of so and so group?" However, it is often not made clear what the phenomenological significance of lived experiences is or in what ways research into lived experiences provides a research outcome with phenomenological credibility.

Van Manen (2017) argued that the founders of phenomenology intended a method for recovering the lived meanings of the moment free from preconceptions and abstractions. Further, he asserted that phenomenology originally aimed at bringing past experiences into focus so that people could "reflect phenomenologically on the living meaning of the lived experience" (p. 813). Reviewing the foundational literature, it is, however, not exactly clear how he comes to these conclusions. Consequently, Zahavi (2018) argued that van Manen misrepresented the literature in this respect.

However, adding "lived" in front of experience does signify that researchers are addressing a subject matter that is different from just experiencing and perceiving. From a phenomenological psychological perspective, experience is the phenomenon of meanings that arise when perception and subjectivity make contact, which can be seen as a mental "indoor" process. The notion of lived experience, however, indicates that something more involved is happening.

Heidegger (2010) argued that the analysis of Dasein is prior to any psychological analysis (p. 44). He posited that a person exists only in the sense of carrying out intentional acts and that these acts represent certain ways of being. Where Husserl and Merleau-Ponty often took their cue from perception when engaging in a phenomenological analysis, Heidegger (2010) found that any attempt to conceptualize acts in a psychological sense, "is identical to depersonalization . . . thus psychical being has nothing to do with being as a person" (p. 47). Therefore, Dasein is not a psychological or mental phenomenon, but an ontological structure that resides in this world and encounters things and other Dasein. It is in the engagement with the world that Dasein reveals the phenomenology of the being of what and whom people encounter. Thus, Heidegger (1988) argued, "The thing does not relate to a cognitive faculty interior to the subject; instead, the cognitive faculty itself and with it this subject is structured intentionally in their ontological constitution" (p. 66). By this, he meant to say that Dasein is in the world, relating to things, and that Dasein is not an "indoor" cognitive event, and, consequently, neither is meaning. While transcendental phenomenologists and phenomenological psychologists posit a connection between perception and subjectivity, Heidegger (1988) proposed that Dasein is not perceiving but happening in temporality (see p. 278). This happening has its own kind of seeing (i.e., circumspection; Heidegger, 2010, p. 69), which is a particular way of experiencing where Dasein uncovers the beings of things by attending to objects in a practical manner and relating to them in terms of their usefulness. Consequently, circumspection should be understood as a modification of Husserl's notion of intentionality by introducing lived experience as part of its structures. Thus, *lived experience* sums up the comportment of Dasein to the outside world (see Luchte, 2008, p. 30). Therefore, the thematic description of these lived experiences is not the end-goal of phenomenological research, but rather a means to an end (i.e., the interpretation of the possibility of different modes of being for Dasein; Luchte, 2008, p. 41). Thus, Heidegger (1988) posited that "Every being has a way of being," but raises the question whether "this way of being has the same character in every being" (p. 18). This, in turn, is what concerns applied phenomenological researchers, drawing from Heidegger's existential tradition, when they sample and investigate the lived experiences of several individuals.

Temporality and meaning

Van Manen (as cited in Patton, 2002) argued that phenomenology is backward looking and that "a person cannot reflect on lived experience while living through the experience. . . . Thus, phenomenological reflection is not introspective but retrospective" (p. 104). In this connection, objective time would be what one can measure on a clock while subjective time can be understood as what the passing of time feels like. Thus, van Manen (2016) argued that phenomenological time is lived time that can be experienced differently depending on what a person is doing; for example, some days just feel longer than others (see p. 306). However, the notion of phenomenological time still presents time as a succession of "nows," and the idea of projecting past experience into future anticipations is typically how psychologists relate to the connection between time and experience.

In contrast, when phenomenologists such as Heidegger or Merleau–Ponty spoke of time, they collapsed the notion of time and subjectivity into what is referred to as temporality. Heidegger (2010) posited that "Dasein does not exist as a sum of momentary realities of experiences that succeed each other and disappear" (p. 357). Temporality should therefore not be understood as an actual succession of events in the manner of sequences in a movie. Instead, temporality is to be understood as the "unity of future, past and present," which presents an uninterrupted horizon from which Dasein can understand the meaning of the world (Heidegger, 1988, p. 266).

Merleau-Ponty (1978) argued that the peculiarity of temporality is that both what we, in memory, consider to be something we recall from the past and what we project into the future actually only exist in the present (see p. 413). He therefore argued that the mind is not

> the bodily storage of the past. . . . A preserved perception is a perception, it continues to exist, it persists in the present, and it does not open behind us that dimension of escape an absence that we call the past.
>
> *(p. 413)*

Accordingly, contemporary neuropsychology posits that memories of past experiences are not reproductions of what actually happened. The appearance that memories represent an experience from the past is essentially the phenomenology of retrospection. It is therefore argued that what is recalled is not an actual memory, but current beliefs about what is remembered, which serves the purpose of the individual's dealings with challenges in the present (Ofengenden, 2014).

For example, reflect on the expression "back in the good old days." This statement illustrates the unity of the past, present and future. It can be construed as a speech–act that conveys an implicit critique of the present. At the same time, this statement is embedded with a hope for a future molded in the image of a past that never actually was. Therefore, the understanding and interpretation of what these good old days are all about do not exclusively depend on people's knowledge about any particular point of time in history.

An understanding of temporality as the horizon of meaning is relevant for social researchers because their main source of data is interviews. Thus, understanding that subjects possess a privileged position in disclosing their lived experiences in time should lead researchers to interpret what is being disclosed from a perspective of temporality and not actual time. Therefore, the disclosures speak more to the centrality of the present than anything in the past (Ricoeur, 1979).

From Heidegger's philosophical perspective, the meaning of Dasein's being should be understood as temporality. This notion, coupled with Ricoeur's hermeneutic perspective, provides theoretical justification for the phenomenological researcher; when stating the assumption, the horizon of temporality allows subjects to interpret lived experience similarly to a plot in a storyline. Thus, the researcher is in a position to posit that scattered memories of events are fused together into a fictional narrative, which is a manifestation of the subjects' attempts to understand their own being.

Phenomenology as a philosophy and as an empirical research paradigm

As indicated earlier, phenomenology was not developed for the purpose of social research, and the methods and concepts that we have encountered so far served a philosophical project. Applied phenomenological research is confronted with several challenges: How to bridge the first-person perspective of phenomenological philosophy with the third-person reality of empirical research. In other words, how to justify substituting one's perceptions and intuitions with those of other people and, more specifically, how to do so while still achieving a credible phenomenological outcome. Consequently, the challenge is also how to bridge the phenomenological doctrine of pure description with the need for some form of interpretation of the other person's lifeworld.

In the following, we will briefly consider how these challenges are met by phenomenological psychology that draws from Husserl and Merleau-Ponty as well as contemporary hermeneutic thoughts on the interpretation of lived experiences. The aim is not to review a wide range of applied phenomenological schools, but to consider the theoretical justification for what we could call the naturalization of phenomenology (i.e., phenomenology as a social research methodology).

Phenomenological psychology

Husserl (2017) thought of psychology as a science of facts and realities and that the phenomena that psychology is concerned with are real events that occur with real people in time and space (see p. 44). Phenomenologists came to be quite critical of empirical psychology because, influenced by behaviorism, it was seen to approach perception only in terms of causality. Thus, Merleau-Ponty posited,

One does not see how a social psychology would be possible. . . . If one really thinks that perception is a function of exterior variables, this schema is applicable only to the corporeal and physical conditioning, and psychology is condemned to . . . considering man as only a set of nervous terminations upon which physio-chemical agents play.

(Merleau-Ponty et al., 1968, p. 23)

In Merleau-Ponty's view, a more expansive understanding of the psychology of perception requires a phenomenological perspective as well.

Husserl elaborated at length on why and how phenomenology is not psychology and sometimes seemed very critical of psychology. He nevertheless saw a close connection between the two fields and even a mutually beneficial relationship. Therefore, when attempting to demonstrate a valid naturalization of Husserl's ideas, descriptive phenomenological psychology has a clear advantage because Husserl continuously contrasted his phenomenological project with that of psychology and, therefore, also provided detailed insights into what kind of psychology he had in mind.

Husserl identified the "touch point" between phenomenology and psychology by noting that these paradigms are used to investigate the same thing, but from different perspectives. Phenomenological psychologists make the dimensionality of the experienced phenomenon the theme of description, whereas phenomenologists, after the phenomenological reduction, transcend the concrete experience and make the modes of experiencing the theme of the investigation. Thus, Husserl (2017) stated, "We have thus a remarkable thoroughgoing parallelism between a phenomenological psychology and a transcendental phenomenology . . . to each empirical determination on the one side there must correspond a parallel feature on the other" (p. 15). In other words, the same phenomenon is subject to either a phenomenological psychological or a transcendental phenomenological investigation depending on whether or not the researcher has performed the epoché and reduction.

Thus, without the epoché and reduction, empirical psychology, according to Husserl (1970), is not equipped to explore transcendental subjectivity, and he therefore argued that due to its "capture" by natural scientific method, empirical psychology remains focused on what can be seen and measured (p. 203). Hence, the phenomenological psychologists' research domain is what Husserl referred to as the surplus of data beyond the immediate perception, which can best be described as *apperceptions*. Consequently, Husserl (1970) proposed that the psychologist may engage in thematic reflections of the self, the apperceptions of other people, as well as recollection and inquiry into the development of the self and others, with or without a theoretical perspective, which leads to categorization and labeling of phenomena (see p. 209).

However, Husserl pointed out that psychologists may, from their vantage point, at any time, execute the transcendental epoché. Upon returning from the phenomenological to the psychological domain, their perspectives on apperception will be changed. This is because they have had direct experience with transcendental subjectivity and therefore are cognizant of the constituting role of intentionality. In this manner, transcendental phenomenology plays a role in enriching phenomenological psychology by broadening the horizons of the researchers. Thus, Husserl (1970) stated,

> all the new sorts of apperceptions which are exclusively tied to the phenomenological reduction together with the new sort of language – all this, which before was complete hidden and inexpressible . . . becomes apperceived as its newly revealed intentional background of constitutive accomplishment.
>
> *(p. 210)*

It is for that reason some phenomenological psychologists propose a transcendental reflection prior to engaging in phenomenological psychological analysis.

The hermeneutic bridge to phenomenology

The critique of phenomenology as a research paradigm rests on the argument that, from an empirical standpoint, researchers do not have the ability to truly access anybody's first-person point of view. When subjects communicate their observations, their words do not open a door into their minds through which the researcher can see subjectivity in action. Further, Dennett (1991) raised the question of the credibility of such disclosures because scholars have no way of really knowing if subjects are misrepresenting their experiences or simply fabricating the whole thing from imagination. Consequently, he stated, "We can't be sure that the speech-acts we observe express real beliefs about actual experiences; perhaps they express only apparent beliefs about nonexistent experiences" (Dennett, 1991, p. 78). In qualitative research, scholars often write their way out of this by stating that their assumption is that subjects are truthful and reasonably accurate in their disclosures of their lived experiences. This is honorable, but, in itself, this assumption does not provide the phenomenological research with any degree of theoretical credibility. The question remains, how can we theoretically justify substituting a first-person perspective of our own thoughts and intuitions with the researcher's perspective on another person's disclosures?

Heidegger (2010) argued that Dasein is not only to be understood as being in the world, but also as being with others (see p. 116). In other words, other people are not perceived just as objects in the world. However, they are encountered in the world in their ways of being, such as being an artist, being a writer, etc. Therefore, being with something and being with others is the existential mode of Dasein. Heidegger (2010), hence, posited that the being of Dasein is dominated by "the others" (p. 123). Nevertheless, Heidegger did not mean others in the sense of specific people. He referred to others as a general notion of the social rules of interaction that people have internalized and which guides most everyday decisions (i.e., "the they"). He emphasized, "we enjoy ourselves and have fun the way *they* enjoy themselves, we read, see and judge literature and art the way *they* see and judge" and therefore "everyone is the other and no one is himself" (p. 124).

Ricoeur (1994) further argued that, despite the phenomenological reduction, where the transcendental ego is isolated from the natural world, "it" still knows that it is not alone, but within the reduction the transcendental "ego" can only constitute the other based on itself. Therefore, people already know that the other person is not an object in the world, but a subject such as themselves. Consequently, Ricoeur (1994) posited that "presupposition of the other is contained . . . in the formation of the very sense of the sphere of ownness" (p. 332). Therefore, conceiving of the other person is not the same as conceiving of, for example, a kangaroo. The other person is not an object, but another subject. The difference is that while "I," the subject, can never really get to know a kangaroo, I can achieve a pretty good grasp of another subject through a very intimate form of apperception because I am perceiving somebody like me.

Merleau-Ponty asked

> how could I conceive, precisely as, his colors, his pain, his world, except as in accordance with the colors I see, the pains I have had, the world wherein I live? But at least my private world has ceased to be mine only; it is now the instrument which another plays, the dimension of a generalized life which is grafted onto my own.
>
> *(Merleau-Ponty et al., 1968, p. 11)*

Consequently, the notion that oneself is like the other opens a door to an approach in which researchers' own lived experiences are part of the reflective process, ending up in a synthesis of meaning.

Ricoeur (2019) posited that "human sciences may be said to be hermeneutical inasmuch as their object displays some of the features constitutive of a text, and inasmuch as their methodologies develops the same kind of procedures as those of *Auslegung* or text-interpretation" (p. 159). The subject matter of phenomenological research is almost always verbal accounts of lived experiences. Consequently, a hermeneutic analysis of the first-person disclosures acquires a similarity to the analysis of a "text," where researchers try to tease out "the meaning implied from the literal meaning" (Scott-Bauman, 2012, p. 78).

In this connection, Heidegger (2010) argued that communication is the primary mode of being in the world (see p. 59). In other words, everyday understandings of what is going on are disclosed in communication by the normative they-self, which projects an "average" interpretation of reality, as it is experienced by most people. Communication and the comprehension of the meaning of what is being talked about thus require a shared, by all parties, a priori understanding. The central theoretical argument is that understanding is fundamentally grounded in interpretation, and "Dasein is therefore entrusted to interpretation" and "speech-acts" reveal the being of oneself and of others (Heidegger, 2010, p. 162). It is therefore through the interpretation of words and sentences that the researcher can gain insights into the meaning-making of subjects. Ricoeur's legacy to the field of phenomenology would therefore become the exploration of the hermeneutic dimension of phenomenology in a manner that can be more readily applied for the purpose of social research.

In contrast, Dennett (2003) proposed an approach he called heterophenomenology ("the phenomenology of others as opposed the transcendental phenomenology of oneself"). Dennett (1991) argued that it does not matter whether disclosures of lived experiences are accurate and that instead of assuming that the subjects are "truthful," researchers should assume the stance that "the uttered noises are to be interpreted as things the subjects wanted to say, of propositions they meant to assert for various reasons" (p. 76). Dennett did not reference Ricoeur in his elaborations, but there is a striking similarity except the fact that Dennett did not attempt to connect the sense of the other to transcendental consciousness. Accordingly, Dennett proposed that instead of treating the subjects as conveyers of first-person experiences, researchers should approach their disclosures as if they were a story. This does not mean scholars should assume that the subjects are not truthful, but simply treat their accounts as one would treat a novel. Dennett (1991) thus defined the true subject matter of empirical phenomenological research as "speech-acts" (p. 76).

Dennett (1991) proposed that

> the heterophenomenologist, lets the subject's text constitute the subject's heterophenomenological world, a world determined by fiat by the text. . . . This permits the heterophenomenologist to postpone the knotty problem of what the relation might be between that fictional world and the real world.
>
> *(p. 81)*

This is, however, a somewhat confounding statement because it is never really the phenomenologist's objective to determine such relations. The phenomenologist's objective is to elucidate the meaning of the experience with regard to the realm of subjectivity they are exploring. The challenge is not to discard the troublesome parts of phenomenological philosophy, but to build a bridge where the research is not only intuitively reasonable, but also phenomenologically credible.

Summary

The takeaway from our short account of Husserl, Heidegger and Merleau-Ponty ought to be that phenomenology is not a unified philosophy but fragmented along distinct epistemological and ontological domains. If we were to summarize the essence of phenomenology, then it is a study of subjectivity and existence from the perspective of epistemology and ontology. Husserl spoke of the walled-off consciousness and transcendental subjectivity in terms of the overarching meaning-giving structures (i.e., intentionality). Merleau-Ponty followed Husserl but found that it is not possible to separate consciousness from the body, and therefore scholars cannot speak only of the transcendental ego as the conveyer of meaning without factoring in the body as the mediator.

Heidegger's domain, while related to consciousness, is quite different as he assumed a distinct ontological stance and therefore saw phenomenology primarily as a method. Heidegger's focus was on the meaning of being, and he noted that being is always being in this world. His endeavor therefore aimed at a hermeneutic interpretation of Dasein, its comportment and modes of being. Where Husserl's conceptualization of intentionality is challenging to grasp due to the influence of psychological ideas and commonly held notions of cause and effect, Heidegger's notion of Dasein is complex and challenging to decode from the literature. Our reading of Heidegger arrives at the following insights: Dasein is a phenomenon of human beings; therefore, the essence of Dasein is existence. Dasein experiences are derived from circumspective dealings with things; therefore, the being of Dasein is "taking care of." The meaning of Dasein's being is temporality (i.e., potential possibilities of being).

The illustration below is an attempt to summarize the phenomenological philosophies that we have encountered in this chapter (see Figure 1.6). We can see that the literature presents two quite different phenomenological perspectives: one that takes its starting point in perception and another that takes its cue from lived experiences, which brings us back to our Cartesian starting point in *cogito ergo sum*. However, both orientations bring the first-person perspective back to the social research agenda.

Phenomenology was not intended for empirical research purposes, and consequently, there is no instruction to be found in the works of Husserl, Heidegger or Merleau-Ponty on how to conduct social research. It is up to the social researcher to draw on the aspects of phenomenology that can inspire and inform research into the meaning of lived experiences. In this connection, it is important to point out that phenomenology asserts that there are universal truths, which are embedded in the structure of intentionality or transcendental subjectivity that constitutes how the world is given to people in cognition. This does not mean that reality is socially constructed, which implies that truth is relative. Therefore, the idea of social constructivism rests on a misunderstanding of the relationship between subjectivity and objectivity as one of causality. Further, social constructivists confound knowledge with mere deductive descriptions of reality. These descriptions are, of course, socially constructed, but this fact does not cause objectivity to be socially constructed as well.

The issue of subjectivity and meaning becomes somewhat more complex when addressing Heidegger's phenomenology because it is so different in the

Realm of Consciousness	The world in the mind "Epistemological"		Being in the world "Ontological"
Realm of Consciousness	Transcendental Consciousness	Embodied Consciousness	Dasein
Method	Epoché & Phenomenological Reduction	Epoché & Limited Reduction	Interpretation
Orientation	Transcendental Philosophy	Philosophycal Psychology	Hermeneutics
Domain	Intentionality	Apperception	Lived Experiences
Data Source	Thinking Acts	Perception	Circumspection
Scope	Transcendental Subjectivity	Embodied Subjectivity	Being of Beings
Advocate	Husserl	Merleau-Ponty	Heidegger

FIGURE 1.6 Characteristics of Phenomenological Philosophies

sense that he did seek the meaning in some mental processes and that meaning is not an event, but already out there, ready to be discovered. Consequently, researchers must (from the very beginning) have their phenomenological orientations clearly defined in order to avoid confusing terminologies, scopes and domain, which in turn threatens the credibility of the research. In short, the researchers should make it clear whether they are studying one of the regional subjectivities or studying the existential phenomenon of being in this world and consequently how this affects their choice of methodology in the sense of analysis versus interpretation.

The foundational literature, while not straightforwardly transferable to research, does provide the social researcher a philosophical basis and a conceptual framework to work with. Specifically, the literature points to apperception as an empirically researchable domain that ultimately is connected with transcendental subjectivity, give or take a phenomenological reduction or two. Further, the considerations that allow phenomenology to connect with hermeneutics provide the researcher with a productive framework to study lived experiences in much the same manner as if it were a text. The illustration below is an attempt at demonstrating the naturalization of phenomenology when drawing from the foundational literature we have encountered in this chapter (see Figure 1.7).

The world in the mind	Dasein in the world
Phenomenological Psychology	Hermeneutic Phenomenology
Phenomena	**Beings**
Psychological subjectivity	Dealings and coping
Apperceptions	Speech-acts
Retention and protection horizon	Perceivedness of the perceived
Phenomenological reflections	Interpretation of the "text of lifeworld"
With or without theory	Interpretation in temporality
Thematic categorization	Reflection on oneself as the other person
Labeling	Synthesis of meaning
Psychological meaning	**Meaning of being**

FIGURE 1.7   Illustration Demonstrating the Naturalization of Phenomenology

Note: Hermeneutic phenomenology in this figure is Heidegger's notion of phenomenology.

References

Berger, P. L., & Luckmann, T. (1966). *The social construct of reality: A treatise in the sociology of knowledge.* Anchor Books. ISBN: 978-0-385-05898-8

Cohen, J. (1994). The earth is round (p < 0.5). *American Psychologist, 49*(12), 997–1003. https://doi.org/10.1037/0003-066X.49.12.997

Creswell, J. W. (2007). *Qualitative inquiry & research design: Choosing among five approaches.* Sage Publications.

Dahlstrom, D. O. (2018). The early Heidegger's phenomenology. In D. Zahavi (Ed.), *The Oxford handbook of the history of phenomenology* (pp. 211–228). Oxford University Press. ISBN-13: 978-0198755340

Davidsen, A. S. (2013). Phenomenological approaches in psychology and health sciences. *Qualitative Research in Psychology, 10*(3), 318–339. https://doi.org/10.1080/14780887.2011.608466

Dennett, D. C. (1991). *Consciousness explained.* Back Bay Books. Little Brown Company. ISBN-10: 0316180661

Dennett, D. C. (2003). Who is on first? Heterophenomenology explained. *Journal of Conscious Studies, 10*(9), 19–30.

de Sá, F. L. F. R. G., Henriques, M. A. P., & Velez, M. A. M. R. B. A. (2019). A presença da fenomenologia na investigação em enfermagem: Mapeamento das teses de doutoramento em Portugal; La presencia de la fenomenología en la investigación en enfermería: mapeo de las tesis doctorales en Portugal (Phenomenology in nursing research: Mapping of doctoral theses in Portugal). *Revista de Enfermagem Referência*, 4(23), 9–19. https://doi.org/10.12707/RIV19038

Flynn, S. V., & Korcuska, J. S. (2018). Credible phenomenological research: A mixed method study. *Counselor Education & Supervision*, 57, 34–50. https://doi.org/10.1002/ceas.12092

Giorgi, A. (2004). A way to overcome the methodological vicissitudes involved in researching subjectivity. *Journal of Phenomenological Psychology*, 35(1), 1–25. https://doi.org/10.1163/1569162042321107

Giorgi, A. (2006). Concerning variations in the application of the phenomenological method. *The Humanistic Psychologist*, 34(4), 305–319. https://doi.org/10.1207/s15473333thp3404_2

Goodwin, C. J. (2010). *Research in psychology: Methods and design*. Wiley. ISBN: 978-1-119-33044-8

Gringeri, C., Barusch, A., & Cambron, C. (2013). Examining foundations of qualitative research: A review of social work dissertations, 2008–2010. *Journal of Social Work Education*, 49(4), 760–773. https://doi.org/10.1080/10437797.2013.812910

Heffernan, G. (2015). The paradox of objectless presentations in early phenomenology: A brief history of the intentional object from Bolzano to Husserl, with concise analyses of the positions of Brentano, Frege, Twardowski, and Meinong. *Studia Phaenomenologica*, 15, 67–91. https://doi.org/10.5840/studphaen2015155

Heidegger, M. (1968). *What is called thinking?* Harper & Row. ISBN-10: 006090528X

Heidegger, M. (1988). *The basic problems of phenomenology*. Indiana University Press. ISBN-10: 0253176875

Heidegger, M. (1989). *Die grundprobleme der phaenomenologie*. Vittorio Klostermann. ISBN-13: 978-3465034193

Heidegger, M. (2010). *Being and time*. University of New York Press. ISBN-10: 1438432763

Husserl, E. (1960). *Cartesian meditations*. Springer-Science. ISBN: 978-94-017-4662-5

Husserl, E. (1970). *The crisis of European sciences and transcendental phenomenology: An introduction to phenomenological philosophy*. Northwestern University Press. ISBN: 081010458X

Husserl, E. (1973). *The idea of phenomenology*. Martinius Nijhoff. ISBN: 9024701147

Husserl, E. (2001). *The shorter logical investigations*. Routledge. ISBN: 9780415241922

Husserl, E. (2017). *Ideas: General introduction to pure phenomenology*. Unwin Brothers Ltd. ISBN-10: 0415519039

Kant, I. (2007). *Critique of pure reason*. Penguin Group. ISBN: 9780140447477

King, D. B., Viney, W., & Woody, W. D. (2009). *A history of psychology: Ideas and context*. Pearson Education, Inc. ISBN-10: 0205512135

Lopez, K. A., & Willis, D. G. (2004). Descriptive versus interpretive phenomenology: Their contributions to nursing knowledge. *Qualitative Health Research*, 14(5), 726–735. https://doi.org/10.1177/1049732304263638

Luchte, J. (2008). *Heidegger's early philosophy: The phenomenology of ecstatic temporality*. Continuum. ISBN: 9781847062970

Luft, S. (2018). Kant, neo-Kantianism and phenomenology. In D. Zahavi (Ed.), *The Oxford handbook of the history of phenomenology* (pp. 45–67). Oxford University Press. ISBN-13: 978-0198755340

Merleau-Ponty, M. (1967). *The structure of behavior*. Beacon Press. ISBN-10: 0807029874

Merleau-Ponty, M. (1978). *Phenomenology of perception*. Routledge & Kegan Paul. ISBN-10: 0710036132

Merleau-Ponty, M., Lefort, C., & Lingis, A. (1968). *The visible and the invisible followed by working notes*. Northwestern University Press. ISBN: 9780810104570

Moran, D. (2000). *Introduction to phenomenology*. Routledge. ISBN-10: 0415183731

Ofengenden, T. (2014). Memory formation and belief. *Dialogue in Philosophy, Mental and Neuro Sciences, 7*(2), 34–44.

Patton, M. Q. (2002). *Qualitative research & evaluation methods* (3rd ed.). Sage Publications. ISBN-13: 9780761919711

Proietti, M., Picksont, A., Graffitti, F., Barrow, P., Kundy, D., Branciard, C., Ringbauer, M., & Fedrizzi, A. (2019). Experimental test of local observer independence. *Science Advances, 5*(9). https://doi.org/10.1126/sciadv.aaw9832

Ricoeur, P. (1979). The human experience of time and narrative. *Research in Phenomenology, 9*(1), 17–34.

Ricoeur, P. (1994). *Oneself as another*. The University of Chicago Press. ISBN: 0-226-71329-6

Ricoeur, P. (2019). *Hermeneutics and the human sciences*. Cambridge University Press. ISBN-10: 0521280028

Rockmore, T. (2011). *Kant and phenomenology*. The University of Chicago Press. ISBN: 9780226723402

Romdenh-Romluc, K. (2018). Science in Merleau-Ponty's phenomenology. In D. Zahavi (Ed.), *The Oxford handbook of the history of phenomenology* (pp. 340–359). Oxford University Press. ISBN-13: 978-0198755340

Scott-Baumann, A. (2012). *Ricoeur and the hermeneutics of suspicion*. Continuum. ISBN-13: 9781441170392

Tan, H., Wilson, A., & Olver, I. (2009). Ricoeur's theory of interpretation: An instrument for data interpretation in hermeneutic phenomenology. *International Journal of Qualitative Methods, 8*(4), 1–15. https://doi.org/10.1177/160940690900800401

van Manen, M. (2016). *Phenomenology of practice*. Routledge. ISBN-10: 1611329442

van Manen, M. (2017). Phenomenology in its original sense. *Qualitative Health Research, 27*(6), 810–825. https://doi.org/10.1177/1049732317699381

Woo, H., & Heo, N. (2013). A content analysis of qualitative research in select ACA journals (2005–2010). *Counseling Outcome Research and Evaluation, 4*(1), 13–25. https://doi.org/10.1177/2150137812472195

Zahavi, D. (2008). Phenomenology. In D. Moran (Ed.), *The Routledge companion to twentieth century philosophy* (pp. 661–692). ISBN: 0-203-87936-8 Master e-book ISBN

Zahavi, D. (2018). Getting it quite wrong: Van Manen and Smith on phenomenology. *Qualitative Health Research, 29*(6), 900–907. https://doi.org/10.1177/1049732318817547

Zahavi, D. (2019). *Phenomenology the basics*. Routledge. ISBN: 978-1-138-21670-9

2

UNDERSTANDING THE PHENOMENOLOGICAL THEORY OF EXPERIENCE (CONSCIOUSNESS, INTENTIONALITY AND ESSENCE)

Objectives

Readers will be able to

1   Conceptualize the phenomenon from different phenomenological perspectives.
2   Conceptualize the experience of phenomena from four different phenomenological perspectives.
3   Understand the connection between consciousness, intentionality and givenness.
4   Understand the connection between psychological subjectivity, apperception and experience horizon.
5   Understand the difference between, on one hand, subjectivity and perceptions and, on the other hand, Dasein and circumspection.
6   Understand the role of temporality in the emplotment of the narrative self.
7   Understand how different phenomenological conceptualizations of the experience align with certain overarching research questions.

What is an object (i.e., a phenomenon)?

In order to visually perceive an object, it must have certain features, such as shape and a surface capable of reflecting certain light waves (see Husserl, 1973, p. XVII). In other words, each object in the real world has its own *thingliness* about it. From an empirical psychological perspective, Eagly and Chaiken (1993) further posited that objects are encoded with certain stimuli traits "that denote the objects and elicit evaluative responses from the beholder" (see p. 5). From this statement, researchers can see reflected the natural scientific preoccupation with cause and effect and a perspective on experience that seems to make little distinction between the actual object and the object as perceived. Therefore, the problem with such conceptualization is the lack of insights into what it means when an object becomes an object of thought because this is the only way people can actually know objects.

Heidegger (2010) pointed out that the literal English translation of the Greek word phenomenon has a double meaning in the sense that it means both an appearance and appearing as something the object in fact is not. Heidegger (2010) thus defined the meaning of the word *phenomenon* in the following manner: "that something which does not show itself but announces itself through something that does show itself" (see p. 28). Thus, scholars have two understandings of the term phenomenon: one that is psychological in nature as it concentrates on how objects appear in the mind and one that is phenomenological, focusing on the meanings. Accordingly, the phenomenology is never just what is perceived or merely lived through, but rather its meaning, which lies beyond people's immediate apprehension of what they encounter and perceive.

In *Critique of Pure Reason*, Kant (2007) stated that it remains doubtful whether the cause of a perception is internal or external. As he elucidated, "Whether in fact all so-called outer perceptions are not merely a play of our inner sense or point to actual external objects as their cause" (p. 74). Kant assumed an idealist position, where he did not deny the fact that objects exist externally from consciousness. However, he argued that such objects are not perceived directly. The idea of the object is in immediate perception. It is therefore not the object that constitutes the experience, but the other way around. It is consciousness that constitutes the object as a phenomenon.

Kant (2007) further posited that while the objects people hold in mind are just appearances of objects, then the manner in which they perceive these are "peculiar to us" (p. 75). Consequently, Kant articulated a distinction between objects as they appear in perception (i.e., phenomena) and objects as meanings (i.e., noumena). Accordingly, Kant referred to *phenomena* as "beings of sense" and *noumena* as "beings of understanding" and posited that noumena is "what understanding must think without reference to the intuition" (Kant, 2007, p. 258). Noumena is therefore not the psychological representation of the object, but certain qualities of a person's understanding, which are necessary in order determine the meaning of the phenomena (p. 262).

From a psychological perspective, Zahavi (2019a) stated that "what we see is never given in isolation but is surrounded by and situated in a horizon that affects the meaning of what we see" (p. 11). In other words, context and temporality is the horizon from which meanings of phenomena appear. The illustration below is an attempt to show how the perception of tones produced by instruments acquires the phenomenal appearance of music, which, simultaneously, may acquire the meaning as art contingent on the spatial and temporal horizons of the experience (see Figure 2.1).

However, phenomenology should not be reduced to merely a thematic description of how objects appear to us in apperception (see Zahavi, 2019a, p. 13). The thematic analysis is only a first step in a process, where the phenomenologists

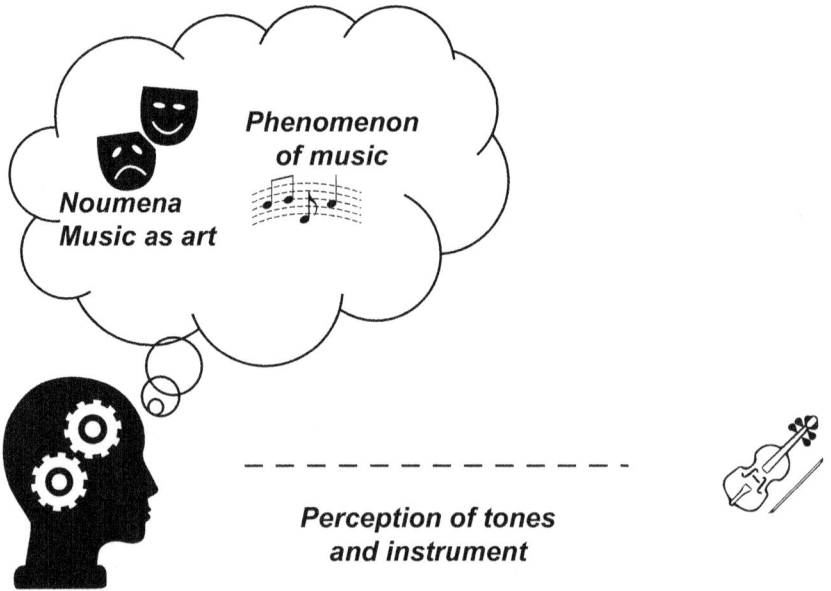

FIGURE 2.1 Demonstration of How the Phenomenon of Music Is Experienced

study objects and their appearances in order to gain insight into what it means for something to be real.

In relation to this concept, Husserl (2001) is famous for stating "We must go back to the things themselves" (p. 88). By this, he meant that people would not be able to gain any firm insights into the meaning of the world by merely focusing on apperceptions. Instead, researchers must study intentionality and try to grasp the meaning of the thinking acts themselves. Husserl (2017) therefore stated,

> It is part of the peculiarity of consciousness generally to be continually fluctuating in different dimensions. . . . The phenomenologically particular object is then just this imagery of the thing in the whole wealth of concreteness, precisely as it participates in the flow of experience . . . now in this aspect now in that.

> *(p. 209)*

Thus, the transcendental perspective is that the meanings are constituted by something that is not found within the objects themselves nor within the horizon of apperception, but in how objects are given to cognition by consciousness.

In contrast, Heidegger (2010) argued that scholars are only "dealing the formal concept of phenomenon" if "we leave undetermined which beings are to be addressed as phenomena" (p. 29). Thus, Heidegger posited that "The phenomenon in the phenomenological understanding is always just what constitutes being" (p. 33). Therefore, "phenomenology is the science of the being of beings" (p. 33). Consequently, Heidegger (2010) argued that it is not only through perception that people encounter objects, but in their dealings with objects in terms of "handling, using and taking care of" them (p. 67). It is therefore in how people handle objects in the world that their being is revealed.

Based on Heidegger's (2010) perspective, the phenomenological interpretation of objects is not their appearing qualities as the perspective of intentionality assumes, but rather the thematic description of their modes of being in the world as, for example, being useful. Heidegger (2010) thus stated,

> the less we just stare at the thing called hammer, the more we take hold of it and use it, the more original our relation to it becomes and the more undisguisedly it is encountered as what it is, as a useful thing.
>
> *(p. 69)*

Heidegger continued this exploration of the hammer by further stating, "the act of hammering itself discovers the specific handiness of the hammer . . . No matter how keenly we just look at the outward appearance of things constituted in one way or the other, we cannot discover handiness" (p. 69).

From the aforementioned text, it becomes clear that there are at least three phenomenological perspectives on people's experiences of objects. The first perspective is what Heidegger (2010, p. 29) referred to as a *vulgar understanding of phenomenology* (i.e., the study of the ways objects appear in the mind as phenomena and how people draw their meanings from spatial and temporal horizons). This conceptualization is what scholars would refer to, within descriptive phenomenological psychology, as the study of apperception. The second perspective unfolds within the *phenomenological reduction*, where the focus is no longer on the phenomena, but on intentionality and the noumena (i.e., the meaning of the thinking act toward the phenomena). This conceptualization belongs to the domain of transcendental phenomenology. Finally, Heidegger's perspective broke with all of the above, by focusing on the *being of beings* in terms of what people's actions and engagement with objects in the world reveal about the meaning of their beings.

Thus, by considering the objects, we have laid our three distinct phenomenological perspectives: psychological, transcendental and hermeneutic. Whereas the first two perspectives are epistemological (i.e., how people can know the meaning of the world around them), the latter is ontological (i.e., what the world around people means). The illustration below shows how the fields of phenomenology have different perspectives on an object, informing how phenomenological researchers conceptualize the experience, which we will consider in more detail in the following section (see Figure 2.2).

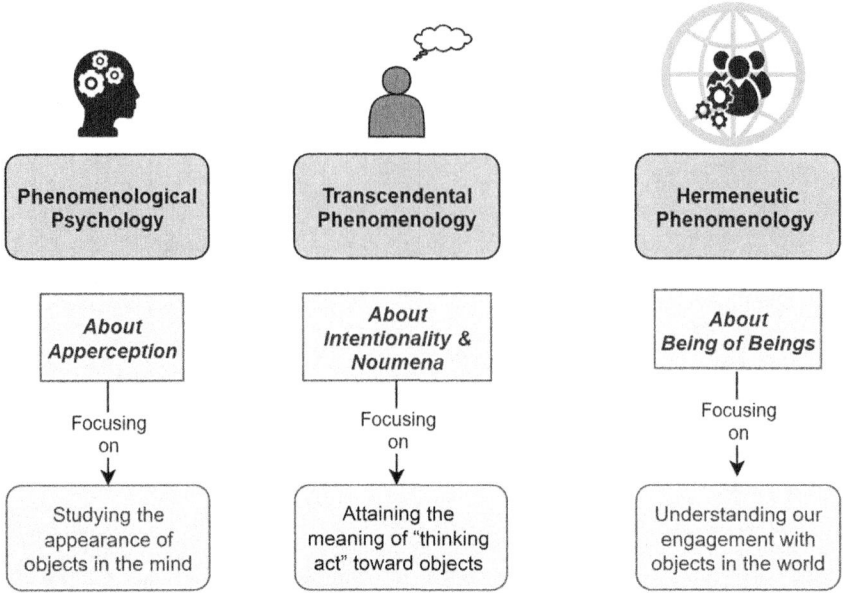

FIGURE 2.2 Fields of Phenomenology and the Respective Perspective About Objects

Note: Hermeneutic phenomenology in this figure is Heidegger's notion of phenomenology.

Understanding the process of experience from a phenomenological perspective

Often, social researchers will propose research questions regarding social phenomena that include the word *perception* and claim to study perceptions of their subjects regarding a specific phenomenon. The interest in perception is clearly influenced by both Husserl and Merleau-Ponty's fixation of this intentional act as a starting point for the investigation of transcendental subjectivity. The problem here is that social researchers are not in the business of studying this region of subjectivity and perception does not actually mean what many social researchers intend it to mean (i.e., the perspective of psychological subjectivity).

In general, perception is not conceived as anything more than just apprehending something. Thus, Heidegger (1988) argued that "perceiving as intentional, falls so little into a subjective sphere that as soon as we wish to talk about such sphere, perceiving immediately transcends" (p. 69). Perceiving is simply an act that allows people to encounter something. Therefore, when social researchers talk about perception, they actually mean what something is experienced like or experienced to be.

Our previous elaborations indicate that the different phenomenological orientations have quite different conceptualizations of experiences. Merleau-Ponty vividly expressed this underappreciated challenge of understanding the nature of experience in the following manner: "If we ask ourselves what this is, what seeing is, and what thing or world is, we enter into a labyrinth of difficulties and contradictions" (Merleau-Ponty et al., 1968, p. 3). In the following, we will try to untangle some of these difficulties by looking at how experience is conceptualized within transcendental, psychological and hermeneutic phenomenology, which hopefully can assist emerging scholars in framing their phenomenological studies appropriately.

The mental look at the transcendental experience

Kant (2007) argued that knowledge is transcendental when that knowledge is not about objects but about how people know these objects (see p. 52). Further, Kant distinguished between empirical knowledge and pure knowledge. While empirical knowledge is always derived from experiences, pure knowledge exists a priori and is not caused by any experiences with objects or phenomena. It is a form of pregiven knowledge that makes it possible to have an experience in the first place. The transcendental phenomenological assumption is that this pure knowledge is ultimately what constitutes the meaning of reality and objectivity and it therefore became the focus of Husserl's investigations. Accordingly, Husserl (2001) stated, "We are plainly concerned with a quite necessary generalization of the question as to the conditions of the possibility of experience" (p. 74). Consequently, the proper realm of investigating the meaning of the world became intentionality, which "excludes the natural performance of all empirical apperceptions and positing" (Husserl, 2001, p. 95).

Thus, from a transcendental phenomenological perspective, objects appear in consciousness not as a consequence of their existence. Instead, experience is the result of objects appearing in a manner correlated with the mode of consciousness (Ashworth, 2017). In fact, it makes no difference to this form of experience whether the objects are real or just imagined (see Husserl, 2001, p. 216). Husserl (2017) believed that through the proper procedures of phenomenological reduction, which we will consider in the following chapter, it is possible to turn the modes of intentionality into objects of phenomenological investigation, where the mental look takes over from the empirical way of investigating phenomena (see p. 133). Husserl (2017) explained the mental look in terms of "replacing the practice of living in perception . . . attention turned towards the perceived object both in observation and in theoretical inquiry, by that of directing our glance on that of perceiving itself" (p. 256).

To demonstrate the distinction between psychology and phenomenology, Husserl emphasized a unique nonpsychological terminology for the purpose of describing the way in which consciousness correlates with the world: noesis and noema. Noesis can be explained as "thinking acts," where noema is "what is thought" (Moran, 2000, p. 55). The thinking acts, or noesis, are the contentless structures of intentionality that make experience possible. According to Husserl (2001), these structures are universal to consciousness and characterized by a certain way reality is given by consciousness to experience (e.g., "presentative in a presentation, judicial in a judgment etc." [p. 212]).

Experience and Judgment (first published in 1939) provides the most lucid example of Husserl's insights in his interrogation of the meaning of *judging*. Judging is clearly a cognitive act that serves the purpose of gaining knowledge about something. Then, according to Husserl (1973), in order for this cognitive act to be possible, this *something* has to be given to cognition in a certain manner (see p. 19). He thus stated, "the act of judgement requires something underlying, about which it judges, an object-about which, it is necessary that the existent be so pregiven that it can become the object of a judgment" (p. 19).

The key word here is givenness, which is the meaning-constituting role played by consciousness. Husserl (1973) attempted to illustrate this by articulating what scholars could call a transcendental phenomenological research question: "How can the pure phenomenon of cognition reach something which is not immanent to it?" (p. 5). With this question, Husserl pondered how it can be that, for example, the cognitive act of judging can find the phenomenon about which it judges in exactly the manner in which it makes judgment possible. In other words, because the phenomenon about which judgment is made is not part of the cognitive act of judging, what then connects the phenomenon with the act? One could perhaps use the example that, while we can observe that the Moon circles Earth, it is only possible if we assume gravitation, which we cannot observe directly.

The two schools of thoughts for understanding consciousness and intentionality

Husserl (2017) posited that "to have meaning or to have something in mind is the cardinal feature of all consciousness" (pp. 261–262). While the concept of *noesis* appears reasonably comprehendible as modes of intention (e.g., judging, appreciating, imagining), researchers tend to wrestle with the concept of *noema*. This is not only due to the ambiguity of the concept, but because it is difficult for the social researcher (who is firmly anchored in the empirical reality) to follow Husserl's transcendentalism. Social researchers can be left somewhat disoriented by his transcendental move, questioning what just happened to the object and phenomenon we elaborated on a moment ago? It is as if when scholars are just at the cusp of grasping Husserl's phenomenology, he moves the proverbial cheese.

Our account of noesis and noema is quite condensed and does not fully capture Husserl's own evolution of thought. Nevertheless, Zahavi (2019b) pointed to at least three distinct conceptualizations of Noema within Husserl's work: "Noema understood as the concrete appearance, noema understood as ideal meaning and noema understood as the constituted object" (p. 93). Consequently, within transcendental phenomenology, there is more than one school of phenomenological thought on the actual meaning of noema, sometimes referred to as the West and East Coast Schools.

West Coast School

Noesis and noema are not to be confused with appearances or the object as an apprehended phenomenon. It is through these concepts that scholars leave the psychologism of the natural world as they turn away from the phenomenon toward the phenomenology of the phenomenon. Noesis can be explained as "thinking acts," which bestow sense, values and meanings, whereas noema represents "what is thought" (Moran, 2000, p. 55), which, in turn, connects the thinking act to the phenomenon (see p. 162). In this conceptualization, the noema is a vehicle for the various modes of consciousness. In addition, it is distinct from both the thinking act and the object/phenomenon. Consequently, the West Coast School conceptualizes intentionality as a mediator theory, while the noema is a meaning abstraction that serves as a go-between for intentionality and objects (see Zahavi, 2019b, p. 84).

The West Coast School's conceptualization of intentionality is thus tripartite, consisting of noesis, noema and the objects. Further, the West Coast School's conceptualization of noema rests on the philosophical notion that there is a form of connectedness between expression, senses and reference to the object. Consequently, the analysis may focus on the connection between the sense of the object and the linguistic reference, where the expression reveals how an object appears to a person's senses. For example, the planet Venus, expressed as the morning star or the evening star, reveals just how that planet appears (Pradelle, 2016).

The West Coast School's attention to linguistic manifestations and references offers the social researchers a bridge from phenomenology to hermeneutics, where the meanings of "thinking acts" can be inferred from how the sense of the experiences reveals itself in the "speech-acts." Thus, "meaningful expressions intend a sense of meaning and therefore through its mediation an object" (Pradelle, 2016, p. 186). Here, we can put Ricoeur's hermeneutics into play by focusing the phenomenological investigation on the structure of intentionality as revealed by the expression–sense–reference nexus. Ricoeur, as noted previously, detranscendentalizes phenomenology by substituting intentionality with intention and thereby focusing the analysis of the accounts of lived experiences on "Who is speaking? Who is acting? Who is the narrator? And who is the subject of moral action?" (van Manen, 2016, p. 137).

East Coast School

The proponents of the East Coast School reject the meditator interpretation of Husserl's noema (see Sokolowski, 1999, p. 223). This is because they find that this reading of phenomenology carries the risk of disconnecting the phenomenological analysis from any kind of reality because the brackets in the Husserlian epoché are being applied in a manner that disregards the natural world altogether (Sonner, 2006). Obviously, both schools can quote phenomenological scripture in support of their ideas, where readers can see that Husserl, in some quotes, shuts the proverbial door between the natural world and consciousness. However, in other instances, he spoke more moderately of simply suspending the validity of the natural world, but not discarding it.

Thus, proponents of the East Coast School interpret the noema as a version of the actual real object, as it is perceived and presented in thought and thereby comes closer to equating the noema with Kant's phenomenon. Zahavi (2019b) therefore argued that the noema "is to be understood neither as an ideal meaning, nor as a concept, nor as a proposition, it is not an intermediary between subject and object; it is not something that bestows intentionality on consciousness" (p. 83). Consequently, from the East Coast School's perspective, meaning is not derived from inside the realm of consciousness, where after it is imposed on the object it emerges in the encounter between intentionality and real-world objects (Sonner, 2006).

This interpretation means that intentionality is mirrored in the noema, and therefore, wrestling with Husserlian notion of noesis, as some phenomenological psychologists do, may be of limited utility for the social researcher. This, however, could be criticized as implying that there is no distinction between the subject "I" and the object and that the intentionality of consciousness can be reduced to that of phenomena (van Mazijk, 2017). Nevertheless, while the distinction between noesis and noema may be an interesting philosophical discussion, it may also be of limited consequence to the actual research. The reason is that noesis and noema always appear in correlation with each other, and therefore, the social researcher is not in a position to make an empirical distinction between them.

Consequently, Zahavi (2019b) argued that "the difference between an object and its meaning is not an empirical distinction" (p. 84). Thus, Sartre (1984) stated that "the object-essence is an organized whole" (p. 8). Moreover, for an applied phenomenological researcher, the most productive perspective is to conceive of some kind of unity between object, phenomenon and noema (meaning). Zahavi (2019a) was careful to point out that the object becomes a noema due to the phenomenological reflective method (which includes steps such as bracketing and epoché; see p. 83). Zahavi's position was therefore that the noema and the object are, in fact, the same thing but differently considered.

The psychological perspective on perceptional experiences

Husserl acknowledged that his transcendentalism is challenging for psychological researchers, as they essentially are forced to distinguish between perceiving as an empirical experience and perception as an idea. Husserl (1973) argued that it is necessary to acknowledge a delimitation between the "pure phenomenon of the mental act" and the "psychological phenomenon" (p. 34). The latter falls under the purview of empirical psychologists. Husserl (1970) states that psychology and transcendental phenomenology are not conflicting disciplines but allied in the sense they study the same thing but in different ways (p. 205). While transcendental phenomenology explores the transcendental ego's intentional modes and their meaning-constituting features, the psychologist is focused on the natural or naïve psychological ego.

In other words, phenomenological psychologists focus on the meaning-constituting role of psychological subjectivity and not on transcendental subjectivity. Phenomenological psychologists focus on how the psychological ego objectifies itself and the world. Another focus is contrasting and comparing past experiences as well as future anticipations (protention) to arrive at the meaning of what is experienced. For example, in a bicycle race with two teams, while the specific race is an object on its own, it also exists in a broader context of racing, the rules governing racing (i.e., a horizon). Further, these teams have likely raced before and therefore the meaning of the current race is also informed by past experiences and anticipated outcomes. Assuming that the spectators are supporters of either of these teams, it is almost certain that one group will appreciate this race as either a loss or a victory. Depending on the significance attributed to the race, whether it is an off-season friendship competition or the Tour-de-France, the victory may be judged as an important or less important victory. It is also quite possible that the supporters of the losing team, at a future point in time, upon discovering that the winning team was cheating by using performance-enhancing drugs, will reevaluate the meaning of the experience, which is then no longer one of loss, but of victory or redemption. It is thus the process of apperception in a horizon of temporality that facilitates meaning by drawing on prior experiences in anticipation of the future.

Consequently, the articulation of the phenomenological psychological research question is somewhat different, with an emphasis on the psychological mode of experiencing. Husserl (1973) argued that, in contrast to the transcendental research question, the psychological phenomenological research question could be: "How can I, this man, contact something in my mental processes that exists in itself, perhaps out there beyond me?" (see p. 5). This is perhaps a somewhat convoluted question, and in contemporary phenomenological psychological research, it is commonly replaced with the more operational: What is it like to experience something? The scope is no longer what makes the experience possible in the first place, but simply an emphasis on what it is like (in the psychological meaning of the word) to experience something, hereunder what is significant about the experience and what that means to the individual (i.e., the experience as a psychological phenomenon [Giorgi, 2019, p. 138]).

Circumspective experiencing of Dasein

Heidegger did not dispute Husserl's discovery of intentionality, but unlike his mentor, he placed less importance on the connection between perception and consciousness in constituting meaning (see Crowell, 2018, p. 232). Heidegger (1988) stated that "the idea of the subject which has intentional experiences merely inside its own sphere is an absurdity that misconstrues the basic ontological structure of the being that we ourselves are" (p. 64). Heidegger (2010) concluded that the most intimate way of experiencing the world is not perception, but "*handling, using and taking care*" (i.e., Dasein [p. 67]). In other words, "practical behavior" has its own form of epistemology (i.e., a form of seeing) that Heidegger (2010) referred to as "circumspection" as opposed to perception (p. 69). It is precisely from this perspective that the often-used phrase lived experiences comes into focus as a research domain.

Circumspection is a particular way of experiencing where Dasein uncovers the "what-for" (Heidegger, 2010, p. 69) of things by attending to them in a practical manner and relating to them in terms of their usefulness. Heidegger (2010) thus stated, "beings are discovered with regard to the fact that they are referred as those beings which they are to something. They are relevant together with something else" (p. 82). In this manner, Heidegger's phenomenology truly assumes a hermeneutic character as it downgrades the role of Husserl's subject–object polarity and, subsequently, the role of subjectivity in meaning-making and instead elevates the notion of context, being with, belonging to and relevance (Ricoeur, 2019, p. 65).

Circumspection is to Heidegger what perception is to Merleau-Ponty. However, instead of perception moving into apperception, circumspection involves noticing references while engaging with objects and people. The references are what come to the forefront when people engage with something in terms of what their beings are to us (e.g., useful objects, useless objects and, very importantly, context). Heidegger (2010) argued that "the structure of being is determined by reference" (p. 74). The distinction between Heidegger's phenomenology and Merleau-Ponty's phenomenology is therefore that in apperception, meaning is found internally in psychological processes, whereas from Heidegger's perspective, the meaning is ontologically already in the world.

The challenge here is to break free of the psychologism of perception as the vehicle for meaning-making. It is of course true that people grasp objects in their surroundings, but Heidegger's perspective is that we grasp the world not in perception and apperception, but in understanding and interpretation. Therefore, an interpretation-mitigated understanding is already there for people to access prior to any thematic apperception when they deal with things that are practical at hand. Thus, Heidegger (2010) argued that in encountering everyday objects such as "a table, a door, a car, a bridge. . . . The seeing of this sight is always already understanding and interpretation" (p. 144).

The notion of lived experience should therefore be understood literally that only by acting, using, producing, consuming, etc., do people reveal the being of things (in the sense of what these things mean to them) when they engage with them. For example, how can someone know that driving their own car bestows a sense of freedom without doing so. A person cannot discern the being of "freedom" from just perceiving the car. In other words, the being of Dasein is revealed in action and references and not in apperception. Heidegger (1988) posited, "We understand ourselves by way of things" (p. 289). Dasein is understood from the ability to be that is determined by the success and failure, the feasibility and unfeasibility, of its commerce with things. Therefore, "Dasein thus comes toward itself from out of the things" (p. 289). In other words, the meaning of being is not projected from within subjectivity but is discovered in circumspective dealings.

With this perspective in mind, the research question that Heidegger (2010) articulated is therefore different from what we encountered within transcendental phenomenology and descriptive phenomenological psychology, as he asks, "Whom is this Being that in its being is concerned about its very being?" (p. 11). In contemporary phenomenological research, this is most often articulated as What does it mean to be . . .?

The unity of experience and narrative self

Ricoeur advanced the hermeneutic phenomenological tradition. Similar to Heidegger, he questioned the relationship between subjectivity and experience that Husserl proposed in transcendental phenomenology and that the perspective of phenomenological psychology also reflects. Ricoeur (1994) found that to conceive of a "substratum of subject in which thoughts have their origin" is simply an illusion as it somehow "aligns the inner experience with external causation" (p. 15). Thus, the problem with transcendental phenomenology and phenomenological psychology is that these theoretical perspectives assume there is some form of accurate factual experience that can serve as the starting point for a scientific investigation (Ricoeur, 2019, p. 64). This may be true if the field of inquiry narrowly pertains to perception and if researchers subscribe to the idea that perception is the overarching mode of being in the world and, therefore, the starting point of all phenomenological investigations.

In contrast, Heidegger (1968, p. 61) argued that human beings are unique in the sense that we can speak and that we have the ability to confront our existence in language. Words are therefore "vessels of sense" (p. 129). Since Dasein is always preoccupied with being, language has then the meaning of pointing toward that being, and in this connection Heidegger posited that "man is that being who has his being by pointing to what is, and that particular beings manifest themselves as such by such pointing" (p. 149).

Thus, Ricoeur (2019) came to the understanding that "the reference of the linguistic order back to the structure of experience constitutes . . . the most important phenomenological presupposition of hermeneutics" (p. 78). The key point is that language is not only a vehicle that describes experience but contains tropes or certain ideographic structures that signify the experience and its meaning in its own right. In this manner, Ricoeur departed from transcendental phenomenology by focusing on the disclosed intentions of the subjects rather than the intentionality of their consciousness.

However, Ricoeur's essential insight is that these disclosures of experiences, first and foremost, point toward the meaning of self rather than the meaning of the experience. Therefore, Ricoeur (1994) posited that the disclosure of lived experiences takes the form of a "narrative unity" between the self and what is experienced. In this connection, Heidegger (1968, p. 150) suggested that it is a misunderstanding to see these disclosures as simply mentally preserved events. Thus, Heidegger argued that the original meaning of the term memory is more instructive in the sense that it signified "man's inner disposition and devotion" (p. 148). Consequently, Ricoeur (1994) posited that memories manifest "as an unstable mixture of fabulations and actual experience," and speech-acts are nothing more than the subjects' attestations of their beliefs about their experiences (p. 43).

Consequently, temporality is the horizon from where experiences have meaning, but not as recalled experiences consisting of sequences of "nows," but from a perspective where the actual now of the disclosure is the focal point of the subjects' concerns (Ricoeur, 1979). Therefore, hermeneutic phenomenological researchers should understand the experience not as a psychological act, but instead as an attestation of self, where language is a manifestation of a sign that points to a narrative self (see Ricoeur, 1994, p. 23) that needs to be read. Thus, the appropriate question to ask in a hermeneutic investigation of lived experiences is "who?" Thus, Ricoeur (1994) argued that "it is self-attestation that, at every level – linguistic, praxis, narrative and prescriptive – will preserve the question who? From being replaced with the question *what?* or *why?*" (p. 23).

What does the essence of experience mean?

In phenomenological research, the essence is considered the ultimate outcome (see Creswell, 2007, pp. 156–157). Moustakas (1994) thus stated, "The final step on the phenomenological research process is the intuitive integration of the fundamental textural and structural descriptions into a unified statement of the essence of the experience of the phenomenon as a whole" (p. 100).

Because articulating the "essence" is the ultimate goal of the phenomenological researcher, it is essential to clarify what it is and how to find it. Here it is important to understand that Husserl himself evolved on this notion and conceptualized the essence quite differently before and after his transcendental turn. However, this should not be understood as indicating only the latest version of Husserl's thoughts holds relevance because publishing philosophy is not the same thing as publishing newspapers. Hence, drawing from Husserl's combined works, scholars can see the contours of two conceptualizations of "essence" representing Husserl's philosophical journey: an early version that can best be described as psychological and a later version that is transcendental.

Both the transcendental phenomenological and phenomenological psychological conceptualizations of essence are bound to the same notion of intentionality as the mode of consciousness and subjectivity. This is, however, not the case with Heidegger, who emphasized Dasein's ontological nature. In the following, we will try to illuminate the distinctions between what phenomenologists consider to be the essence and where to find it.

Transcendental subjectivity and givenness

Husserl explained the essence in the following manner. If one begins with assuming the natural standpoint then it is a fact that every object and event has its own essence. For example, a musical note has its own essence as a specific tone or acoustics. Subsequently, the perception of a musical note is a psychological event with its own aboutness essence (see Husserl, 2017, p. 114). However, by assuming the transcendental standpoint, the focus is no longer on the phenomenon of the music, nor do people pay attention to the cognitive act toward the object such as perceiving or judging. Instead, people train their attention to the act itself.

Husserl illustrated this with the following example: An observer can have an infinite range of perceptions of an object as they move around it and change their vantage point. The essence of such experience can therefore be called perspective and not furniture. When moving from perception to experience, intentionality of consciousness occupies a similar phenomenological position as perspective (i.e., the intentional act of experiencing purified of the actual empirical experiences).

Further, Husserl (2017) proposed that the phenomenologist, in an iterative process, could attempt to reconstitute an experience with different intentional modes of thinking (see p. 115). The idea is that what manifests as a common theme of such ideation is the essence, and ideally this essence should manifest in the same manner for every person who is capable of executing the phenomenological reduction, and thereby, the outcome of phenomenological analysis should, in theory, acquire a sense of universality.

Husserl (2017) stated that while researchers can analyze and identify the components of a cognitive experience as if it were an object, people's consciousness-intentional experience "harbors meanings," and these meanings are not objects in the empirical sense (p. 257). For example, judging something is a thinking act, but judging itself, bracketed from the object of experience, also has its own meaning structures in the way it gives the objects to cognition. Thus, the essence of experience in the realm of transcendental subjectivity can best be understood as "givenness."

Psychological subjectivity and apperception

While transcendental phenomenology aims at uncovering the essence of the mode of experiencing for the purpose of identifying a universal truth, the psychologist's analysis is not transcendental and remains within the context of the natural world. Thus, Husserl (1970) argued that due to the fact that the psychologist does not perform a complete transcendental epoché, the insights gained are merely "objective-psychological essential insights" (p. 180). Therefore, at the psychological level of analysis, the essence can be understood as essential aspects of what is perceived. Thus, William James viewed the "essence" as the sum of the most important features of an experience and that the individual observer is the only one in a position to bestow importance on anything (Wilshire, 1969).

Husserl (1973, p. 34) argued that it is perfectly legitimate to study the psychological meaning-making of the perceived, which is the phenomenon of apperception, where perceptions become psychologically connected with a body of preexisting knowledge and experiences pertaining to the object as perceived (Husserl, 1973, p. 34). Therefore, according to Merleau-Ponty (as cited in Romdenh-Romluc, 2018),

> an essence is a meaning inherent in a particular set of experiences. It has some claim to universality insofar as it is the essence of a particular

phenomenon, so future experiences of that item (future instances of that phenomenon) will unfold according to that form.

(p. 354)

The phenomenological psychological perspective is therefore that "apperception is the universal law of experience" (Chernavin, 2016)

Dasein's interpretation-mediated understanding

Husserl (2017) defined the world as "the totality of objects that can be known through experience" (pp. 51–52). However, Heidegger (2010) defined the world as "that in which Dasein lives," which means that the world is a public place (p. 65). As we have noted before, Heidegger's approach to phenomenology was quite different because his scope was the being of human beings and not intentionality or subjectivity per se. Consequently, Heidegger (1988) questioned what insights to the being of beings can be gained by adding a subjective act of perception to an object besides the fact that some relationship has now been established between subject and object (see p. 47). Thus, Heidegger (1988) claimed that perception "is at most the mode of access to the existent" and, because perception does not equal being nor does it constitute its existence (p. 49), a thematic analysis of the cognitive acts of perception and apperception does not reveal the meaning of being.

The fallacy of the psychological perspective lies in the notion that the way people's Dasein understands being is in some mode of objectification (see Heidegger, 1988, p. 66). Heidegger (1968) thus stated "within psychology it never becomes clear in any way what it is to which ideas are attributed and referred. . . . Here everything remains in question; and yet, the scientific findings are correct" (p. 41). In other words, Dasein cannot see intentionality as something that exists in a relation between beings; it must cling to the notion of a subject that exists in contrast to an object. Dasein, therefore, has to invent the mysterious walled-off transcendental subjectivity as the ultimate arbiter of objectification. In contrast, Heidegger (1988) argued that because Dasein is ontological in this world and "is always already immediately dwelling among things," Dasein has neither an inside nor an outside (p. 66) and is neither subject nor object. Consequently, the essence of Dasein is its existence and being with others and things.

Therefore, Dasein understands the world and itself through the experiences it has with objects and other Dasein. In this connection, the role of interpretation is that of disclosing the relevance of what is at hand in the world to understand. Heidegger pointed out that interpretation should not be understood as a psychological process, where the mind "throws significance" or "sticks some value" to the objects (p. 145) because interpretation is always oriented toward relevance of objects and therefore draws on the references that belong to the beings of these objects. Consequently, it can be argued that the essence of Dasein's experience is interpretation-mediated understanding.

The emplotment of the narrative self

Ricoeur (1994) concurred with Heidegger on the notion "of being with" and posited that the most significant relationship is with others. He therefore called for a different kind of phenomenology (i.e., a "phenomenology of the self, affected by the other than self"; p. 33). Ricoeur's hermeneutic phenomenological insight is that the Dasein is public and that the Dasein component "the they" is not owned by the individual but merged into the horizon of experiences of others. This is what makes the human being different from any other objects in the world because people are the same as others and, through reflection, can come to understand the shared Dasein. Ricoeur (2019) stated, "We ourselves are what the other is" (p. 16). Therefore, other people are not phenomena in the alien sense, but "*a phenomenological modification of myself*" (Moran, 2000, p. 177). The subject's understanding of the "self" is therefore to be conceived as a belief in sameness with others and being different from others. Hence, it is in the encounters with other people that the subjects form a belief about themselves and thereby acquire an identity.

In contrast to the phenomenological traditions, Ricoeur's method is not introspection but interpretation. Moreover, once again, temporality provides an opportunity to connect hermeneutics with phenomenology in terms of collapsing the past, present and future into a unified horizon. This then allows disclosures to be guided by a plot where the subjects are able to "construe a significant whole out of scattered events" (Ricoeur, 1979, p. 24). This is similar to an author who is able to design a story plot due to the fact that he or she has a privileged fictional time perspective.

In this connection, Heidegger (1968) argued that human beings, through language, confront themselves and construct themselves as persons. However, Heidegger noted that in Latin the meaning of *persona* is "the actor's mask through which his dramatic tale is sounded. Since man is the percipient who perceives what is, we can think of him as the persona, the mask of being" (p. 62). Consequently, Ricoeur (1994) argued that researchers can discern the essence of this "persona" by investigating how subjects recall of memory similar to a story with a plot, where the different agents, including the self, perform actions that reveal their selfhood (see p. 143). Ricoeur (1994) thus stated, "the decisive step in the direction of a narrative conception of personal identity is taken when one passes from the action to the character" (p. 143). The person thus occupies a certain role similar to a fictional character in a storyline with a plot. Consequently, it can be argued that the essence of experience is the emplotment of the narrative self.

Summary

We have, in this chapter, dived further into phenomenology and attempted to provide a structured understanding of the different perspectives on experience that may serve to delimit phenomenological research and inform the articulation of an appropriately aligned research question.

Husserl's project was to identify universal truths through the phenomenological reduction and subsequent analysis of the various modes of intentionality and thereby demonstrate that subjectivity is constituting what scholars in the natural sciences would construe as objectivity. This is the reason why phenomenologists of the Husserlian tradition are preoccupied with the experience, not for the sake of the experience itself, but as a gateway from the natural and psychological realm into the realm of transcendental subjectivity. Through a complex technique of phenomenological reduction, Husserl believed that it would be possible to achieve a form of mental seeing by which he could observe intentionality in its form and the meanings they impose (i.e., the pure essence of the phenomenon). However, Husserl also considered a more ordinary psychological essence. The object of interest is the appearance of the phenomenon in the ordinary psychological sense of its meaning. Transcendental and psychological phenomenologists are therefore looking at the same phenomenon, but from different perspectives.

The more ontological and hermeneutic-orientated phenomenologists, such as Heidegger and Ricoeur, were less interested in the meaning of the experience, but more in what that experience reveals of the meaning of being. Consequently, the notion of perception plays a limited role as the gateway between the actual and the transcendental because the focus is on interaction. It is therefore only by using a hammer that a person can come to understand the essence of the hammer's being as well as the essence of their own being as the one hammering. A person's "seeing" here is therefore better understood as circumspection, where a person considers a range of the possibilities of beings that is only delimited by their interpretation-mitigated understanding of the world and their selves within the world.

The challenge for the social researcher is of course how to naturalize the phenomenological theories without confounding the notions of "Cogito ergo Sum." Social researchers must attempt to grasp the parallelism between the transcendental and psychological realms. They should be aware of the difference in focus from Husserl to Heidegger. Moreover, they need to master the epoché and phenomenological reduction, as they pertain to the domain of subjectivity or being. The illustration below summarizes the different phenomenological perspectives pertaining to experience we have addressed so far and how these perspectives may delimit the research into the meaning (i.e., the essence of the experience; Figure 2.3).

The illustration given later is a demonstration of how the theoretically overarching research questions align with the three different orientations within phenomenology that we have addressed throughout this book (see Figure 2.4). Obviously, social researchers will not be engaged in transcendental phenomenological investigations but will find themselves engaging with their research problem either psychologically or hermeneutically, and to this end, the literature supports two overarching types of research questions that, of course, can be modified and made more specific. A researcher answers either the phenomenological psychological question, what is it like to experience something? or the hermeneutic phenomenological question, what does it mean to be a person that experiences something?

"Cogito"

```
┌─────────────┐                              ┌───────────────┐
│  Givenness  │                              │ Apperception  │
└─────────────┘                              └───────────────┘
        ▲                                            ▲
        │                                            │
        └──────────┐                      ┌──────────┘
          ┌──────────────────┐  ┌──────────────────┐
          │  Transcendental  │  │  Psychological   │
          │   Subjectivity   │  │   Subjectivity   │
          └──────────────────┘  └──────────────────┘
```

```
          ┌──────────┐        ┌──────────┐
          │  Dasein  │        │ Narrative│
          └──────────┘        │   Self   │
       ┌──────┘               └──────┐
       │                             │
       ▼                             ▼
┌────────────────┐          ┌────────────────┐
│  Interpretive  │          │   Emplotment   │
│ Understanding  │          └────────────────┘
└────────────────┘
```

"Sum"

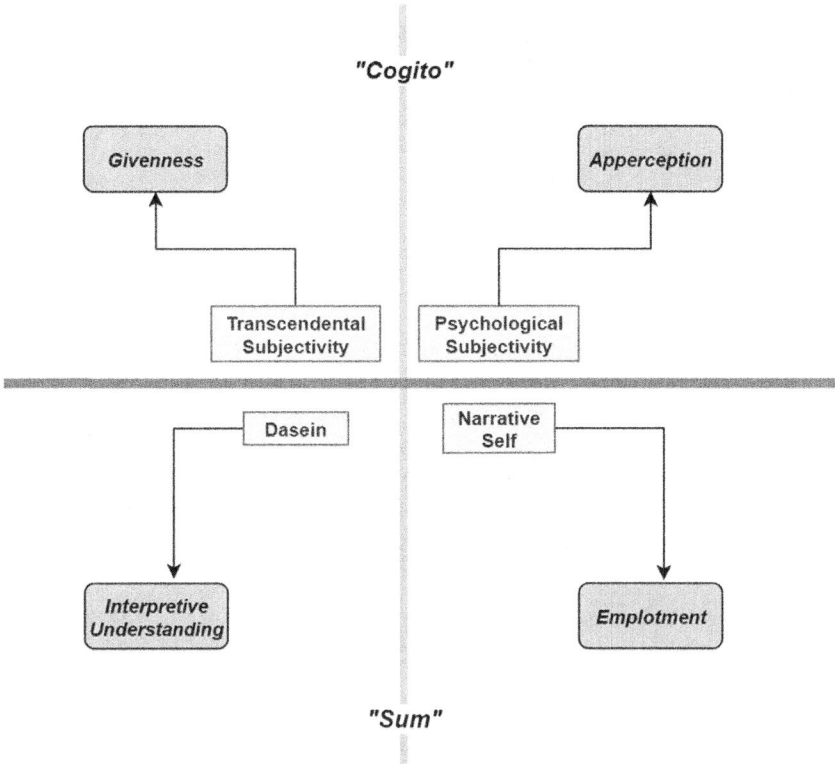

FIGURE 2.3   Phenomenological Perspectives on Experience

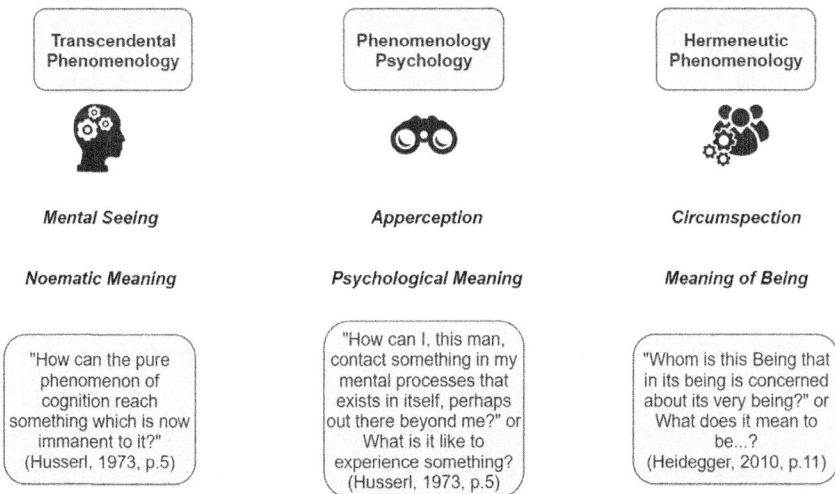

Transcendental Phenomenology	Phenomenology Psychology	Hermeneutic Phenomenology
Mental Seeing	*Apperception*	*Circumspection*
Noematic Meaning	*Psychological Meaning*	*Meaning of Being*
"How can the pure phenomenon of cognition reach something which is now immanent to it?" (Husserl, 1973, p.5)	"How can I, this man, contact something in my mental processes that exists in itself, perhaps out there beyond me?" or What is it like to experience something? (Husserl, 1973, p.5)	"Whom is this Being that in its being is concerned about its very being?" or What does it mean to be...? (Heidegger, 2010, p.11)

FIGURE 2.4   Phenomenological Orientations and Their Respective Research Questions

Note: Hermeneutic phenomenology in this figure is Heidegger's notion of phenomenology.

References

Ashworth, P. D. (2017). Interiority, exteriority and the realm of intentionality. *Journal of Phenomenological Psychology*, *48*(1), 39–62. https://doi.org/10.1163/15691624-12341321

Chernavin, G. I. (2016). The process of sense-formation and fixed sense-structures: Key intuitions in the phenomenology of Edmund Husserl. *Russian Studies in Philosophy*, *54*(1), 48–61.

Creswell, J. W. (2007). *Qualitative inquiry & research design: Choosing among five approaches*. Sage Publications. ISBN: 1412916070

Crowell, S. (2018). What is the "middle" Heidegger? In D. Zahavi (Ed.), *The Oxford handbook of the history of phenomenology* (pp. 229–250). Oxford University Press. ISBN-13: 978-0198755340

Eagly, A. H., & Chaiken, S. (1993). *The psychology of attitudes*. Harcourt Brace Jovanovich College Publishers. ISBN-10: 0155000977

Giorgi, A. (2019). *Psychology as a human science: A phenomenological based approach*. University Professors Press. ISBN: 9781939686268

Heidegger, M. (1968). *What is called thinking?* Harper & Row. ISBN-10: 006090528X

Heidegger, M. (1988). *The basic problems of phenomenology*. Indiana University Press. ISBN-10: 0253176875

Heidegger, M. (2010). *Being and time*. University of New York Press. ISBN-10: 1438432763

Husserl, E. (1970). *The crisis of European sciences and transcendental phenomenology: An introduction to phenomenological philosophy*. Northwestern University Press. ISBN: 081010458X

Husserl, E. (1973). *The idea of phenomenology*. Martinius Nijhoff. ISBN: 9024701147

Husserl, E. (2001). *The shorter logical investigations*. Routledge. ISBN: 9780415241922

Husserl, E. (2017). *Ideas: General introduction to pure phenomenology*. Unwin Brothers Ltd. ISBN-10: 0415519039

Kant, I. (2007). *Critique of pure reason*. Penguin Group. ISBN: 9780140447477

Merleau-Ponty, M., Lefort, C., & Lingis, A. (1968). *The visible and the invisible followed by working notes*. Northwestern University Press. ISBN: 9780810104570

Moran, D. (2000). *Introduction to phenomenology*. Routledge. ISBN-10: 0415183731

Moustakas, C. E. (1994). *Phenomenological research methods*. Sage Publications. ISBN: 0803957998

Pradelle, D. (2016). On the notion of sense in phenomenology: Noematic sense and ideal meaning. *Research in Phenomenology*, *46*(2), 184–204. https://doi.org/10.1163/15691640-12341335

Ricoeur, P. (1979). The human experience of time and narrative. *Research in Phenomenology*, *9*(1), 17–34.

Ricoeur, P. (1994). *Oneself as another*. The University of Chicago Press. ISBN: 0-226-71329-6

Ricoeur, P. (2019). *Hermeneutics and the human sciences*. Cambridge University Press. ISBN-10: 0521280028

Romdenh-Romluc, K. (2018). Science in Merleau-Ponty's phenomenology. In D. Zahavi (Ed.), *The Oxford handbook of the history of phenomenology* (pp. 340–359). Oxford University Press. ISBN-13: 978-0198755340

Sartre, J. P. (1984). *Being and nothingness*. Washington Square Press. ISBN: 0671867806 9780671867805

Sokolowski, R. (1999). Appendix: Phenomenology in the last one hundred years. In *Introduction to phenomenology* (pp. 211–227). Cambridge University Press. https://doi.org/10.1017/CBO9780511809118.016

Sonner, C. (2006). The opening of intentionality. *Chrestomathy: Annual Review of Undergraduate Research, School of Humanities and Social Sciences, School of Languages, Cultures, and World Affairs, College of Charleston*, 5, 227–246. http://chrestomathy.cofc.edu/documents/vol5/sonner.pdf

van Manen, M. (2016). *Phenomenology of practice*. Routledge. ISBN-10: 1611329442

van Mazijk, C. (2017). Some reflections on Husserlian intentionality, intentionalism, and non-propositional content. *Canadian Journal of Philosophy, 47*(4), 499–517. https://doi.org/10.1080/00455091.2016.1255500

Wilshire, B. (1969). Protophenomenology in the psychology of William James. *Transactions of the Charles S. Peirce Society, 5*(1), 25–43.

Zahavi, D. (2019a). *Phenomenology the basics*. Routledge. ISBN: 978-1-138-21670-9

Zahavi, D. (2019b). *Husserl's legacy*. Oxford University Press. ISBN: 978-0-19-885217-9

3

UNDERSTANDING EPOCHÉ AND BRACKETING

Objectives

Readers will be able to

1   Explain the meaning of epoché.
2   Describe the original phenomenological rationale of epoché.
3   Differentiate between the epoché within the psychological and hermeneutic traditions.
4   Appropriately align the application of the epoché and reduction with choice of phenomenological conceptual framework.
5   Identify limitations of the applied versions of epoché and reduction.

Origin and meaning of epoché

At the beginning of this book, we reflected on a general problem pertaining to the credibility of applied phenomenological research, namely a gap in researchers' understanding of phenomenological methodological concepts. Concerning this problem, the epoché and the phenomenological reduction are likely the most consequential. Quite often, researchers will simply state that they have executed the epoché and talk a bit about bias and be done with it, and of course there is much more to it than that (Butler, 2016).

The epoché is associated with various schools of ancient Greek philosophy with slightly different meanings. In a direct translation, the epoché could be understood as suspending judgment or withholding judgment. Husserl subsequently appropriated this term as the central concept for the method of phenomenological inquiry, and it has since inspired phenomenological researchers of all stripes to the degree that the epoché has become almost synonymous with phenomenology itself, but it is nevertheless often poorly understood in the context of applied phenomenological research.

As mentioned in chapter 1, Immanuel Kant's (1724–1804) rigorous system of philosophy served as an inspiration for Husserl. Thus, in *Critique of Pure Reason*, Kant (2007) alluded to an a priori knowledge that makes experiences possible, and for Husserl it became essential to develop the epoché into a scientific method that could enable a "mental seeing" of this knowledge (i.e., the essence). Consequently, Husserl (1970) referred to the epoché as the breakthrough method that would reconstitute modern philosophy as a discipline grounded in self-evident truths (see p. 70). He proclaimed that his overarching project is "that of pressing forward through the hell of an unsurpassable, quasi-skeptical epoché towards the gate of the heaven of an absolute rational philosophy, and a construction of the latter systematically" (Husserl, 1970, p. 77). This may all sound a bit high-minded, and of course it is, but that should not distract readers from understanding that Husserl was trying to reconfigure the modern philosophy of the meaning of the world by building from a base of self-evident truths, which are that thoughts exist, and that we think.

Building on Descartes' insight that only thinking acts are self-evident, Husserl believed that these acts of thinking contained an essence of meaning that constituted all other forms of meanings. Moreover, due to the transcendental nature of consciousness, this essence would be universal irrespective of whose consciousness it is. Husserl therefore posited that through a methodical application of the epoché and phenomenological reduction, it would be possible to separate out thinking from thought, like oil from water. In other words, the purpose of the epoché was to disconnect the validity of the content of thinking acts, hereunder all notions of theorizing about cause and effect that normally guide people's everyday lives. Husserl (2017) thus stated "the disconnexion from nature was for us the methodological means whereby the direction of the mental glance upon the pure transcendental consciousness becomes at all possible" (p. 171).

Husserl wanted to see intentionality in its pure form as he believed this to be the meaning-constituting function of consciousness. In other words, if thoughts are fish then thinking is the river, and he wanted to find a way of removing the fish from the river to study the flow of water without the fish confusing his gaze. Husserl (1973) stated:

> Every intellectual process and indeed every mental process whatever, while being enacted can be made the object of a pure "seeing": and understanding and is something absolutely given in this "seeing." It is given as something that is, that is here and now, and whose being cannot be sensibly doubted.
>
> *(p. 24)*

It is important to understand that the epoché is not a denial of the real world or a philosophical position where scholars doubt its existence, as some of the classic Greek scholars proposed. Within the epoché, thinkers do not discard the natural world with its objects and scientific ideas; they simply place those things in brackets. This means that people are aware of them, but do not use their notions of cause and effect for investigations. Thus, Husserl (2017) stated:

> I am far from any thought of objecting them (sciences) in the least degree, I disconnect them all. I make absolutely no use of their standards; I do not appropriate a single one of the propositions that enter into their systems, even though their evidential value is perfect, I take none of them, no one of them serves for a foundation. . . . I have placed it in a **bracket**.
>
> *(p. 111)*

As the reader may recall from chapter 1, the reason for this bracketing is not a denial of science, but the recognition that consciousness cannot be submitted to empirical investigation because it is transcendental subjectivity that constitutes the meaning of such objectifications in the first place. Significant intellectual resources of different phenomenological schools have been allocated to procedural arguments about the exact nature of the epoché. One of the reasons for these enduring disagreements lies in the fact that Husserl, throughout his career, continuously modified and restated the meaning of the epoché (Butler, 2016). For example, in his earlier writings, the phenomenological reduction was part of the epoché (see Moran, 2000, p. 147). Then in later works, it would seem that Husserl thought the epoché was a distinct move that precedes the reduction, where the philosopher first disconnects from the validity of the theoretical assumptions of the real world and then reduces these assumptions to phenomena (Butler, 2016).

The question is whether Husserl advocated an entirely new ontology or simply a radically different point of view from that of empirical science. Zahavi (2019b) supported the latter interpretation and argued that with the epoché and phenomenological reduction, researchers do not ignore the world, but assume an expansive view that allows them to "thematize" the experience of something from a subjective point of view (p. 59). However, Moran (2000, p. 132) argued that Husserl's purpose was to establish a science of essence, and to this end, the phenomenologist must try to access intentionality by eliminating the factual circumstances around the experiences. To use Heidegger's terminology, Husserl wanted to suspend the Dasein to discover the structures of consciousness that make Dasein possible in the first place. This discussion draws back to the discussion of the meaning of the noema, which we reviewed in Chapter 2, and reflects the disagreement between the East Coast and West Coast Schools of phenomenology.

Essence of epoché and bracketing

In *Crisis*, Husserl (1970) stated that

no matter how far I push my doubt, and even if I try to think that every-thing is dubious or even if truth does not exists, it is absolutely self-evident that I, after all, would still exist as the doubter.

(p. 77)

With an understanding of Husserl's Cartesian starting point, the essence of the epoché is, first and foremost, radical doubt, where everything that is not self-evident is placed in brackets, which means that the validity of a natural world view, seemingly governed by cause and effect, is suspended. Thus, the essence of the epoché is to bracket thesis, so that the phenomenologist can have a good mental look at the thinking acts.

Husserl thought that every concrete experience was bound to a larger struc-ture of a priori consciousness, and by engaging in the phenomenological reduc-tion where the experiences, step by step, would be stripped off their empirical content, it would be possible to discern "universal truths" (Moran, 2000, p. 134). In other words, the mode of consciousness, such as perceiving, judging, willing, etc., have their own essence apart from the psychological essence that manifests when these structures engage with the phenomena in apperception. By accessing the pure essences of these intentional structures through the appli-cation of the epoché and phenomenological reduction, Husserl believed that scholars would be able to see how subjectivity constitutes what people experi-ence as objective reality and makes that experience of objective reality possible in the first place. In other words, the essence of the epoché is to be understood as providing credibility for the universality of the outcome of phenomenologi-cal inquiry.

What Husserl proposed was not a subjectivist view of reality, where each person or group of individuals construe reality in their own ways. Husserl in fact challenged the conventional understanding of external validity within science and research by claiming that universal validity can be derived from an N of 1 (Merriam, 1995). In other words, through the epoché and the phe-nomenological reduction, scholars can acquire a mental seeing of the meaning-constituting structures of subjectivity that constitute what is considered real and objective.

The attraction of Husserl's methodology lies in the notion that the epoché and phenomenological reduction is to phenomenology what alpha and rep-resentative sampling is to correlational research. The illustration below is an attempt to illustrate that, in principle, the epoché plays the same role in terms of producing credible findings as the method of inferential statistical analysis (see Figure 3.1). The difference is that phenomenology aims at credible universal findings, whereas correlation research aims at generalizability relative to a larger population. Thus, Husserl (2001) stated "The laws of thought count as natural law characterizing the peculiarity of our mind" (p. 36). It is therefore the func-tion of the epoché and phenomenological reduction to uncover the essence of how consciousness operates.

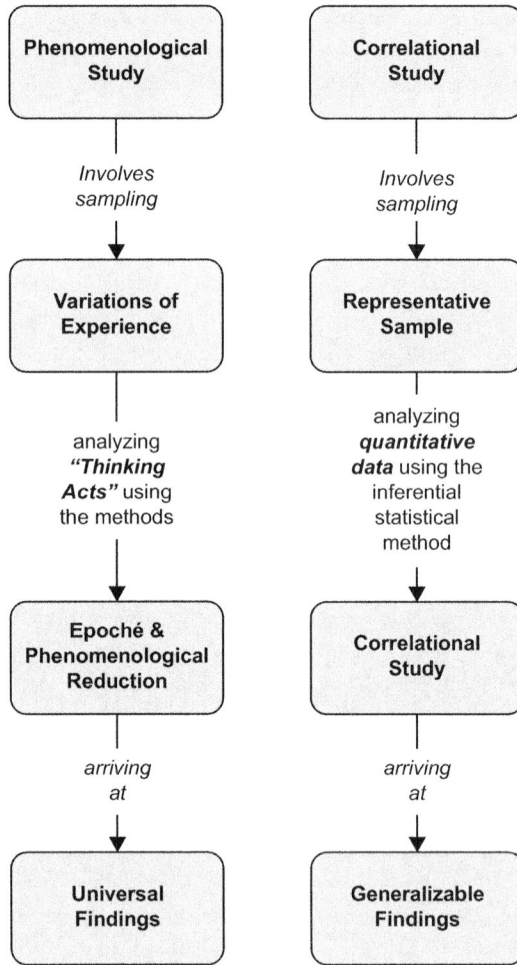

FIGURE 3.1 Parallel Between Phenomenological Study and Correlational Study

Reconciling bracketing of thesis with description

In *Ideas*, Husserl (2017) argued that, while consciousness needs to be purified from the empirical objects and their phenomenal representations, there is a limit to this purification. In other words, if the epoché and reduction are taken too far and all knowledge and presumptions are suspended, scholars would end up in a situation where it would be difficult to even describe their research findings (see p. 175). Thus, Husserl argued that the prerequisite for scientific inquiry is the ability to approach consciousness as an object of research, and with this follows the notion of categorizations, classifications and descriptions. Thus, Husserl (1973, p. 77) proposed that, while the content of thoughts is bracketed, this content still has validity in an ontological sense. By this, he meant that in the epoché, the empirical world and all its ideas and theories have not been deleted, only bracketed, and can therefore be used for descriptive purposes. Therefore, what in the natural world appears to have validity in terms of explaining cause and effect will in the epoché be considered merely as phenomenal content. Thus, Husserl (2017) stated that while phenomenologists avoid conceptual affirmations of the experience, "we for that reason do not cast them away. They are there still and belong essentially to the phenomenon . . . rather we contemplate them ourselves; instead of working with them we turn them into objects" (p. 264). In other words, the essence of the epoché is also that it renders the research descriptive.

It would appear that Husserl's transcendental phenomenology is theory-rich but example-poor, which underscores the challenge of describing what transpires in the transcendental phenomenological reduction with words and concepts that belong to the natural world without directly or indirectly theorizing about causes and effects. Husserl (2001) specifically addressed this problem and stated that:

> it is, in fact, impossible to describe referential acts without using expressions which recur to the things to which such acts refer. One then readily forgets that such subsidiarily described objectivity, which is necessarily introduced into almost all phenomenological description, has undergone a change of sense, in virtue of which it now belongs to the sphere of phenomenology.
>
> *(p. 91)*

What Husserl here indicated is that while an investigation must remain descriptive and grounded in the actual data, the investigator cannot communicate their findings in a transcendental mode but must do so with the terminology that is available in the empirical world. For example, researchers cannot use a theory of perception to explain causes and effects with regard to the psychological experience. Nevertheless, scholars recognize that the components of a theory are also components of the phenomenon they are investigating. Therefore, such theory of perception can be used for descriptive purposes. In other words, researchers do not reject psychological theories when trying to describe what goes on between intentionality and perception. They just do not consider these theories as "psychological realities" (Husserl, 2001, p. 91) and suspend their explanatory validity and apply them more as a heuristic strategy or a lens for the purpose of conveying descriptions.

How epoché is carried out by a phenomenologist

Husserl, after his transcendental turn, was adamant that the epoché and the phenomenological reduction are essential steps necessary for achieving the so-called mental seeing of essence and addressed the steps in great detail throughout his publications. What may be perplexing for budding social researchers as they set out to acquaint themselves with Husserl is likely the realization that Husserl's epoché has nothing to do with social and psychological research in the empirical sense but has been repurposed by different social researchers with very different perspectives. Therefore, there is not one authoritative approach to the applied epoché, which can be both confusing and liberating because many novice researchers look for a 1–2–3-step approach to their qualitative data analysis. On the contrary, it is liberating because the confusion is also a license to develop a unique approach relevant to the specific study. In the following, we will provide an authentic Husserlian account of the epoché with an assorted range of scholarly interpretations, which at least may serve to inspire do-it-yourself phenomenologists.

Husserl's transcendental epoché and phenomenological reduction

Husserl's transcendental phenomenology aimed at understanding how the transcendental subject objectifies the world and thereby constitutes its meaning. To this end, the purpose of the epoché is to separate transcendental subjectivity from the more contextual and personal subjectivism. In other words, to separate the thinking act from what is being thought about in order to describe the essence of the act on its own.

In *The Train of Thoughts Lectures*, Husserl (1973) attempted to describe the process of disconnecting from the natural way of thinking. First, he invoked the philosophical notion of Cartesian doubt. Husserl (1973) referred to this as a "phenomenological orientation," where he encouraged the audience to ponder what the various mental acts actually do and how thoughts manage to reach the objects that people are thinking about. However, in order to achieve this phenomenological orientation, scholars must disconnect all transcendent knowledge, which is what they know about an "object" that is not strictly found in that object. Husserl explained this as "assigning every transcendent knowledge to index-zero" or "the phenomenological reduction" (p. 4).

In *Ideas*, Husserl (2017) was quite specific and listed a range of examples of what phenomenologists must disconnect when making the transcendental move into the study of pure consciousness. As he stated:

> In the first place it goes without saying that with the suspending of the natural world, physical and psychological, all individual objectivities . . . all varieties of cultural expressions, works of the technical and of the fine arts, of the sciences also, aesthetic and practical values of every shape and form. Natural in the same sense are also realities of such kind as state, moral custom, law, religion. Therewith, all the sciences natural and mental.
> *(Husserl, 2017, p. 171)*

At the next level, Husserl (1973) urged scholars to "abandon the psychological standpoint even of the descriptive psychology" (p. 5). He demonstrated this move by stating that in the psychological mindset people would ask themselves, "How can I, this man, contact something in my mental processes that exists in itself, perhaps out there beyond me?" (p. 5). This question essentially addresses the process of meaning-making in the form of apperceptions. However, in abandoning the psychological mindset with its orientation toward the cognitive process of meaning-making informed by spatial and temporal horizons, Husserl suggested that the earlier question be replaced with "How can the pure phenomenon of cognition reach something which is not immanent to it?" (p. 5). In other words, in what ways does consciousness give objects to cognitive meaning-making?

The final transcendental move is an attempt at understanding the essence of thinking acts, such as perceiving and judging, by contemplating how objects are given by these modes of consciousness. In other words, the essence is already part of people's intentional structures, but needs to be isolated from the psychological meaning of a specific experience by an analytical or reflective procedure (see Moran, 2000, p. 134).

The epoché and the phenomenological reduction can thus, in its final analysis, be understood as a thematic analysis of modes of consciousness (noesis). Husserl (2017) explained the outcome of the epoché by stating that:

> in the stream of our experiences, we find embedded empirical connections and systems of theorizing reason and by bracketing these, the experience will be modified, however the consciousness and the experiential systems will not be fundamentally altered, but remain as a residue and subsequently the sole focus of our acts of reflection.
>
> *(p. 152)*

Husserl's epoché does not even require an actual lived experience but can be executed with imaginary objects in exactly the same manner because it is neither the object nor its phenomenological representation that is important; it is the reduction that counts. To that end, the absence of any real experiences or object may even be helpful in preventing the natural world from sneaking back in during the epoché.

Moustakas' repurposing of transcendental phenomenology

The Husserlian epoché is an exercise that does not lend itself well to empirical research, especially when it comes to other people. This has, however, not prevented scholars and researchers from attempting to naturalize phenomenology (i.e., modify its procedures for empirical investigations). The problem of bridging Husserl's phenomenological philosophy with empirical social research is demonstrated by Moustakas' (1994) seminal work *Phenomenological Research Methods*. Creswell (2007) referred to this work as an ***empirical*** transcendental phenomenological method, which is confusing because Moustakas did not actually use the term empirical in connection with transcendental, and empirical and transcendental are contradictory terms (see p. 59).

However, Creswell was not unreasonable in his predication because the purpose of Moustakas' work was to establish a link between Husserl's phenomenology and empirical research. However, instead of constructing a unique applied methodology, Moustakas (1994) approached the challenge of naturalizing phenomenology by simply repurposing Husserl's philosophical concepts of epoché, reduction, imaginative variations and essence into a five-step method that Moustakas posited can be applied for the purpose of elucidating the essence other people's lived experiences. For example, Moustakas (1994) emphasized an epoché where the researchers bracket their "prejudgments, biases and preconceived ideas of things" (p. 85). It is then followed by the phenomenological reduction, which, in his reconceptualization, "takes on a character of graded pre-reflection, reflection and reduction" (p. 91). The next step is imaginative variation, where the researcher seeks possible meanings of the subjects' experiences through the researcher's own imagination and "varying the frame of reference" (p. 99).

Siewert (2007) argued that the problem with approaches such as Moustakas' is that the third-party observer perspective leads to a situation in which meanings regarding a subject's experience are derived from the theoretical preconceptions of the observer, and therefore such research is not phenomenology. This is perhaps a bold statement because there is no single authority with editorial control over the doctrines of phenomenology. However, legitimate concerns can be raised regarding the credibility of research findings based on Moustakas' interpretation of the epoché, phenomenological reduction and imaginative variation. Specifically, it is difficult to see how Moustakas' bracketing of preconceptions is not immediately nullified by the suggestion that the researchers use their own imagination as a means to elucidate the subjects' experiences.

It is of course correct that Husserl proposed this technique but with the important difference that the imaginative variation was done in regard to one's own perceptions and not the conceived perceptions of others. Therefore, it would seem that Moustakas' (1994) approach to the epoché and phenomenological reduction wades into what William James referred to as the "psychologist's fallacy," where researchers confuse their own perspective with that of their subjects and "forget" that the experiences of the subjects must be understood on their own terms and not on the terms and frame of reference of the researcher (Ashworth, 2009).

It appears that Moustakas' (1994, p. 41) approach was informed as much by theoretical phenomenology as it was by therapy, where practitioner and client coconstruct narratives and meanings (see p. 41). It is not uncommon for scholars to attempt to adapt phenomenology to their particular fields of expertise. While Moustakas' narrative is compelling and demonstrates deep knowledge of Husserl, it is not immediately clear what his research domain actually is. From his methodological considerations, it appears to be neither psychological subjectivity nor intersubjectivity, but more an artificial intersubjectivity defined by the relationship between researcher and subject.

Giorgi's psychological epoché

Moustakas simply repurposed Husserl's concepts of epoché and phenomenological reduction to mean something other than what Husserl intended and thereby gravely contributed to the confusion among social researchers as to what these methodological moves are all about. However, a more credible approach can be found within phenomenological psychology because phenomenology originates from psychology, and Husserl recognized the parallelism between the two fields as they study the same phenomenon, but from two different perspectives. Therefore, in contrast to Moustakas' approach, there exists a solid theoretical basis in Husserl's writings for a limited psychological epoché as a waystation from the psychological realm, which is part of the natural world, toward the transcendental phenomenological realm.

Phenomenological psychologists find solace in Merleau-Ponty's incomplete reduction (Kee, 2019). Although Merleau-Ponty believed that there is a meaningful connection between perception, subjectivity and transcendental subjectivity, his skepticism of the role of transcendental subjectivity in constituting the meaning of reality is a logical consequence of his view of the embodied consciousness. Merleau-Ponty (1978) thus stated that the subject is not a "God who posits the world," but "a man who finds himself thrown into it" (p. 218). Consequently, he believed that the thematic reflections of both consciousness and objects lead people to the concepts of meanings. In other words, Merleau-Ponty's thoughts indicated that the phenomenological reduction does not exclude the phenomenal presentations of objects in thought. We can therefore argue that he does not buy into what we referred to as the West Coast School's purist interpretation of the noema as some sort of meaning vehicle of intentionality that can be isolated by the reduction. Thus, Merleau-Ponty (1978) stated, "No, the noema is the object itself considered in the phenomenological reflection" (p. 220).

In this vein, Giorgi (2006a) explained that "meaning is the determinate relationships between an act of consciousness and its object, which the intentional relationship establishes" (p. 315). Take, for example, Stalin as an intentional object. Depending on the mode of intention, he is Stalin the revolutionary, Stalin the leader, Stalin the dictator or Stalin the murderer. In this example, the meaning of Stalin is correlated with a specific perspective of intentionality. However, a full phenomenological reduction has not been completed because the object of Stalin is still present in the analysis as a phenomenon.

Giorgi et al. (2017) recognized that the main difficulty in adapting Husserl's epoché to empirical research is that the description of lived experiences comes not from the first-person perspective, but from a researcher's observations and recordings of someone else's experiences. They therefore argued that in order to apply Husserl's paradigm to descriptive psychology, the epoché and phenomenological reduction must be adapted to empirical research. Consequently, they emphasized a psychological reduction instead of the phenomenological reduction. Giorgi et al. (2017) proposed a prescriptive five-step procedure for pretranscendental phenomenological psychological research, which rests on the assumption that researchers can naturalize Husserl's phenomenological philosophy by replacing thoughts with speech.

The researcher therefore operates from an interview that has been transcribed verbatim. First, they read the transcript in its entirety to get a sense of the narrative. Second, the researcher assumes the psychological phenomenal perspective in the sense that the objects of the experiences are not assumed to necessarily exist in reality, but only as objects in thought (i.e., phenomena). This form of epoché and phenomenological reduction is therefore a partial reduction. This involves reducing the descriptions of our subjects' experiences to mere phenomena within consciousness. Third, the researcher proceeds with deconstructing the narrative into specific psychological meaning units. Fourth, they transform the meaning units in a "phenomenological psychological sensitive way" (p. 17). This entails, on the one hand, that the researcher articulates a psychologically informed understanding of these meanings and, on the other hand, a decontextualization in the sense that the meanings are articulated more generally and are therefore easier to compare with meanings derived from other subjects. This needs to be done as explicitly as possible in order to satisfy the aforementioned empirical scientific criteria. Fifth, the researcher now has transformed the narrative of the interview into a web of meanings or meaning structure, where the last step is to determine the meanings that are essential for this narrative in the sense that they are overarching.

It could be argued that phenomenological psychology's limited epoché is what Husserl referred to as a vocational epoché, which is what all professions do in order to focus on their subject matter. Giorgi (2006b) appeared to confirm this by stating that for the purpose of research, a specific disciplinary outlook must be infused with the phenomenological methodology, otherwise the analysis will simple be too unruly. In other words, "the data will always be richer than the perspective brought to it, but it is the latter that makes the analysis feasible" (Giorgi, 2006b, p. 354). The limited psychological epoché means that researchers confine themselves to the realm of the subjective experience with little consideration of the actual lived experience, which helps researchers avoid the trap of imposing theoretical explanations that make unsubstantiated psychological claims regarding cause and effect (Ashworth, 2009).

Heidegger's reduction, construction and destruction

As we have noted in the previous sections, Heidegger's perspective significantly diverged from Husserl's, but although Heidegger seemed to downgrade the importance of perception and intuition and instead elevated hermeneutic circumspection, both thinkers shared in the purpose of trying to discover a meaning that is not immediately accessible through mere observation. Therefore, the meaning discovery process requires some form of epoché and reduction. Dahlstrom (2018) argued that Husserl's methodology in principle is suitable for the analysis of the being of Dasein because "Heidegger's project requires the exclusion of any attempt to understand what to be means by referring some being" (pp. 216–218). Thus, Heidegger (1988) stated that "Being is always being of beings and accordingly it becomes accessible at first only by starting with some being" (p. 21). Subsequently, the task of the phenomenological method is to elucidate the existent being's way of being in this world and to figure out "whether this way of being has the same character in every being" (p. 19). Heidegger thus argued that turning the gaze from actual beings toward their ways of being is in fact a form of phenomenological reduction.

Nevertheless, this comparison of Husserl's and Heidegger's methods is perhaps more of an attempt to situate Heidegger within the phenomenological tradition (which Husserl began) than reckoning with the fundamental differences between these two thinkers. Heidegger's focus was on investigating the meaning of Dasein's being and not intentionality. Thus, in contrast to intentionality, Dasein is not related to the ego or subjectivity but is happening (Heidegger, 1988, p. 278). Dreyfus (1995, p. 163) argued that it is easier to understand the difference using the verb *Daseining*, meaning coping with being in the world, and argued that Dasein is "not a matter of private experiences" (p. 145)

Dasein's coping is, however, devious toward itself, and the researcher as well, in the sense that Dasein attempts to cover up its own authentic being and resists its uncovering. Therefore, the reduction cannot simply entail suspensions of presumptions and changing of the mental gaze from the actual human to its being, but, as Heidegger (2010) puts it, "the existential analytic constantly has the character of doing violence" (p. 298) because Dasein does not want the disturbance of coming face-to-face with its authentic self. Thus, Dreyfus (1995) argued that

> our understanding of our being is never fully accessible . . . Since everyday Dasein does not want to face up to its own interpretive activity and the consequent unsettledness of human being, it uses its everyday understanding to conceal the truth about itself.
>
> *(p. 35)*

In this connection, Heidegger 1968), in his later work *What is called thinking*, quotes Aristotle:

> just as it is with bats' eyes in respect to daylight, so it is with the mental vision with respect to those things which are by nature most apparent. The being of being is the most apparent; and yet, we normally do not see it – and if we do, only with difficulty.
>
> *(p. 110)*

Heidegger exemplifies this challenge with the notion of standing in front of a cathedral, where "we are faced not just with a church, a building, but with something that is present, in its presence" (p. 98). This presence is Christianity or religion in general, but it is difficult for us to see, because "we are standing within in it" (p. 110). Is this not indeed what social researchers are often preoccupied with? Uncovering the presence within the present? The presence of bias and privilege within present structures of society?

Indeed, it is difficult to have an outside perspective on what we stand within, and instead of a phenomenological reduction, which is central to transcendental phenomenology as well as phenomenological psychology, Heidegger (1988, p. 23) proposed a phenomenological method that goes beyond the reduction of the physical being to its phenomenal being by proposing a further move of destruction or deconstruction of existing conceptualizations and assumptions regarding the being of beings. Heidegger further proposed that people, in equal measure, need a positive move that guides them toward being due to the fact that the reduction and deconstruction alone do not make the being of human beings pop out. Consequently, Heidegger (1988, p. 23) suggested that deconstruction should take place in conjunction with phenomenological construction, and thereby posited "that the methodological meaning of phenomenological description is interpretation" (Heidegger, 2010, p. 35).

As we have noted in Chapter 1, the being of Dasein can be understood as "taking care of" (Heidegger, 2010, p. 347), which should not only be understood as taking care of things, but also as taking care of itself. Thus, taking care is ultimately always for Dasein's own purpose. Thus, Heidegger stated that Dasein can be understood from "the way its for-the-sake-of-it-self is connected with some current in-order-to" (as cited in Dreyfus, 1995, p. 245). Dreyfus (1995) further posited that because this in-order-to is always directed toward some future outcome (see, p. 244), the interpretation of the meaning of Dasein's being that Heidegger called for is always from the perspective of temporality.

Thus, Heidegger's notion of temporality is in fact an epoché and phenomenological reduction of natural time. The meaning derived from lived experience is found within a horizon where the chronological past, present and future have been reduced to mere phenomena and collapsed into temporality. This notion is important because it implicitly reduces the apparent recall of experiences to mere memory beliefs situated in the now and thereby also reduces speech to intentional speech-acts that can be studied hermeneutically like a text in which the researcher can elucidate the "who" and the meaning of being understood as projected possibilities of being for-the-sake-of and in-order-to.

Ricoeur's hermeneutic distanciation

Perhaps the real problem in translating Husserl's epoché and phenomenological reduction into social research lies in what we previously discussed in Chapter 1 (i.e., the third-person challenge). This is where researchers have to theoretically contend with the difference between personally grasping the essence of one's own thoughts and grasping the essence of other people's experiences in a phenomenological way based on the subjects' verbal disclosures. To this end,

Dreyfus (1995) argued that the problem is overblown in the sense "that in our everyday activities inner experiences play a decidedly secondary role" (p. 148). In other words, Dasein is not an ego, and Dasein always "interprets its being in terms of for-the-sake-of-which" (p. 148) and can therefore only understand itself in relation to other beings. Therefore, researchers do not engage with another mind, but with a publicly accessible Dasein. This fact is clearly demonstrated in a shared language (p. 155). Therefore, the problem of the other person in research only arises when researchers attempt to psychologize their experiences and meanings because that does presuppose some form of mind-to-mind access.

Consequently, Ricoeur (2019) departed from Husserl's phenomenology as he came to see that transcendental phenomenology, despite the epoché, was still too intertwined with psychology in its dogmatic focus on subjectivity (see pp. 72–73). Ricoeur, similar to Heidegger, thought that the discussion of whether meaning was constituted in consciousness or in cognition was beside the point because meaning lies outside in the world and not primarily in intentionality. Ricoeur (1994) therefore argued that attempting to draw a more stringent epoché for the purpose of isolating the "I" from the "others" simply does not lead to the meaning of being because from the publicness of Dasein follows that the meaning of the world is shared and not individually construed.

Consequently, Ricoeur (1994) claimed the "others," or rather the view they have of us, belongs to the constituting force of sense-making. Therefore, at the phenomenological level, a dialectic process plays out where, on the one hand, the ego posits itself, but the self only recognizes and understands itself through "the affection of others" (Ricoeur, 1994, p. 329). Consequently, it is this "the other" that is revealed in the epoché like a form of public Dasein that links the "I" with the community of others. Merleau-Ponty (1978) expressed this sentiment quite well by stating that "the phenomenological world is not pure being, but the sense, which is revealed, where the paths of my various experiences intersect, and also where my own and other people intersect and engage each other like gears" (p. xx).

Ricoeur (1994) bridged the textual tradition of hermeneutics with a more contemporary social research tradition by positing that "speech actions can be treated as a text and the interpretation of motives as reading" (p. 64). To this end, Ricoeur (2019) introduced an analytical move with a similar function as the epoché (i.e., distanciation), which serves to transfer autonomy to the "speech-acts," away from the actual speaker, so that people can behold these acts of speech as a form of imaginative variation of reality (pp. 76–77). Thus, hermeneutic distanciation is a way of interrupting the account of the lived experience where researchers take a step back and reduce the disclosure of these lived experiences to mere phenomena (see van Manen, 2016, p. 138). Therefore, scholars no longer consider the phenomenon of speech to be real in the sense that it is an accurate representation of what actually transpired. The intention is similar to Husserl's (i.e., grasping the essence through phenomenological reduction; MacAvoy, 2016), but because social researchers are not in the transcendental realm, the purpose is to thematize and signify meanings of speech-acts beyond what is the subjects' immediate intention to disclose.

In practical terms, Ricoeur appeared to introduce a double hermeneutic approach, where researchers first interpret the narratives from a mindset of belief, which means that they reflect on what is being actually disclosed. Researchers subsequently switch to an attitude of suspicion, where they approach the interpretation of the same disclosures from perspectives outside the "text." Dreyfus (1995, p. 37) argued that Ricoeur's hermeneutics of suspicion drew directly from Heidegger's notion of "doing violence" to interpret Dasein. By this, we are not implying the subjects are lying or trying to deceive us. The perspective of suspicion takes aim at the everydayness of the language that, similar to the everydayness of Dasein, covers up the authentic self. While words are "vessels of sense" (Heidegger, 1968, p. 129), Heidegger argued that the language we have learned to speak "plays with our speech – it likes to let our speech drift away into more obvious meanings of words" (p. 118). In other words, our speech becomes "usurped by common terms" (p. 119) like Dasein by "the-they." Heidegger thus argued that "this floundering in commonness is part of a high and dangerous game and gamble, in which, by the nature of language, we are the stakes" (p. 119).

Consequently, Heidegger (1968) proposed that we must try to listen to what is actually being said but admits that "this is particularly difficult for us moderns, because we find it hard to detach ourselves from the at first of what is common; and if we succeed for once, we relapse all to easily" (p. 130). To this end, Ricoeur enlisted heuristic strategies by employing, for example, Freudian psychoanalysis and Marxism as a lens of suspicion (Langdridge, 2008). This is because Freud, but also Marx, tended to view the content of consciousness as false (Ricoeur, 2019) or, at the very least, misleading.

The final step is quite the opposite of distanciation (i.e., appropriation of meaning), which, according to Ricoeur (2019), implies the struggle of the hermeneutic researcher against cultural distance and historical alienation for the purpose of making what is alien one's own (see p. 147). Ricoeur emphasized that it is neither a freewheeling spiritual process nor is it considering the intended audience. It is simply to "understand the author better than he understands himself . . . beyond the limited horizon of his own existential situation" (p. 147) by way of references in the text.

Appropriate way of practicing epoché and bracketing in a phenomenological study

It is a fact that a significant amount of published research claims to be phenomenological but without really engaging with the foundational literature in a manner that could demonstrate the phenomenological credibility of the research findings (Flynn & Korcuska, 2018). It is simply not sufficient to state that a study is phenomenological when researchers are studying "lived experiences" because a mere thematic description of a group of people's experiences with a phenomenon does not provide any particular phenomenological insights on its own. Dennett (2003) argued that, rather than trying to interpret what Husserl really meant, researchers should focus on the right way of doing phenomenology. However, understanding Husserl's overarching purpose with the epoché does inform the applied phenomenologists how, at least in principle, they can align with phenomenological philosophy and thereby, with some credibility, argue for the universal character of their research findings.

Bentz and Shapiro (1998) stated that in order to conduct social research from a phenomenological perspective, the researcher should first become a philosopher, which is an unrealistic proposition for most social researchers. Nevertheless, a purposeful engagement with the phenomenological literature should not require a degree in philosophy. The most important thing is to ensure the researcher realizes that phenomenology is not only a method, but also a broad theoretical framework with both epistemological and ontological features. Also, they should be aware that phenomenology could provide a theoretical lens to the study of experiences. Further, it can assist the researcher with alignment toward an appropriate method that can be justified in the literature and bestow credibility on the research outcomes. Therefore, the appropriate way of working with the epoché and phenomenological reduction is not by simply appropriating Husserl's terminology and reinventing its meanings as Moustakas (1994) appeared to do. The appropriate way should take its starting point as what the phenomenological research questions actually intend to uncover, either the meaning of an experience with a phenomenon or the meaning of being a person having such an experience.

The notion that the epoché and reduction provide phenomenological research with credibility in terms of the universality of findings is in fact not that different from similar considerations regarding how to avoid type 1 and type 2 errors in statistics. For example, if the population is not sampled correctly and alpha in a correlation study is set too lax, then the outcome would not be generalizable. In both cases, the researcher relies on subjective judgment calls regarding the analytical procedures, but whereas the phenomenological approach is validated in philosophy, the quantitative approach is validated by a mathematical formula. However, this does not mean that the inferences are any more objective than in the phenomenological example. In both cases, researchers are still just dealing with inferences, but they arrive at these in different ways. Arriving at a probability (which is what correlation studies do) does not represent any form of knowledge, just an assumption of chance that a hypothesis may not be supported.

The problem with much phenomenological research is that researchers often do not grasp the credibility that an appropriate adaptation of the epoché and reduction may bestow on the outcome. It is often the case that, instead of demonstrating how the adapted epoché and reduction lead to a phenomenological meaningful outcome, researchers resort to issuing formal antibias statements and, in some cases, list their own possible biases as a way of demonstrating fealty to the phenomenological paradigm (Creswell, 2007). While such exercise may hold therapeutic value for the researcher, Englander (2016) argued that novice researchers mostly misunderstand bracketing by assuming that it means nothing more than being an unbiased observer. Instead, the epoché ought to be understood as a change in viewpoint where focus is on subjectivity. Moran (2000) therefore argued that "phenomenology is a science of the essence of consciousness. . . . How to arrive at these essences without construing them psychological is the function of the epoché and the phenomenological . . . reduction" (p. 145).

Relatedly, Spaulding (2018) argued that a research design with less rigor in the application of the epoché risks falling prey to the dynamic of intersubjectivity. The procedure of member check, where the researchers, on the one hand, seek validity of their findings in the feedback from their subjects and, on the other hand, attempt to use this feedback as a safeguard against researcher bias, may in fact reinforce the dynamics of intersubjectivity. Spaulding (2018) thus argued that some phenomenological studies are nothing but a manifestation of simulation theory, which posits that the researchers simply derive their interpretations from imaginatively placing themselves in the position of the subjects. Consequently, this may lead to a situation where the outcome of the phenomenological research neither speaks to the universality of the phenomenon nor represents an ideographic account of the subjects' lived experiences, but in fact says more about the bubble universe that researcher and subjects have cocreated. In particular, the approach advocated by Moustakas (1994) and Bentz and Shapiro (1998) would risk falling prey to intersubjectivity, as they advocated a process of active engagement and coconstruction of meanings and seemingly forgot that they are conducting research, not doing therapy.

Ashworth (2009) therefore cautioned that an "impoverished account of the experience" (p. 6) may lead to a research outcome, which does not reflect actual lived experiences of the subjects. For example, a discourse psychological case study of coaching conversations with female executives demonstrated that the dialogue was not contextualized within the actual organizational and employment circumstances of these executives, but instead situated within a broader and more theoretical discourse regarding gender and leadership. Thus, the coaches did not appropriately consider the lived experiences of their clients, but instead fell victim to theoretical hegemony and, instead of meaningful insights, ended up reproducing abstract themes not directly relevant for these executives' lifeworlds (Graf & Fleischhacker, 2020).

What this case illustrates is the confusion of phenomena with actualities, where gender discrimination in the workplace, instead of being considered as a phenomenon, was considered as an empirical fact. However, only observable behaviors can be considered to be real; what those behaviors appear as or appear to be in apperception is then the phenomenon of experience. Therefore, the purpose of the epoché is to avoid the fallacy where researchers assume the phenomenon is some external real factual situation (Ashworth, 2009). Instead, researchers should consider the phenomenon in terms of the potential meaning of those actualities. This can be a challenging conversation with emerging researchers, who may feel that the phenomenon is real in the empirical sense of the word because the meaning of something feels true. Meaning and facts are, however, not the same thing, and scholars should be careful not to treat one as the other in research. Thus, Husserl (2001) stated,

> We must, above all, dwell upon the enigmatic double sense or manner, the two-sided context, in which the same experience has a content, and the manner in which in addition to its real and proper content, an ideal, intentional content must and can dwell in it.
>
> *(p. 94)*

The schematic below is an attempt at creating an overview and alignment model for the various phenomenological theoretical perspectives on experience and what meanings can be derived from studying them (see Table 3.1). Further, this overview attempts to convey the distinct approaches with regard to the epoché and reduction that the literature indicates are appropriate for each theoretical domain of experience investigations. They serve the purpose of moving the study from an initial ideographic description to a nomothetic research outcome that speaks to a depersonalized meaning transcending the individual. While this is not a comprehensive account of the phenomenological method, our hope is that this overview can at least serve as a starting point for a meaningful engagement with the foundational literature, much of which is referenced in this book.

Strengths and limitations of practicing epoché and bracketing in phenomenological research

The epoché both solves and creates problems for the researcher. It solves problems in the sense that it orientates researchers' attention toward a realm of the human experience (i.e., meaning), which is underappreciated by the more positivist scientific approaches. By suspending assumptions of causality between the objective reality and the experience, researchers gain new ground in the quest to humanize the social sciences. However, the application of the epoché gives rise to much methodological confusion because this concept is not only ambiguous in philosophical phenomenology, but also not intended for social research in the first place. Consequently, scholars have proposed a plethora of approaches inspired by the foundational literature, but often with little consideration as to how those approaches either confuse or enhance the specific research project.

Van Manen (2016) provided an entire catalog of epoché and reduction methods such as "epoché-reduction" (p. 222), which he interpreted as a form of openness: "heuristic reduction" (223), which he introduced as a sense of wonder; "hermeneutic reduction" (p. 224), which is also to be understood as openness; etc. Here, the problem is similar to that of Moustakas' (1994) empirical

TABLE 3.1 Theoretical Domains and Their Respective Features

Domain	Proponent	Data	Paradigmatic Lens	Experience Domain	Epoché and Reduction Procedures	Outcome
		IDEOGRAPHIC →				NOMOTHETIC
Transcendental subjectivity	Husserl & Merleau-Ponty	Thoughts/ Perception	Transcendental phenomenology	Givenness of transcendental subjectivity & intentionality	1. Epoché 2. Reduction (phenomenon) 3. Variation 4. Thematization	Essence: Meaning of acts of intentionality
Psychological subjectivity	Husserl & Giorgi	Disclosures of experiences	Phenomenological psychology	Apperception: Retention/ Protection Horizon Lived time	1. Epoché 2. Psychological reduction 3. Deconstruction 4. Transformation 5. Decontextualization 6. Abstraction	Psychological essence: Meaning of phenomenal experience
Beings	Heidegger	Disclosure of lived experiences	Dasein (Existential or ontological phenomenology)	Understanding/ Interpretation Temporality	1. Reduction (being) 2. Construction 3. Destruction	Meaning of being as possibilities
The self— affected by others	Ricoeur	Speech–acts	Hermeneutic phenomenology	Emplotment Narrative self Temporality	1. Distanciation 2. Interpretation: Belief and suspicion 3. Appropriation	Selfhood: Sameness Otherness Character

phenomenology, in the sense that van Manen appeared to take poetic license with the foundational literature, for example, the "epoché-reduction." It is not entirely clear from where van Manen acquired this term and how he arrived at his specific operational definition.

Based on what we have learned so far regarding the purpose of the epoché and reduction, it is somewhat confounding that van Manen introduced the epoché-reduction by stating "The basic idea of the epoché and reduction is to return to the world as we live it in the natural attitude" (p. 222). First of all, return from where? Second, how is reduction to be equated with "to open oneself to experience as lived" (p. 222)? Further, van Manen's account of the hermeneutic reduction as a method of "bracketing all interpretation and explicating reflectively" and to be aware of not being led by "preunderstandings" is equally confounding (p. 224). First of all, the purpose of hermeneutics is interpretation, and Heidegger's hermeneutic phenomenology does in fact operate with preunderstanding as the basis for circumspective seeing. Finally, it would have been relevant for van Manen to consider Ricoeur's hermeneutic phenomenology and his modification of the epoché and reduction (i.e., distanciation or suspicion).

Zahavi (2019) posited that phenomenological research does not need an epoché in order to analyze the meaning of experiences from a subjective personal perspective and argued that most qualitative researchers do just fine in exploring the lived experiences without having to go through the rigmarole of the epoché. In fact, he questioned whether it is reasonable to demand that applied phenomenologists engage in metaphysical considerations prior to investigating educational or health-care topics. In contrast, van Manen (2016) encouraged scholars and researchers to "receive their insights and inspiration from original phenomenological sources" (p. 16).

To this end, our reading of the foundational literature points to an understanding of the epoché and phenomenological reduction along the following dimensions: (a) an *attitude* of radical Cartesian doubt and questioning; (b) a *descriptive psychological methodology* with prescribed analytical steps and (c) a *hermeneutic distanciation*, which orients toward the being of beings and reduces disclosures to the phenomenon of speech-acts that can then be interpreted. In our previous elaborations, we have accounted for how this works in theory. How this works in practice is, however, another matter, which we will consider in the following.

The attitudinal epoché

When we consider epoché as an attitude, we should consider Husserl's Cartesian inspiration in terms of the doctrine of radical doubt. What is it then that social researchers doubt, and how do they operationalize doubt into method? Researchers doubt their own senses; they doubt that they are able to be open-minded and neutral; they doubt that their theories of mind and theories of lived experiences are suitable for the purpose of conducting research. Thus, Davidsen

(2013) articulated the epoché as "the idea of putting oneself philosophically in a position to hear and understand what is said" (p. 335).

In this way, van Manen (2016) argued that the epoché and reduction are more a style of thinking, where the researcher reflects on what makes life meaningful, than a concrete method (see p. 52). Van Manen expanded on this notion by arguing that the epoché is a form of opening up to life as it is lived, where researchers try to make contact with the lived experience (see p. 222). In other words, the ideal of the attitudinal epoché appears to be one where researchers assume a position of unbiased naïveté relative to the disclosures of lived experiences by their subjects.

For the purpose of applied phenomenology, Creswell (2007) therefore suggested that researchers could begin with describing their own experiences with the phenomenon in order to neutralize any biases before embarking on a study of other people's experiences. In concrete terms, Chan et al. (2013) suggested researchers should examine whether they are suitable or humble enough to actually engage with the proposed research topic, and the authors further discussed the possibility of delaying or minimizing the literature review prior to data analysis. Finally, they argued that researchers should allow for the research findings to be reviewed by the subjects in order to secure that the outcome accurately reflects their experiences. This interpretation of the epoché shows the reasoning behind member-check triangulation, simply because these scholars believed that validity ultimately rests with the subjects and not with the application of the methodology. It can therefore be argued that some scholars, in this way, approach epoché as an "anti-method."

Bentz and Shapiro (1998) took the attitudinal orientation one step further by suggesting that the researcher assumes the observer–participant role not only through extended interview sessions, but also by "imitating the movements or facial expressions" of the subjects while joining with them in their tasks and social activities. Essentially, the researcher is supposed to gain an understanding of the lived experiences through personal immersion and self-questioning. The research outcome would be the researcher's personal understanding of the phenomenon (see Bentz & Shapiro, 1998, p. 96). Further, they argued that "any analysis will delimit the meaning of an observation" and therefore, suggested delaying, for as long as possible, the structuring of the data (p. 99), for example, by retaining the interviews on a recorder instead of transcribing.

The fundamental problem with the attitudinal epoché in research is that phenomenological researchers' claim of having assumed the position of naïve observers can never really be verified. Although researchers may state that they have bracketed out their preconceptions and refrain from imposing theoretical explanations, readers cannot actually know if this is true (Giorgi, 2006b). One could compare this with promising your spouse not to admire other people at the beach. While we may have the best of intentions, there may be reasons to anticipate that such a promise may not be kept because of the inverse relationship between the inherent temptation and the available means of verification. It is simply not believable that a trained social scientist can set aside all theoretical assumptions with a jedi mind-trick. Thus, people never encounter something or someone from the perspective of nowhere (see Davidson, 2016, p. 162). In fact, it is easy to disguise a covert theoretical bias by simply choosing one set of terminology over another. The issue is even more potent when the researcher farms out the thematic analysis to a computer program, especially when conducting automatic text analysis (see Adu, 2020). Does software perform epoché or is software in fact pure coded bias?

Turning our attention to the subjects, researchers should realize that being a naïve observer only goes so far, as the accounts of lived experiences are naïve as well. However, what researchers are dealing with is likely far from that. In fact, a specific subject's and a specific researcher's attempts to engage with each other are an act of intersubjective understanding in the context of a research project. In other words, the subject's disclosure of lived experiences might have been quite different had it been conveyed over breakfast at home. For example, Luan and Li (2020) demonstrated through seven experimental studies that subjects are significantly more likely to construe objects based on their conceptual features (80%) when they are observed than when they are in private (57%). Thus, research subjects choose a more intellectual conceptual form of communication when they know a researcher is observing. Therefore, the notion that the ideal of the attitudinal epoché is unbiased naïveté is compromised as a method if researchers assume that subjects, instead of recalling lived experiences, are engaging in speech-acts, which are in part motivated by the research context. It is therefore somewhat misplaced to only worry about bracketing of the researchers' preconceptions if the data are not memory recall but experience beliefs (Tuffour, 2017).

The elaboration given earlier has demonstrated that executing the attitudinal epoché from a position of naïveté likely invites bias in the form of intersubjectivity between subject and researcher, which defies the purpose of phenomenology in terms of elucidating some form of universality of meaning that holds true beyond the immediate context. Giorgi (2006b) specifically cautioned researchers in the mold of Moustakas and Bentz and Shapiro, when he reminded researchers that they are not doing therapy but research, in the sense that the method of coconstructing reality with a single client undergoing therapy serves a different outcome than phenomenological research. In other words, while a phenomenological investigation into research subjects' experiences of being with others is exactly what both Heidegger and Ricoeur were advocating for (as a way of revealing the meaning of Dasein), if the intersubjectivity between the researcher and subject supersedes this due to lack of methodological rigor, there is an obvious threat to the credibility and trustworthiness of the research outcome.

Epoché as a methodology in descriptive psychology

Giorgi (2009) saw phenomenology as a foundational discipline that can provide descriptive psychology with a conceptual framework for conducting empirical research. He emphasized the necessity of a rigorous research methodology that can demonstrate alignment with phenomenological philosophy and, at the same time, respect empirical scientific standards. Giorgi (2010) therefore argued that "no claim for phenomenological status can be made if some legitimate type of reduction is not used" (p. 18) and that the reduction as well as other relevant steps in this type of qualitative research must be prescribed to the degree that the other researcher can either replicate the study or verify the outcomes.

Phenomenological psychology distinguishes itself methodologically from the more interpretative phenomenological approaches by proposing an epoché and reduction that profess a specific disciplinary psychological sensitivity with prescribed steps that borrow directly from Husserl's transcendental phenomenology. While Husserl did refer to a psychological reduction, it was a much less consequential move than the transcendental phenomenological reduction. For example, in *Crisis*, Husserl (1970) argued that every professional field applies some form of epoché in order to work consistently within its own unique paradigm. Therefore, Zahavi (2019a, p. 35) argued that the epoché and bracketing proposed in phenomenological psychology has only the name in common with Husserl's transcendental phenomenological epoché.

While phenomenological psychology claims to be a descriptive scientific approach, the application of the epoché and reduction moves this approach in the direction of idealizing the experience at the expense of the individuality and uniqueness found in the actual lived experience. However, in contrast to the hermeneutic approach, phenomenological psychology does not attempt an actual interpretation of subjects' disclosures, but does attempt to generalize the experiences and restate these in a psychological, disciplinarily informed way. In this connection, Englander (2016) argued that the epoché is the move that allows researchers to study intentionality instead of causality, and, at a minimum, researchers need to perform a psychologically informed epoché. This means that they disconnect from the actual experiences and reduce these to mere phenomena.

However, the problem of naturalizing phenomenology is still that scholars have to rely on subjects' recall of what their experiences were. Therefore, phenomenological psychology needs to work under the assumption that the subjects' disclosures are naïve and can be taken at face value. It is therefore suggested that the researcher should assume an attitude of equal unbiased naïveté in order to process and describe these allegedly naïve accounts of experiences without interpretation. Consequently, scholars run into the same problem as described under the attitudinal epoché, where van Manen (2016) argued that Ricoeur's hermeneutic analysis demonstrates that the phenomenological grounding in so-called pure description is compromised by interpretation from the get-go (see p. 137). Thus, the naïve attitude fails to take into account the fact that research subjects are not uneducated, and many subjects are quite familiar with common psychological concepts such as depression, burnout and codependency. Therefore, their accounts of lived experiences may not be pure, but be intertwined with conventional psychological theoretical wisdom that explains their experiences.

What further weakens Giorgi's argument for the epoché in phenomenological psychology is that Husserl introduced the epoché precisely as a method to escape the framework of descriptive psychology. In addition, many of Husserl's followers did not embrace the epoché or the phenomenological reduction, and their ideas are still considered to be situated within the phenomenological tradition. For example, Jean Paul Sartre declared that the reduction is "useless and disastrous" because the approach only measures the world by the knowledge that the individual may have of it, and obviously there is more to the world than just one person's horizon (see Sartre, 1984, p. 318).

However, if the essence of the applied methodological epoché is simply to focus on the subject matter at hand, then every academic discipline could in fact have their own vocational epoché, where the prescribed steps are informed by the peculiarities of their respective fields. Nevertheless, by approximating Husserl's technique, researchers may acquire an understanding of a more empirically based psychological essence of the phenomenon. It could therefore be argued that the phenomenological psychological epoché and reduction are characterized by ideation, depersonalization and generalization, like peeling an apple. On the surface, apples come in different shapes and colors, but once a person removes the peel and a few layers of flesh, at the core, apples share a similarity that was not observable at first glance.

The hermeneutic epoché

From a hermeneutic phenomenological perspective, the object of the study is not subjectivity, but rather the study of what it means to be in this world or what being is. The implications here are that the epoché may in fact not bring us in contact with the pure subjective experience. Ricoeur, therefore, understood the epoché as a reflective redirection and focusing of our perspective (Moran, 2000).

While there does not appear to be a universally agreed-on analytical framework for hermeneutics, Ricoeur (1994) posited that hermeneutics has three defining features: the self, the selfhood as sameness and the selfhood of otherness (see p. 16). The hermeneutic interpretation begins with identifying, "who is speaking, who is acting, who is recounting about him or herself and who is the moral subject" (p. 16). Consequently, scholars can say very little with regard to the meaning of the experience, but a lot more about the narrative self from the plot that is conveyed by the subjects. Therefore, instead of applying an attitude of naïveté, researchers approach these accounts with circumspection and reduce them from propositions of truth and facts to the phenomenon of "speech-acts." By doing so, the disclosure is not readily accepted as recollection about past experiences, but merely statements expressing subjects' theorizing about the meaning of these experiences and therefore is a manifestation of our subjects' ways of dealing with or coping with the present.

In this connection, Davey (2008) specifically pointed to Ricoeur's double hermeneutics, where researchers, when interpreting the disclosures of our subjects, should be open to their authenticity but, at the same time, be suspicious of the hidden symbolic meanings in their statements (see Itao, 2010, p. 15). Scott-Baumann (2012) argued that Ricoeur's emphasis on suspicion should be understood as a way to distance researchers from the text and maintain a dispassionate attitude, while still challenging the content in much the same way as a therapist would challenge the illusion of consciousness in psychoanalysis (see p. 70). Scholars therefore execute a limited reduction, where the disclosures are reduced to the phenomenon of speech-acts. Likewise, researchers also reduce the theories pertaining to real-word occurrences to phenomena. In practical terms, this means that both the disclosures and related theories lose their explanatory validity, which makes it possible for the researcher to begin a process of interpretation and reflection.

What about the bias and the influence of preexisting assumption that the attitudinal epoché tried to eradicate? Here, the hermeneutic argument is that this idea is somewhat misguided because presupposition, under all circumstances, is the foundation of understanding and that there is no such thing as a perspective from nowhere in research. Van Manen (2017) therefore suggested that the applied hermeneutic approach relies on "inseeing," which he defined as "the grasping of the primal structure of meaning of something" (p. 822). The challenge is that reflection, by nature, is quite personal and difficult to codify while at the same time exposing the researcher to the criticism of bias and prejudice. Dreyfus (1995) pointed out that "since we must begin our analysis from within the practices we seek to interpret, our choice of phenomena to interpret is already guided by our traditional understanding of being" (p. 36). Under all circumstances, there is a clear gap in the interpretative phenomenological literature pertaining to how researchers can more clearly demonstrate their "reflexive actions" as part of the interpretative process (Engward & Goldspink, 2020).

The outcome of the epoché may therefore be influenced by the context in time and space of the researcher and risks speaking more to the nature of the researchers' own lived experience with the subject material than the lived experiences of the subjects. Thus, without a guiding lens of theoretical framework or hermeneutics of suspicion that can serve as a lens, the researcher may unwittingly end up applying a "folk-psychological" frame of reference when trying to analyze the data and convey the research findings. In this connection, an often-overlooked weakness in the hermeneutic approach is that the focus on the speech-act phenomenon also reduces the scope of the experiences to just what is being said. The question is whether there is more to the experience than just what is signified in language and whether poor language skills, limited vocabulary or cognitive impediments means that the hermeneutic approach favors the well-articulated and, therefore, will present a somewhat elitist interpretation of the lived experience.

Summary

In the previous chapters, we have identified two overarching phenomenological schools: a transcendental phenomenological school, originated by Husserl, and an existential and hermeneutic school, based on Heidegger's ideas. Both schools share an interest in investigating experiences for the purpose of elucidating either the meaning of the world or the meaning of being. Subsequently, we attempted to account for how various phenomenological orientations associated with these two great thinkers conceived of the experience. We found that to be an absolute necessity because explicating exactly what it is we are studying is the first step in achieving a credible research outcome.

The second step in our quest for credible phenomenological research is to articulate analytical or reflective procedures that are congruent with how we choose to conceptualize the experience. To this end, we have demonstrated that each of the phenomenological conceptualizations of experience we have considered in this book has its own version of epoché and reduction. It is relevant for the social researcher to grasp these nuances because the methodological choices provide the consumers of phenomenological research a structure against which to assess the phenomenological credibility of the research outcomes and thereby the extent to which the findings can be said to lay claim to some degree of universality. In principle, the credibility of phenomenological research outcomes expressed by a statement of an essence hinges on the researchers' ability to:

- Avoid confounding different types of phenomenology;
- Conceptualize exactly what in the study is meant by experience;
- Explain, apply and justify an epoché and phenomenological reduction congruent with the first two points.

In studies where the researcher either does not address these techniques or does not manage them very convincingly, it would be fair to argue that the research findings only apply to the sample of subjects and therefore do not speak to the universality of the phenomena in question. Because research is often used to justify policies, interventions or treatments relative to a larger population than just the sample, it would, in theory, be problematic if the researcher is unable to demonstrate an understanding of the research domain within which they are operating. Moreover, it would be problematic if the researcher is unable to justify the universality of the research findings on the basis of a thoughtful and theoretically consistent application of the epoché and phenomenological reduction. If the essence of experiencing is meaning, then social researchers must clearly articulate their theoretical conceptualization of experience in order for their research outcome to have phenomenological credibility. The choices of epoché are therefore not just a free-for-all because each approach reflects quite distinct ontological and epistemological orientations.

Research designs need to make sense within their own frames of references. We cannot use the murky waters of qualitative research as an excuse for not fully clarifying ontological and epistemological perspectives. Researchers should not accept "lived experiences" as magic words that absolve them from intellectual and theoretical rigor. Therefore, as a minimum requirement, the researcher must be able to explain how the design and the chosen phenomenological approach

TABLE 3.2 Phenomenological Orientations and Their Respective Key Terms

Transcendental Phenomenology	Phenomenological Psychology	Existential Phenomenology	Hermeneutic Phenomenology
• Epoché • Phenomenological reduction • Imaginative variation • Intentionality • Brackets • Universality • Transcendental subjectivity	• Psychological reduction • Perception • Apperception • Meaning units • Vocational epoché • Subjectivity • Intersubjectivity • Retention • Protention	• Reduction • Construction • Destruction • Being of beings • Dasein • Circumspection • Understanding • Uncovering • Interpretation • Temporality	• Distanciation • Appropriation • Suspicion • Attestation • Emplotment • Narrative self

make sense for the purpose of the specific research project. In other words, can the design credibly answer the research question? To this end, Table 3.2 is a reminder of the key terms associated with the different phenomenological orientations we have examined so far.

References

Adu, P. (2020). Understanding the applications, strengths and limitations of automatic qualitative coding (conference presentation) [PowerPoint slides]. *SlideShare*. www2. slideshare.net/kontorphilip/understanding-the-applications-strengths-and-limitations-of-automatic-qualitative-coding-conference-presentation

Ashworth, P. D. (2009). William James's "psychologist's fallacy" and contemporary human science research. *International Journal of Qualitative Studies on Health and Well-being*, *4*(4), 195–206. https://doi.org/10.3109/17482620903223036

Bentz, V. M., & Shapiro, J. J. (1998). *Mindful inquiry in social research*. Sage Publications.

Butler, J. L. (2016). Rediscovering Husserl: Perspectives on the epoché and the reductions. *The Qualitative Report*, *21*(11), 2033–2043.

Chan, Z. C., Fung, Y., & Chien, W. (2013). Bracketing in phenomenology: Only undertaken in the data collection and analysis process. *The Qualitative Report*, *18*(30), 1–9. https://nsuworks.nova.edu/tqr/vol18/iss30/1

Creswell, J. W. (2007). *Qualitative inquiry & research design: Choosing among five approaches*. Sage Publications. ISBN: 1412916070

Dahlstrom, D. O. (2018). The early Heidegger's phenomenology. In D. Zahavi (Ed.), *The Oxford handbook of the history of phenomenology* (pp. 211–228). Oxford University Press. ISBN-13: 978-0198755340

Davey, N. (2008). Twentieth century hermeneutics. In D. Moran (Ed.), *The Routledge companion to twentieth century philosophy* (pp. 693–735). ISBN: 0-203-87936-8 Master e-book ISBN

Davidsen, A. S. (2013). Phenomenological approaches in psychology and health sciences. *Qualitative Research in Psychology*, *10*(3), 318–339. https://doi.org/10.1080/14780887.2011.608466

Davidson, S. (2016). Intersectional hermeneutics. In S. Davidson & M. A. Vallée (Eds.), *Hermeneutics and phenomenology in Paul Ricoeur: Between text and phenomenon* (pp. 159–174). Springer International Publishing. ISBN: 978-3-319-33424-0

Dennett, D. C. (2003). Who is on first? Heterophenomenology explained. *Journal of Conscious Studies, 10*(9), 19–30.

Dreyfus, H. L. (1995). *Being-in-the-world: A complimentary on Heidegger's being and time, division 1.* The MIT Press. ISBN: 0-262-54056-8

Englander, M. (2016). The phenomenological method in qualitative psychology and psychiatry. *International Journal of Qualitative Studies on Health and Well-being, 11*(1). https://doi.org/10.3402/qhw.v11.30682

Engward, H., & Goldspink, S. (2020). Lodgers in the house: Living with the data in interpretive phenomenological analysis research. *Reflective Practice, 21*(1), 41–53. https://doi.org/10.1080/14623943.2019.1708305

Flynn, S. V., & Korcuska, J. S. (2018). Credible phenomenological research: A mixed method study. *Counselor Education & Supervision, 57*, 34–50. https://doi.org/10.1002/ceas.12092

Giorgi, A. (2006a). Concerning variations in the application of the phenomenological method. *The Humanistic Psychologist, 34*(4), 305–319. https://doi.org/10.1207/s15473333thp3404_2

Giorgi, A. (2006b). Difficulties encountered in the application of the phenomenological method in the social science. *Analise Psicologica, 3*(24), 353–361. https://doi.org/10.1080/20797222.2008.11433956

Giorgi, A. (2009). Phenomenological psychology: A brief history and its challenges. *Journal of Phenomenological Psychology, 41*(2), 145–179. https://doi.org/10.1163/156916210X532108

Giorgi, A. (2010). Phenomenology and the practice of science. *Journal of the Society for Existential Analysis, 21*(1), 3–23.

Giorgi, A., Giorgi, B., & Morley, J. (2017). The descriptive phenomenological psychological method. In C. Willig & W. Rogers (Eds.), *The SAGE handbook of qualitative research in psychology* (pp. 176–192). Sage Publications. https://doi.org/10.4135/9781526405555

Graf, E. M., & Fleischhacker, M. (2020). "Wenn ich es nicht schaffe, liegt es an meiner Person und nicht an meiner Leistung" – Die Individualisierung struktureller Probleme im Coaching weiblicher Führungskräfte. Genderlinguistische und gendertheoretische Erkenntnisse für die Praxis. *Coaching Theorie & Praxis.* https://doi.org/10.1365/s40896-020-00034-0

Heidegger, M. (1968). *What is called thinking?* Harper & Row. ISBN-10: 006090528X

Heidegger, M. (1988). *The basic problems of phenomenology.* Indiana University Press. ISBN-10: 0253176875

Heidegger, M. (2010). *Being and time.* University of New York Press. ISBN-10: 1438432763

Husserl, E. (1970). *The crisis of European sciences and transcendental phenomenology: An introduction to phenomenological philosophy.* Northwestern University Press. ISBN: 081010458X

Husserl, E. (1973). *The idea of phenomenology.* Martinius Nijhoff. ISBN: 9024701147

Husserl, E. (2001). *The shorter logical investigations.* Routledge. ISBN: 9780415241922

Husserl, E. (2017). *Ideas: General introduction to pure phenomenology.* Unwin Brothers Ltd. ISBN-10: 0415519039

Itao, A. D. S. (2010). Poaul Ricoeur's hermeneutics of symbols: A critical dialectic of suspicion and faith. *Kritike an Online Journal of Philosophy, 4*(2), 1–17. https://doi.org/10.25138/4.2.a.1

Kant, I. (2007). *Critique of pure reason.* Penguin Group. ISBN: 9780140447477

Kee, H. (2019). Phenomenological reduction in Merleau-Ponty's the structure of behavior: An alternative approach to the naturalization of phenomenology. *European Journal of Philosophy, 28*, 15–32. https://doi.org/10.1111/ejop.12452

Langdridge, D. (2008). Phenomenology and critical social psychology: Irections and debates in theory and research. *Social and Personality Psychology Compass, 2*(3), 1126–1142. https://doi.org/10.1111/j.1751-9004.2008.00114.x

Luan, M., & Li, H. (2020). How do people construe objects when being observed? *Journal of Personality and Social Psychology, 119*(4), 808–823. https://doi.org/10.1037/pspa0000197

MacAvoy, L. (2016). Distanciation and epoché: The influence of Husserl on Ricoeur's hermeneutics. In S. Davidson & M. A. Vallée (Eds.), *Hermeneutics and phenomenology in Paul Ricoeur: Between text and phenomenon* (pp. 13–30). Springer International Publishing. ISBN: 978-3-319-33424-0

Merleau-Ponty, M. (1978). *Phenomenology of perception.* Routledge & Kegan Paul. ISBN-10: 0710036132

Merriam, S. B. (1995). Theory to practice: What can you tell form an N of 1?: Issues of validity and reliability in qualitative research. *Journal of Lifelong Learning, 4*, 51–60.

Moran, D. (2000). *Introduction to phenomenology.* Routledge. ISBN-10: 0415183731

Moustakas, C. E. (1994). *Phenomenological research methods.* Sage Publications. ISBN: 0803957998

Ricoeur, P. (1994). *Oneself as another.* The University of Chicago Press. ISBN: 0-226-71329-6

Ricoeur, P. (2019). *Hermeneutics and the human sciences.* Cambridge University Press. ISBN-10: 0521280028

Sartre, J. P. (1984). *Being and nothingness.* Washington Square Press. ISBN: 067186780 69780671867805

Scott-Baumann, A. (2012). *Ricoeur and the hermeneutics of suspicion.* Continuum. ISBN-13: 9781441170392

Siewert, C. (2007). In favor of (plain) phenomenology. *Phenomenology and Cognitive Sciences, 6*, 201–220. https://doi.org/10.1007/s11097-006-9035-x

Spaulding, S. (2018). *How we understand others: Philosophy and social cognition.* Routledge. ISBN: 9781138221581

Tuffour, I. (2017). A critical overview of interpretative phenomenological analysis: A contemporary qualitative research approach. *Journal of Healthcare Communication, 2*(52). https://doi.org/10.4172/2472-1654.100093

van Manen, M. (2016). *Phenomenology of practice.* Routledge. ISBN-10: 1611329442

van Manen, M. (2017). Phenomenology in its original sense. *Qualitative Health Research, 27*(6), 810–825. https://doi.org/10.1177/1049732317699381

Zahavi, D. (2019). Applied phenomenology: Why it is safe to ignore the epoch. *Continental Philosophy Review*, 1–15. https://doi.org/10.1007/s11007-019-09463-y

Zahavi, D. (2019a). *Phenomenology the basics.* Routledge. ISBN: 978-1-138-21670-9

Zahavi, D. (2019b). *Husserl's legacy.* Oxford University Press. ISBN: 978-0-19-885217-9

4

NAVIGATING THROUGH THE TENETS OF PHENOMENOLOGY

Objectives

Readers will be able to

1 Distinguish between the dominant applied schools of phenomenology
2 Understand methodological differences between phenomenological psychology and IPA
3 Understand the shortcomings of aligning with a specific school
4 Conduct a study with no affiliation with a specific school of phenomenology

Schools of phenomenology within social science research

The nature of qualitative research is such that there are no universally agreed-upon approaches similar to what one would find in quantitative research. Nevertheless, two approaches to phenomenological research have emerged as dominant within the field: IPA (Norlyk & Harder, 2010). Descriptive phenomenological psychology draws its theoretical credibility from Husserl's earlier writings and has psychological subjectivity as its research domain. In contrast, IPA aims to describe and interpret lived experiences. This approach draws on a broad range of phenomenological ideas, and proponents of IPA select the tenets that suit their purposes rather than building on a particular school of thought. In the following, we will examine the differences between these two applied approaches and subsequently consider the possibility of conducting phenomenological research unaligned with any particular school of thought or established method.

Scope of phenomenological psychological research

For most researchers, psychological and transcendental phenomenology are somewhat intertwined, and even Husserl (2017) stated that "psychology is implicitly contained in transcendental phenomenology" (p. 23). Relatedly, Zahavi (2019b, p. 157) acknowledged that the lines between phenomenology and psychology are blurry, and during the early days of Husserl's career, the influence of Brentano's philosophical psychology still appeared to be significant. For example, in Husserl's *Logical Investigations* from around 1900, he initially defined phenomenology as a form of descriptive psychology before his transcendental turn (see Husserl, 2001, p. 96). However, later, Husserl rejected the notion that phenomenology is a form of descriptive psychology because phenomenology has a transcendental character and differs from psychology by disengaging the preconceptions of the "natural attitude" (Zahavi, 2008, p. 668).

Ashworth (2017) posited that phenomenological psychology aims to study the meanings that constitute experiences and that the "intentional realm is the only appropriate venue" (p. 41). He further argued that the West Coast and East Coast dichotomy, regarding the significance of internal and external sources of meaning-making, is of no major significance. This is because the notion of a "reality distinct from experience does not play a part in the realm of intentionality" (p. 55). In other words, whether objects in people's experiences are real and external or simply internal noema matters little for how consciousness intends them. In phenomenological psychological research, researchers therefore focus on the meaning of a particular experience to the self (Ashworth, 2016). Thus, Ashworth (2017) defined the research scope of phenomenological psychological research in terms of investigating the different modes of intentionality through detailed descriptions of subjects' "*identity, sense of agency, feelings and sense of presence and voice in the situation as they appear*" (p. 54). Therefore, according to Ashworth (2016), the psychological perspective entails an attempt to uncover the meanings people ascribe to everyday experiences, and Ashworth illustrated this using an instructive example of a phenomenological research question, "*what is it like to experience something like this?*"

In addition, Englander (2016) argued that within phenomenological psychology, the focus of research is the phenomenon and not the specific population. It could therefore be argued that the lived experiences are a means to an end for phenomenological psychologists and that the focus of this discipline is the "mental indoors."

Phenomenological psychological research method

Contemporary phenomenological psychologists attempt to draw closer to Husserl's transcendental phenomenology and seem not to be content with their field's being relegated to merely thematizing apperceptions. They have therefore attempted to bring the focus back to the transcendental realm and the role of intentionality (i.e., all subjective mental processes that constitutes how an object is presented in mind; van Mazijk, 2017).

In this way, Applebaum (2012) firmly criticized the position of the qualitative researcher, who, in his view, mistakenly believes that the scientific method, where the various steps of the research procedure can be reproduced, is only relevant in quantitative research and therefore can be discarded in phenomenological studies. Applebaum argued that in order for qualitative research to be considered scientific, the research design and approach must demonstrate "a collectively understood means of access to the phenomenon under investigation and must be appropriate to the phenomenon investigated" (p. 47). Giorgi (2019) therefore argued that it is "by means of the methods of reflection and description, the intentional relation of consciousness can be discovered" (see p. 138).

The epoché and research credibility

As we have seen in Chapter 3, phenomenological psychologists attempt to formulate a research approach that is both rigorous and congruent with Husserl's philosophical epoché and phenomenological reduction. Husserl's method of epoché and phenomenological reduction are techniques designed to isolate the transcendental subjectivity from the empirical psychological subjectivity. Moreover, it is therefore a defining feature of phenomenological research that scholars must relate to. The reason is quite simple but admittedly difficult to grasp. Without some form of technique to facilitate direct contemplation of subjectivity, researchers will not be in a position to argue that research findings have universal credibility. Thus, the difference between psychological and transcendental phenomenology is that the psychologist remains focused on the phenomenon, whereas the phenomenologist focuses on intentionality. Therefore, the function of the epoché in applied research becomes that of turning toward the phenomenon and distancing from the individual. Consequently, the role of the epoché is that of a method that demonstrates the credibility of the research findings within the specific domain of subjectivity with regard to a specific phenomenon Giorgi, 2006).

However, there is nothing preventing the psychologist from executing a transcendental turn and thereby considering intentionality on its own terms. Subsequently, when returning from the transcendental mode, the insights the researcher may have acquired will (in the natural mode of thinking) expand the psychologist's insights into the phenomenon. In this manner, the noema (meaning) will, in the natural psychological realm, belong to the phenomenon as yet another quality that only came to light due to the phenomenological reduction. Thus, transcendental phenomenology can serve to enrich psychological research, when the researcher has grasped not only meaning as constituted in the horizon of apperception, but also the hidden meaning of givenness (Husserl, 1970, p. 210). Is this like crossing the river to collect water? Perhaps, and such an approach suffers from the fact that it is impossible to demonstrate and verify in research and likely more relevant for those psychologists who are engaged in therapy.

In contrast, some qualitative researchers who are unfamiliar with or skeptical about the phenomenological method will often emphasize that the credibility of the research outcome can be derived from in-group verification or member check. In such cases, the researchers present their findings to their subjects in order to secure validation of their findings (Merriam, 1995). However, Giorgi (2010) rejected the fact that validation of research findings can be derived from such a procedure and argued that proponents of member-check confound therapy with research and that phenomenological psychologists should not attempt to derive validity from their subjects' opinions about their research. Giorgi (2006) argued that while the essence is derived from the subjects' first-person accounts, the articulation of the essence should be considered a disciplinary endeavor and not a collaborative effort between researchers and subjects.

Thus, Giorgi (2006) stated that "the purpose of research is not to clarify the experience that the individuals have for their own sake, but for the sake of the discipline" (p. 358). Consequently, the articulation of the psychological essence is a process where the researcher attempts to develop thematic headlines that capture the descriptive content of the experience from a distinct psychological perspective. For example, if the subjects retold an experience as horrid, brutal and terrible, it would make sense for the phenomenological psychologist to thematize such disclosures under the headline of *traumatic experiences.*

Descriptive or interpretative? Lifeworld fractions

Phenomenological psychologists maintain that their approach remains descriptive and not interpretative because the analysis only makes subtle modifications to the interview transcripts for the purpose of generalization. Nevertheless, phenomenological psychologists lay claim to a distinct privilege in elucidating the essential meaning of the experience of others (Giorgi, 2010). The problem is how to justify such claims when psychologists do not actually share the consciousness of their subjects. Husserl (2017) pointed out that people have immediate access to their own inner and outer perceptions, but not to the perceptions of others (see pp. 51–52). Likewise, Merleau-Ponty argued, "If it is already difficult to say that my perception, such as I live it, goes unto the things themselves, it is indeed impossible to grant access to the world to the others' perception" (Merleau-Ponty et al., 1968, p. 9). People can observe the behaviors and reactions of other people, but not through perception, only through intuition. Consequently, when the researcher assumes a psychological phenomenal perspective, it could be argued that it is a form of idealization of the experience (Giorgi et al., 2017). Obviously, these idealizations of an experience must draw from some conceptual framework, which makes the claim of pure description somewhat questionable.

From our elaborations on Husserl's views regarding descriptive psychology in Chapter 2, we could see that he acknowledged that the study of apperceptions could be conducted with or without a theory. Further, our elaborations in Chapter 3 on the epoché and phenomenological reduction also indicated that Husserl found there was a limit to how far people could take the reduction if they were still to be able to describe their findings. Finally, while phenomenologists' perspectives may be transcendental, their reporting of findings will always take place in the natural world. Accordingly, Ashworth (2017) posited that in so far that focus remains on intentionality, it is justifiable to apply interpretation, "just so far as it can be seen to stay with and illuminate lived experience" (p. 59).

Similar to Husserl's (1970, p. 91) view in *Logical Investigations* that suspending ontology would make the description of the essence of intentionality difficult, Ashworth (2016) argued that suspending the lifeworld is equally impossible in descriptive phenomenological psychology because the experience is situated within that reality. Consequently, Ashworth (2016) stated that

> The presupposition of a lifeworld seems to go against the bracketing procedure of the epoché. However, the lifeworld is a necessary exception. Were we to bracket it, it would inevitably reappear as soon as an experience was opened up for description.
>
> *(p. 23)*

Ashworth (2016) thus proposed what he called eight fractions of the lifeworld that the researcher can utilize as a vehicle to connect the phenomenon back to the lifeworld. The fractions of the lifeworld that can assist descriptions are concepts such as: "*self, sociality, embodiment, temporality, spatiality, project, discourse and moodness*" (p. 23). The concept of self that Ashworth introduced is quite similar to the notion of Dasein that we considered the past chapters. He thus stated that lifeworld informs the subject's notion of self and "it is often explicitly (and always implicitly) the case that my selfhood or identify is bound up with my relationships with others" (p. 25). Thus, sociality, understood as the relationship with others, is essential for people's identities, and with this notion we can draw parallels to Ricoeur's (1994) call for a "phenomenology of the self, affected by the other than self" (p. 33).

The notion of embodiment draws from Merleau-Ponty's insight that the experience is mediated by the body, and in phenomenological psychology, this could, for example, be relevant in the study of an individual's experience of their gender. Temporality, although philosophically complex, acquires in phenomenological psychology the meaning of apperception that we have discussed in Chapter 2. Similar to the notion that apperception occurs on a temporal horizon or retention and protention, lived experiences also take place in a spatial horizon. For example, studies of the perceptions of crime and vulnerability have, in the past, demonstrated a connection between that experience and architectural design (Holzman et al., 1996). With the notion of project, Ashworth drew on Heidegger's (2010) conceptualization of the being of Dasein as "taking care of" (p. 67).

In Chapters 2 and 3, we specifically discussed how Dasein understands the meaning of its being from the activities and copings it is engaged in. The notion of discourse invokes our previous elaborations on speech–acts and the insight that the language available to people possesses its own a priori interpretation of reality. Thus, Heidegger (2010) emphasized that "the human being shows itself as a being that speaks" and argued that discourse is constitutive for Dasein's being in the world (p. 159). Further, Gadamer saw that speech is the most consequential mode of being in the world and being with other people and that language therefore embodies the symbols of existence (Moran, 2000). The final fraction of the lifeworld Ashworth (2016) considered was moodness. He did not consider moodness to be an emotional response to an experience, but more in terms of an "atmosphere" (p. 30). Dreyfus (1995, p. 170) further clarifies the concept of moodness by arguing that moods are not only private, but also public, and should be "understood as specifications of a dimension of existence, i.e. of affectedness as a way of being in the world" (p. 172) and pointed to cultural sensibilities, norms and social moods as examples.

Each abstraction or fraction is relevant for every phenomenon, but not every abstraction may be equally relevant for every study. It is easy to see how this notion opens the door for psychological conceptual frameworks to assume the role of heuristic strategies that can assist with focusing the researcher's exploration of the experiences with a phenomenon (see Figure 4.1).

Scope of IPA

Smith, one of the founders of IPA, stated that "the primary goal of IPA researchers is to investigate how individuals make sense of their experiences" (Pietkiewicz & Smith, 2014, p. 8). In this manner, Smith (Eatough & Smith, 2017) suggested that IPA is engaged in phenomenological psychological investigations

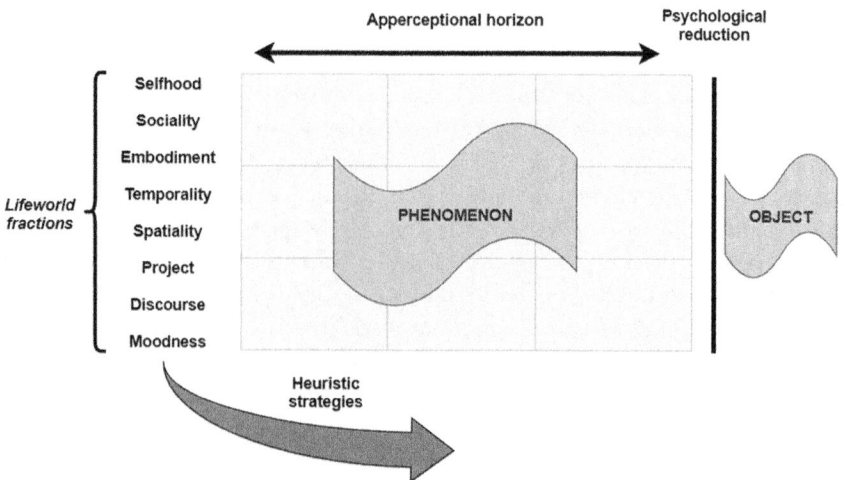

FIGURE 4.1 How Lifeworld Fractions Are Used to Connect Phenomenon to the Object in the World

of experiences. It is, however, not the typical psychological understanding of experience as a cognitive event that IPA researchers are interested in. It is more the perceived significance of the experience that is within the scope of IPA. Thus, Smith et al. (2009) stated, "When people are engaged with and experience of something major in their lives, they begin to reflect on the significance of what is happening and IPA research aims to engage with these reflections" (p. 3).

IPA is often associated with studies within the fields of nursing and educa-tion, where there is great interest in understanding the actual experiences of stakeholders in order to improve institutional outcomes. Thus, the ideographic nature of IPA provides rich and detailed descriptions of concrete experiences of, for example, patients' access to health-care services or practitioners' approaches to decision-making with regard to treatments and interventions (Anderson et al., 2019). Ideographic findings like these may not speak to the broader understand-ing of a phenomenon but can be transformed into immediate and meaningful institutional changes.

Methodology of IPA

Eatough and Smith (2017) argued that "without phenomenology, there would be nothing to interpret, without hermeneutics, the phenomenon would not be seen" (p. 5). Thus, their justification for IPA was that this approach combines two pow-erful schools of thought for one purpose: to elucidate the broad meaning of lived experiences. Smith argued that IPA is situated within the phenomenological tra-dition because of its focus on lived experiences in a nonbiased manner. Thus, IPA is, in contrast to Giorgi and Moustakas, not an attempt to operationalize Husserl's transcendental phenomenology for the purpose of research but draws on multiple ideas, ranging from Husserl to Merleau-Ponty to Heidegger (Smith et al., 2009).

Smith claimed that the purpose of IPA is to elucidate what lived experiences mean to human beings (Eatough & Smith, 2017). To this end, proponents of IPA attempt to integrate both phenomenological and hermeneutic perspectives into one approach, but because these theoretical orientations are so different, the price IPA pays is the loss of a coherent methodology. Thus, Smith et al. (2009) emphasized that there are no right or wrong ways to carry out IPA and encour-aged researchers to develop their own methods (see p. 80).

Nevertheless, Smith et al. (2009) argued that IPA applies "a double hermeneu-tic" approach in the sense that "the researcher" attempts "to make sense" of the sense their subjects made of their experiences (p. 3). Essentially, this is accom-plished through an interpretative process where researchers imagine themselves in their subjects' shoes. This is a significantly different conceptualization of double hermeneutics compared with Ricoeur's shift between attitudes of faith and suspi-cion. It is quite similar to Moustakas' reinterpretation of transcendental imagina-tive variation, where researchers and subjects, in reality, co-construct meanings.

Although IPA proponents claim that they have an interest in psychology, this methodology is quite different from what Giorgi proposed, in the sense that IPA does not operate with any recognizable form of epoché and reduction.

Consequently, the analysis of the experience stays within the context of the subjects' lifeworld, and IPA thereby acquires a distinct ideographic character similar to an in-depth case study of an individual. Thus, Smith et al. (2009) stated that IPA "wants to know in detail what the experience for this person is like, what sense this particular person is making of what is happening to them" (p. 3). Naturally, IPA operates with quite a small and homogeneous sample of subjects in order for such detailed inquiries to be doable.

Due to the ideographic character of IPA, it is an open question if this approach is phenomenological. In contrast, phenomenological psychology approaches the experience in the reduction for the purpose of understanding the phenomenon in new ways and not the subjects' lifeworld. In other words, while an ideographic approach may be a starting point in a phenomenological investigation, phenomenology eventually acquires a **nomothetic** character as it seeks the universal within the actual. Thus, Churchill (2014) argued that "the phenomenologist shifts the attention away from the individual experience grasped for its own sake and towards the category or class of experiences of which the individual experience is now taken as merely an example" (p. 4).

While IPA is interested in the subjects' lived experiences and how they signify them, a mere thematic description of lived experiences with a phenomenon is not a phenomenological description. In phenomenology, researchers search for the idealized meaning of the experience. Thus, IPA is essentially a researcher's do-it-yourself project without prescribed steps that normally characterize scientific approaches to research. This is, however, not to say that the outcomes of IPA research are not valuable for understanding a particular group of people. It can help researchers understand the sense individuals make of their experiences, which in turn, may inform best practices in, for example, health-care and educational settings in relation to specific clients.

Main contentions between the schools of phenomenology

Due to the increasing use of phenomenology in social research, in recent years, there have been ongoing and often spirited discussions between philosophical and applied phenomenologists as well as debates between proponents of the various applied traditions as to what constitutes legitimate and credible research. In the following, we will revisit the gist of these arguments, as they are illustrative of the limitations inherent to the various approaches. This is relevant for emerging social researchers, as they have to delimit the scope of their studies and identify methodological limitations that may influence the credibility of their research findings.

Contention regarding the epoché and phenomenological reduction

Although alien to many researchers and even disputed by Husserl's own followers, the notion of the epoché and phenomenological reduction has been tremendously influential in the attempts to establish an applied phenomeno-logical research method. Consequently, the proponents of the phenomenological psychological school (Giorgi et al., 2017) argue that only qualitative researchers who embrace and apply the epoché and bracketing can claim that their research is phenomenological.

This is a somewhat confounding position because descriptive phenomenologi-cal psychology is exactly the discipline Husserl's epoché and phenomenological reduction was intended to move the researcher beyond. Cairns (2010), who in his time was considered one of Husserl's followers, stated this in the following manner:

> A psychological interpretation of Husserl's results is a simplification. The most abstruse of his methodological theories, *the theory of transcendental phenomenological reduction, is disregarded when his results are interpreted psychologically* . . . . phenomenology is not meant to be anybody's psychol-ogy. It has left unnecessary difficulties in the way of the psychologist who wants to discover in Husserl's writings whatever is relevant to psychology as a natural science.
>
> *(p. 2)*

This should not be construed as an argument against phenomenological psy-chology. It is, however, a critique of the modified psychological reduction, which should ensure that the researcher is focused on phenomena rather than the ideo-graphic content of the lifeworld disclosures that comprises the research data. It is not entirely clear exactly why it is not possible for the researcher to maintain focus on the phenomenon without the steps that Giorgi prescribed (Giorgi et al., 2017)

Giorgi's argument was that the psychological reduction allows the researcher to explicate the meaning of the experience using psychological terminologies for the purpose of producing knowledge for the discipline of psychology. How-ever, all scientific disciplines use their own terminologies without engaging in philosophical moves, which is exactly what Husserl meant when he alluded to a vocational reduction. Further, Ashworth (2016) argued that phenomenological researchers should use the same terminology their subjects use when describing their experiences and the meanings of these experiences.

Van Manen (2016) argued that the step-by-step approach of Giorgi's phe-nomenological psychological analysis may appeal to novice researchers in need of methodological scaffolding but using "rule bound methods leads to a shallow insight" (p. 211). While such step-by-step approaches are easy to follow and in much demand among students, they suffer from focusing on technique over a broader engagement with the phenomenological ideas. Thus, Zahavi (2019c) argued that it is likely to be counterproductive when researchers attempt to mimic Husserl's philosophical procedures because most qualitative researchers end up "choking on methodological meta-reflections" and "misrepresent the intricacies of the philosophical phenomenology" (p. 10). Van Manen therefore promotes what is sometimes referred to as an esthetic approach to qualitative research, which relies more on the poetic than the technical skills of the researchers (Applebaum, 2012).

Does IPA lack scientific rigor?

Within the applied schools of phenomenology, there are contentious exchanges between the originators of contemporary phenomenological psychology and IPA. The gist of the argument is that Giorgi (2011) believed IPA does not secure an appropriately developed theoretical and philosophical underpinning and takes poetic license with the foundational literature. While IPA scholars frequently quote the foundational literature, it is not obvious how the phenomenological theories actually inform IPA research designs. For example, the notion of epoché and phenomenological reduction is not integrated in an IPA methodology.

Thus, Giorgi (2011) argued that because IPA does not have a prescribed method, it is not possible to replicate an IPA study or verify its procedures against a commonly agreed-to standard, and IPA therefore is unscientific. In fact, Giorgi went as far as positing that the founders of IPA simply developed a pragmatic but generic qualitative research approach and then subsequently attempted to connect it to the field of phenomenology by picking and choosing quotes from the foundational literature. Because very few emerging scholars would ever read this literature, IPA's interpretation of key concepts would therefore not be questioned. For example, proponents of IPA often state that the human being is a Dasein, which is to misconstrue Heidegger's philosophy because Dasein is more accurately understood as existence (see Heidegger, 2010, p. 36). Thus, Heidegger's phenomenology is not the interpretation of lived experiences for their own sake, but for the sake of understanding the meaning of being and not the actual human being.

The critique is perhaps a bit overblown because Giorgi's own version of the epoché and reduction appears to be nothing more than what Husserl (1970, p. 137) identified as a vocational epoché that allows workers to focus on the goals of their professions. Consequently, Zahavi (2019c) argued that Husserl's foundational work did not provide a strong case for why phenomenological psychology must operate with an epoché and reduction. Nevertheless, Zahavi (2019a) did point out that Husserl would likely consider the ideographic feature of IPA to be inauthentic phenomenological research and thus stated, "It is no coincidence that a purely descriptive endeavor devoid of systematic ambitions was dismissed by both Husserl and Scheler as a mere picture book phenomenology" (p. 34).

Limitations of aligning with a specific school when conducting a study

Merleau-Ponty (1978) argued that empirical sciences have a tendency to "force the phenomenal universe into categories, which makes sense only in the universe of science," where these worldviews and paradigms present a false narrative of a detached external objectivity with a causal relationship to the mind (p. 11). A similar critique could be leveled against applied phenomenological research approaches. In a manner of speaking, phenomenological research is unique in the sense that the researchers already know beforehand what the outcome will be (i.e., the meaning). Thus, the research question together with the choice of phenomenological framework predefines whether researchers will find the meaning of the experience or the meaning of being.

Our previous elaboration has demonstrated how Husserl's phenomenology tends to inspire a psychologization of the experience, while Heidegger's orientation seems to inspire a somewhat more hermeneutic and ontological approach. Accordingly, qualitative researchers tend to find what they are looking for, while tending to ignore data that do not conform to their theoretical and methodological filters. Thus, aligning with a specific school or applying a specific phenomenological framework may enhance overall alignment for the research components, but at the same time, also limit the researcher's perspective on the experience.

For example, consider a hypothetical study of nurses' experiences with caring for patients hospitalized with COVID-19. If the research framework aligns with Husserlian phenomenology, the starting point of such inquiries would begin with perceptions. Because scholars cannot directly access other people's immediate perceptions, the researcher would instead identify essential features of nurses' experiences and describe these thematically. Nevertheless, the underlying theoretical assumptions of transcendental phenomenology would lead the researchers toward psychologizing the research findings.

If the research perspective instead was informed by Heidegger or Ricoeur, the study would acquire an existential and hermeneutic character. In this case, the role of perception and apperception would be diminished. Thus, the focus shifts from psychologizing the experience to personalizing it. Consequently, the data which the researcher would be interested in would relate to the subject's doings, copings and dealings with the situation.

The difference is essentially between experiencing as a psychological phenomenon and lived experiences as happening in the world. The problem is that the subjects themselves do not make these subtle distinctions; these are analytical categories that delimit research and not an accurate reflection of what it means to experience something. Nevertheless, when the researchers align themselves with one school, they are limited with respect to what insights may be produced (see Table 4.1).

It is an ongoing discussion whether phenomenology, especially Husserl's transcendental phenomenology, is limited in the sense that it struggles to address intersubjectivity, social structures and cultural meanings. This accusation against phenomenology is based on the notion that subjectivity and the first-person perspective are always front and center in any analysis and that lived experience, in fact, means direct experience with something. In contrast, philosophers such as Schutz (Deep, 2020) have argued that there are other realities than just the

TABLE 4.1 Schools of Phenomenology and Their Respective Characteristics

School of Phenomenology	Focus of Inquiry	Methodology	Goal of Inquiry
Transcendental phenomenology (Husserl)	Intentionality, transcendental subjectivity and subjectivity in general	Phenomenological reduction in order to turn from the phenomenon toward subjectivity	• Attain the essence of experience • Epistemological explication of experiencing
Phenomenological psychology (Husserl/ Giorgi)	Psychological subjectivity	Reduction in order to turn from actualities toward the phenomenon.	• Essential themes of apperceptional experiences
Existential phenomenology (Heidegger)	Dasein	Attain an interpretation-mediated understanding of being through human beings' copings and dealings with the world	• Uncover the meaning of being from a horizon of temporality • Ontological explication of experiencing
Hermeneutic phenomenology (Ricoeur)	Identity	Distanciation and suspicion Reflective interpretation of the narrative plot	• Uncovering the narrative self

immediate experience. While phenomenologists such as Husserl have focused on the givenness of objects and reality, Schutz argued that lived experiences are constructed and that race, caste, class, etc., are not phenomena, but social facts. People may or may not have a direct experience with such social facts, but they are nevertheless part of social reality. Precisely because social facts are constructed, their meanings are found not only in a first-person lived experience, but also in the collective perspective of groups of people and their histories. In this way, Eidelson (2003) argued that collective beliefs can distort experiences when data that do not confirm core beliefs are simply ignored. He especially singled out beliefs such as superiority, injustice, helplessness, vulnerability and distrust. These beliefs may be culturally transmitted and are therefore not always derived from direct experiences, but nevertheless still play a significant role in perpetuating social conflicts.

The purist argument would be that phenomenology explains any and all objectification of the natural world and that it is constitutive of sociology as well. Thus, Zahavi (2018, p. 734) consistently argued that Husserl was not a solipsist and that his philosophical exploits addressed the problem of intersubjectivity as well. While this is correct, it is perhaps fair to say that the social realities of class, race and gender were not within the scope of Husserl's investigations. In contrast, Heidegger's notion of Dasein being public and his elaboration on the dictatorship of "the-they," as well as Ricoeur's call for a phenomenology of the effect of others on the I, clearly pointed to a phenomenological orientation toward the collective.

Phenomenology can be undecided as to whether it is a kind of descriptive psychology, epistemology, ontology or methodology, but it is quite clearly not sociology. Further investigations into the role of belief systems should be considered when exploring lived experiences with contentious social phenomena. The question is whether such beliefs should be treated as actualities (i.e., social facts) or as part of the experience horizon alongside other phenomena.

Conducting a study with no affiliation to a specific school of phenomenology

We encourage novice researchers to engage with the foundational literature, make it their own and select a heuristic strategy informed by a continuum of phenomenological ideas, ranging from the preeminence of transcendental subjectivity over psychological subjectivity toward the existential and hermeneutic paradigms. The key point is to ensure alignment between the major components (i.e., research question methodology and theory; Adu, 2019).

It worth remembering that a scientific community maintains the relevance of a worldview (i.e., theories, models, assumptions and practices) by successfully applying it to different situations, behaviors or occurrences (Adu, 2019). In some cases, to avoid the abandonment of a worldview, the scholarly community (a discipline) makes the necessary adjustment to the paradigm, increasing its ability to address/explain observations. If it fails to address the challenges it encounters, an unsatisfied scientific community member could either form a new community with a new worldview or join another existing community (Kuhn, 1996).

In this way, social researchers may have no interest in affiliating with any particular phenomenological school of thought and, consequently, throw out the entire framework of phenomenology and replace it with conventional conceptual frameworks drawn from social psychology or sociology. This is a trend seen in many doctoral dissertations, where students prefer a framework that is aligned with their topic rather than the phenomenological research methodology. This could of course be construed as undermining the credibility of the phenomenological research outcomes, but instead of opposing this trend, we choose to provide guidance on how an unaffiliated design can still be phenomenological.

Arguing from the pragmatic perspective, we believe in nonaffiliation with any school of phenomenology. "Pragmatists focus on evaluating existing models, theories, paradigms and research methods, and selecting appropriate ones for their inquiry" (Adu, 2019, p. 2). As a nonaffiliate, you could select any inquiry strategy informed by one of the two main schools (i.e., either transcendental or interpretative phenomenology), provided it is consistent with the research plan. Another important recommendation is that researchers should be aware of the assumptions associated with the strategy or method selected and make sure the presumptions are taken into consideration when using the approach (Adu, 2019).

Toward a nonphenomenological framework

One of the most significant consequences of attempting to naturalize the Husserlian epoché is what we could call "theory-anxiety" among researchers. In contrast to what is considered the norm within quantitative research, many qualitative researchers oppose the use of theories and advocate that researchers bracket themselves and focus solely on the data and the emerging themes of their inductive analysis (Tuffour, 2017). Consequently, an analysis of 55 published peer-reviewed qualitative studies demonstrated that the theoretical framework was absent in 29 of the studies, implied in 11, partially implied in 15 and only in nine cases were the theoretical frameworks consistently applied (Bradbury-Jones et al., 2014).

While the position of theory-shy researchers is informed by Husserl's epoché, it is misguided because it is never really the case that phenomenological researchers can engage in social research that is not somehow informed by theoretical perspectives. In other words, the perspective from nowhere does not exist in the natural world. Thus, Collins and Stockton (2018) argued that theory is embedded in qualitative research either as clarification of the researchers' epistemological orientations, in the assumptions underpinning the methodological choices or as a heuristic strategy for the studies. In practical terms, we can identify covert theoretical positions in the researchers' use of terms such as "perceive," "make-sense of," "attitude to," "believe," etc. (Bradbury-Jones et al., 2014). The choice of these descriptive terms is not accidental and implies a theoretical understanding of cognitive processes.

Grant and Osanloo (2015) argued that theoretical frameworks are necessary in order to guide and align the components of a study including the problem statement, the research questions, the data analysis, as well as the conceptualization of the findings. Applying purposefully a conceptual framework will provide the researcher with several advantages. A consistently applied or even partially applied theoretical framework helps the researcher explain the problem and allows the audience the opportunity to critically evaluate the research design and its outcomes. A theoretical framework provides a bridge to existing knowledge, which has actual value for the purpose of addressing everyday problems. Finally, on a pragmatic level, Lederman and Lederman (2015) pointed out that a lack of or a poorly articulated theoretical framework is a common reason why journals reject research articles because research that is not theory-driven is often seen as less valid or unscientific. It is worth reflecting on the fact that social researchers are caught up in institutional structures and academic traditions, where they have to draw from the existing body of knowledge as they try to expand this very same body of knowledge. This is not heresy because the social researcher is always conducting research within the natural attitude.

The epoché and heuristic strategies

While Husserl (2017, p. 207) argued that theoretical ideas cannot be utilized for the purpose of conveying an authentic description of an experience, he was not anti-science. He was merely attempting to delimit the phenomenological domain. Husserl conceded that "we must further realize that exact and purely descriptive sciences can indeed unite their efforts" (p. 208). In *Ideas*, Husserl (2017) opened the door for an approach where an "idealizing procedure may be adopted side by side with the descriptive . . ., which might then indeed serve as the fundamental nexus for a mathesis of experiences and as counterpart to descriptive phenomenology" (p. 211).

Husserl argued that "the bracketing of thesis should not hinder our description, we just refrain from setting into action said thesis" (Husserl, 2017, p. 265). The issue Husserl here pointed to is how to work with theoretical lenses without simultaneously imposing a theoretical hegemony on the lived experiences. Relatedly, van Manen (2016) suggested that researchers working within the interpretative paradigm should review theories that are deemed relevant to the concrete experiences that are being studied (p. 226). Davidsen (2013) took this one step further and, inspired by Ricoeur, argued that the interpretative mode of suspicion precludes the naïve description subjects' lived experience. Therefore, a "theoretical perspective is applied and the interpretation of what one sees is through that lens" (p. 333)

Thus, parts of Husserl's writings can be interpreted to imply that theoretical concepts can be used as heuristic strategies, and he stated that:

> It follows from what we have said that all deductive theorizing is excluded from phenomenology. Mediate inferences are not positively denied it; but seeing that all knowledge is descriptive and must be purely adjusted to immanent requirements, it follows that inferences, unintuitable ways and means of every description have only the methodological meaning of leading us towards the facts which it is the function of an ensuing direct essential insight to set before us as given. Analogies, which press upon us may, prior to real intuition supply us with conjectures as to the essential relations of things, and from these may be drawn inferences that lead us farther forward; but in the end the conjectures must be redeemed by the real vision of essential connexionsa. So long this is not done we have no result that we can call phenomenological.
>
> *(Husserl, 2017, p. 210)*

The meaning of heuristics can be understood as discovery or exploration. Heuristic inquiry is related to the field of phenomenology, but counter to the idea of the detached researchers, in this context, researchers have significant knowledge and experience with the phenomenon. In a manner of speaking, the expert researcher is the key instrument of the data gathering, as they apply knowledge for the purpose of elucidating the experience with a phenomenon (Patton, 2002). We use the notion of heuristics to signify an informed strategy of discovery. We could, perhaps, just as well have borrowed Heidegger's notion of *circumspection*, as we propose to engage with the phenomena with our experience and knowledge in play.

From a heuristic perspective, the epoché and phenomenological reduction simply mean that the bracketed theories have been reduced to phenomena that exist in conjunction with and belong to the central phenomenon under investigation. The methodological implication can perhaps best be understood as a form of horizontalization, where the disclosures of subjects and theoretical positions are reduced to mere phenomena of speech–acts and descriptive conceptual tools, respectively. Accordingly, researchers, operating within the epoché, situate these phenomena on the same horizon as the central phenomenon they explore in their research.

For example, Maslow's theory of the hierarchy of needs contains several steps from bottom to top. Each step is a concept. What makes this a theory is that the conceptual steps are connected in a hierarchy, and the theory posits that while people can move up and down in the hierarchy, they cannot skip a step. Within the epoché, the notion of hierarchy is suspended, and only the steps and mere conceptual phenomena remain. Consequently, researchers can apply these concepts for descriptive purposes in so far as they are parsimonious with the data.

However, the risk of applying a theoretical framework as an organizing lens in a phenomenological study is *theoretical hegemony*, where the lens, instead of acting as a descriptive resource, obscures the data findings or forces the thematic analysis into predetermined categories that may not reflect, but suppress, underlying meanings in the data (Maxwell, 2005, p. 51). The suspension of validity means that researchers use the theories for descriptive purposes only because any introduction of deductive perspectives in inductive research would lead to an outcome that is neither deductive nor inductive, but instead a product of the researcher's abductive reasoning. In short, scholars must pay heed to Husserl's (2017) notion that conjectures must be redeemed: "self-evident data are patient, they let theories chatter about them, but remain what they are. It is the business of theories to conform to the data" (p. 89).

How to phenomenologize an unaffiliated research design

From our earlier elaboration, we can see that there is not exactly a consensus as to what makes a study phenomenological. On one hand, Giorgi argued that phenomenological credibility is acquired using a certain prescribed methodology and thus proceeded with adapting Husserl's epoché and phenomenological reduction to empirical research. Moustakas (1994), in principle, did the same, but in a more intuitive way. On the other hand, proponents of interpretative phenomenological analysis (IPA) argue that it is the subject matter that defines whether a study is phenomenological (i.e., lived experiences with a specific phenomenon). However, instead of pursuing these lines of argument, it may be more productive to propose a minimum list of features. We recommend that a phenomenological study should have the following minimum criteria:

1   The study should be based on inductive reasoning.
2   Theories (in the theoretical/conceptual framework) can be used to inform data analysis but should solely be used for a descriptive purpose.
3   An experience should be involved.
4   A phenomenon should be involved.
5   The main data collection strategy should be an interview.
6   It should have some form of epoché and/or reduction.
7   The goal of attaining meaning should be achieved.
8   The study should be based on broad range of foundational literature.
9   The research design should be justified by foundational literature.

1. Utilizing inductive reasoning

When carrying out research, deductive reasoning is associated more with a quantitative study than a qualitative study. In general, an inductive process involves recording observations to arrive at a conclusion that may lead to the development of abstract concepts that represent observations in the data or generation of a theory that explains the phenomenon of the study. Similarly, a phenomenological study focuses on examining experiences with the aim of arriving at the essential themes. Further analysis of the themes could lead to the emergence of an underlying meaning of the experiences under a study informed by transcendental phenomenology. Alternatively, the analysis could also lead to unearthing the meaning of being under a study informed by interpretative (existential) phenomenology. Therefore, due to the exploratory nature of a phenomenological study, its inquiry-related decisions and actions should be informed by inductive reasoning. This is consistent with having a theory play a descriptive role in a phenomenological study, informing the generation of codes and themes rather than using the data to confirm or reject the theory.

2. Limiting theory to play a descriptive role

A theory used in the phenomenological study should play a descriptive role, suspending its explanatory features. To prevent a theory from explaining and unduly dictating the meaning of participants' experiences, it should not play a confirmatory role (which involves using the data to validate it) in a phenomenological study. With the descriptive purpose, concepts associated with the theory are used to inform the development of codes and themes representing relevant extracts selected from participants' experiences.

3. Focusing on experience

A phenomenological study should focus on subjects' experience. With this kind of study, data are gathered from participants who are having or have had a direct experience of the phenomenon of interest. These participants are expected to disclose or give an account of their experiences from a first-person perspective. Borrowing from Merleau-Ponty et al. (1968), let us assume you are painting (which is considered a lived experience). The transcendental phenomenological aspect of that experience would be based on the question, "what is the meaning of the experience?" While with the existential (interpretative phenomenological) perspective, you can discover the meaning of two beings. One of the beings could be the paint, which could be described as a wonderful and useful material. Similarly, you could discover yourself as another being, seeing yourself as the finest painter or a remarkable artist. With this perspective, you reveal your being through engagement with the paint (i.e., the phenomenon).

4. Involvement of a phenomenon

A phenomenon should be involved in a phenomenological study. In this context, we are not referring to the phenomenon (object) of participants' experiences but focusing on what the researcher is investigating or researching. It would be either a phenomenon of an experience or a phenomenon of being for a transcendental phenomenology-informed study or an interpretative (existential) phenomenology-informed study, respectively. With the phenomenon of experience, the researcher is interested in getting to the meaning (essence) of participants' experience. This falls under the philosophical assumption of epistemology because it deals with examining knowledge. However, the researcher focusing on the phenomenon of being seeks to explore the nature of participants' existence through the examination of their interaction with objects (phenomena) in the world. This kind of inquiry has the characteristics of ontology, which is the philosophical assumption which focuses on studying an existence.

5. Using interview as the main data collection strategy

The main data collection strategy used in a phenomenological study is an interview. Conducting interviews is the most appropriate way of extracting first-hand accounts of participants' experiences. With this strategy, participants are asked specific questions related to their experiences to elicit rich attestations needed to help meet the goal of the study.

6. Applying epoché and/or reduction

A phenomenological study should have some element of epoché and/or reduction. As shown in Table 3.1 (in Chapter 3), any of the main phenomenological perspectives/schools discussed encourages some sort of epoché and/or reduction procedure. One of the common forms of epoché and reduction is the one Husserl (2017) asserted. He claimed the need to move from a natural to a phenomenological attitude, meaning suspending ordinary ways of looking at issues and embracing phenomenological procedures so as to attain the meaning of an experience. It also involves bracketing the explanatory (validity) characteristics of theories associated with the phenomenon of study and adopting descriptive features to help make sense of participants' experience.

7. Attaining meaning

The ultimate goal of a phenomenology is not just to obtain thematic meaning of participants' experience but to reach the psychological meaning of the experience or the existential meaning of an individual's being. To put it differently, at the data analysis stage, codes are generated and categorized, leading to the development of emerging themes. These themes are further analyzed, arriving at essential themes and meaningful themes, for studies informed by transcendental phenomenology and interpretative (existential) phenomenology, respectively (see Chapter 7). Essential themes are themes shared across participants' experiences or best represent most of the participants' experiences. It is important to note that essential themes are not the essence (underlying meaning) of the experience. They should be examined to create psychological meaning of the experience. Psychological meaning normally addresses a meaning-seeking experience research question such as "What is it like to experience academic success?" With this question, the researcher's role is to examine, understand and describe participants' experiences of attaining academic success.

However, an existential meaning addresses a question pertaining to the being, such as *what does it mean to be a student who has experienced academic success?* Looking at this question, it is expected that researchers examine participants' intentions and actions with appropriate background and context—generating emerging themes and transforming them to meaningful themes. Based on further examination of the meaningful themes, researchers come up with a conclusion depicting the meaning of the being of a student who has experienced academic success (see Chapter 7 for more elaboration on this data analysis process).

8. Being informed by a broad range of foundational literature

When providing a rationale for the decisions and actions researchers take in a phenomenology study, it is not sufficient to present their assertions based on one or two pieces of foundational literature. It is important to get broad-range foundational literature to make a case for the study. We suggest researchers engage with the phenomenological literature. This would help in providing a substantial and balanced description of phenomenological-related issues. It is challenging to do meaningful and rigorous phenomenological research without knowing much about phenomenological literature.

9. Justifying the research design

It is important to use foundational literature to justify a research design. It is not sufficient to rely on one foundational work because most of the proponents' ideas in their writings are not static. For instance, Husserl's and Heidegger's writings are dynamic. Their assertions keep evolving over time and across topics and context. This does not mean that their last books are the most important and have the final answers to understanding phenomenology. Therefore, we recommend that scholars read considerable numbers of both earlier and later foundational books and lectures. Some of the literature is easier to read than others. We hope our book will help digest most of the tenets and concepts related to phenomenology.

Features of a phenomenological study

Based on the nine minimum characteristics, here are descriptions of the features of some sections when writing about phenomenological research.

Background of the study

This is about setting the stage for the presentation of a study, seamlessly preparing the minds of readers for the consumption of detailed information about the study. This is about being creative with respect to introducing the topic and situating it in a particular context. The background section of a study has a unique purpose of igniting the interest of readers and making them feel that it is worth the time to get to the body of the research article/document.

When writing the background, researchers can infuse the introduction with assumptions associated with phenomenology, hereunder notions of subjectivity and experiences. It is often here that confusion arises because it is not always entirely clear what the applied phenomenologist aims to study. Some terms we could consider using are *experiences, lived experiences, apperceptions, understanding* and *meanings*. It is quite common that all of the above is folded into a layperson's understanding of the term *perception*. However, being concise and choosing a consistent terminology that clearly indicates the phenomenological orientation and what the subject matter at hand actually is may help the author align the components of the research and ensure credibility.

Besides creatively incorporating the associated assumptions and features related to phenomenology, there are three main elements a good background should have (Adu, 2017). First, the topic (phenomenon and/or experience of interest) should be anchored to a broad topic, narrative, conversation, situation or concept. Second, the topic should be contextualized when being introduced.

Last, after reading the background, readers should have an understanding about why is it important to conduct a study on the topic.

Situating the topic

Readers learn very well when the communicator relates or connects a new idea or information to the existing knowledge. Establishing this kind of link promotes readers' interest in the topic. It is also a way of legitimizing the phenomenon of study. The process of situating the topic within an existing narrative is like moving from a broad narrative to a narrow one, which is what the focus of the research is. Researchers could use historical facts, current trends and events, stories, theories, quotes from prominent writers, findings of research articles and/or even statistics to introduce the topic (see, Yin & Zeng, 2020, pp. 157–158). These introductory prompts could be related to any aspects of the topic. Let us take the *nurses' experiences of caring for COVID-19 patients* as an example. The writer could:

- Describe the current trends of COVID-19 cases, recovery rates and the roles of health-care providers, including nurses.
- Present how the increase in COVID-19 cases is having a toll on nurses and reference up-to-date sources to support this assertion.
- Narrate a story of a nurse (or stories of a group of nurses) depicting their experience in this pandemic.
- Provide statistics to support how nurses view their jobs and the level of stress experienced.
- Creatively articulate how Husserl (1973) or Heidegger (2010) could have explained the meaning of the experience of nurses when caring for COVID-19 patients.

Contextualizing the topic

Contextualizing the topic means situating the topic in a particular context to help readers understand the scope of the topic, hinting the potential parameters of the study. There are five main ways of contextualizing a topic. The topic could be put in a conceptual, demographical, geographical, historical and/or situational context. With respect to *conceptual context*, a writer presents the broad issue in which the topic is nested and connects it to the topic. For instance, if the topic is domestic violence against women, the author could start by presenting general information such as violence against women and then make a smooth transition to the topic.

Putting your topic into a *demographic context* involves describing the characteristics of the large group to which the research sample belongs and making the connection between the subgroup in the study and the large group. For example, if the sample will be nurses, a researcher could first talk about health-care providers in general and then zoom in to focus on nurses. Alternatively, a writer could use the *geographical context* to position the topic by discussing the characteristics of the location of the research. Another option is to provide events of the past/present and merge them with the topic of interest (i.e., bringing to light the *historical context* as the writer introduces the topic). Last, the researcher could utilize *situational context* by addressing the question, in what situation do issues related to the topic occur? Below are context-related questions researchers could consider when introducing a topic:

- *Conceptual context:* In which aspect of the broad concept/phenomenon is the topic situated?
- *Demographic context:* What are the characteristics of people whom the topic revolves around?
- *Geographical context:* What specific geographical location is the topic connected to?
- *Historical context:* What is the history surrounding the topic?
- *Situational context:* Within what situation is the topic situated?

Justifying the topic

A background statement should contain information supporting the need to conduct research on the topic. This is where the skill of persuasive writing comes in. With this portion, the goal is to help readers understand why is it important to look into the topic. After reading the background, readers should have a view that it would be worth the time and resources to research the topic. Before researchers write the background section, they should note that not all readers are interested in the topic. The goal at this point is not necessarily to boost readers' interest in the topic but to provide a compelling reason(s) why the topic is relevant (Adu, 2017).

Problem of the study

The problem of study is any issue that needs to be directly or indirectly addressed using research findings. To Miles (2017b), "A well-written problem statement defines the problem and helps identify the variables investigated in the study" (p. 2). So, what makes a problem phenomenological? In a phenomenological study, the problem should have something to do with an experience of interest or a phenomenon of study. *Lack of support for domestic violence victims, increased in workplace bullying, limited information about faculty experience of online teaching and unknown experience of people who have lost their job due to COVID-19 pandemic* are examples of a problem one can address by conducting phenomenological research. There are two main kinds of problems: practical and research problems (Creswell, 2009).

Practical problem

A practical problem is a researchable issue people face as we carry out our daily lives (Creswell & Plano Clark, 2011). It should be researchable because not all problems can be studied. Some can be addressed without conducting research and others, due to ethical issues, are less likely to be solved through research. Identifying and articulating a practical problem is the focus when conducting an action research. Action research involves conducting a study to alleviate the problem a researcher/practitioner has encountered, sought or generated (Adu, 2016; Craig, 2009). When carrying out traditional research, scholars can start by coming up with a practical problem before developing a research problem.

One useful technique of arriving at a researchable practical problem is to conduct initial assessment by addressing the following questions (see: Kersulo, 2012):

- What is the problem you have identified?
- What may have been the cause of the problem?
- Who is affected by the problem?
- How do people who are affected experience the problem?
- How do people who are affected perceive the problem?
- What are people doing to resolve the problem?
- What are the consequences of the problem?

A researcher may not have answers to adequately address all these questions, but their response would help them decide which aspects of the problem need further exploration. We want to emphasize that for a phenomenological study, a researcher does not need to have practical problem to determine the research problem, but having a practical problem is a good start when searching for literature to help construct the research problem.

Research problem

The research problem is developed mainly by reviewing existing research literature. It is the problem a researcher plans to address in the study. Because the ultimate goal of carrying out research is to make a contribution to a field of knowledge, it is always advisable to determine what has been done (in terms of research) to know what to contribute to the field of study. Based on the practical problem (which may be broad), scholars search for existing studies, looking into:

- Area of focus;
- Methodology used;
- Findings attained;
- Interpretations arrived at;
- Recommendations made.

At this point, the aim of reviewing the literature is to identify gaps (i.e., potential research problems). The scholar then decides on the specific gap to fill. There are many ways of spotting gaps in the literature. Sandberg and Alvesson

(2011) suggested identifying varied explanations about a phenomenon (i.e., confusion spotting), spotting an area with little or no research (i.e., neglect spotting) and finding an area that needs further studies (i.e., application spotting) as techniques that could be used to identify gaps in literature (see Table 4.2). Table 4.2 shows types of gaps a researcher may arrive at based on conducting gap–spotting (see Miles, 2017a; Müller-Bloch & Kranz, 2014). In this book, because we are focusing on a phenomenological study, we have come up with simplified forms of identifying gaps in the literature. They are *area of focus gap, methodology gap* and *demographic gap* (see Table 4.2).

After researching and reviewing a substantial amount of literature (see Bramer et al., 2018; Keary et al., 2012), a researcher could determine whether the topic, phenomenon or practical problem has been unexplored or underexplored (Sandberg & Alvesson, 2011). Another way of identifying a gap is looking into the methodology used in the studies (i.e., methodology gap-spotting). Based on the methods used previously to study the phenomenon of interest, would a transcendental or interpretative-informed phenomenological approach be a good option? A researcher could argue that an alternative method is needed to gain a fresh insight into the phenomenon of study.

Assuming that the researcher wants to replicate a study in terms of focusing on the same phenomenon and methodology and collecting data from participants with their demographics similar to the existing study, the research problem would be related to a demographic gap. In this case, the ultimate goal is to assess the transferability of the findings of the existing study by comparing them to the findings of the current study. A researcher could replace a study but collect data from participants with demographics that are different from those in the existing study. In this

TABLE 4.2 Gap-Spotting Techniques and Their Respective Gap Outcomes

Gap-Spotting Technique	Types Of Gap Outcomes		
Sandberg and Alvesson (2011, pp. 28–29)	Miles (2017a, p. 5)	Müller-Bloch and Kranz (2014, p. 11)	For a Phenomenological Study
Application spotting	Practical-knowledge gap	Action–knowledge conflict	
Application spotting	Empirical gap	Evaluation void	
Application spotting	Theoretical gap	Theoretical application void	
Confusion spotting	Methodology gap	Methodology conflict	Methodology gap
Confusion spotting	Evidence gap	Contradictory evidence	
Neglect spotting	Knowledge gap	Knowledge void	Area of focus gap
Neglect spotting	Population gap		Demographic gap

TABLE 4.3 Gap–Spotting Checklist

Gap		Question	Answer		
			Yes	No	Not Sure
Area of focus gap	Unexplored area	Is there a phenomenology-related area that has not been explored?			
	Underexplored area	Is there a phenomenology-related area that needs further exploration?			
Methodology gap	Alternative method needed	Should an alternative method be used to study the same phenomenon covered by existing studies?			
	Same method needed	Should the same method be used to study a phenomenon of interest?			
Demographic gap	Similar demographics needed	Should a phenomenon be explored with participants' demographics similar to existing studies which covered the same phenomenon?			
	Different demographics needed	Should a phenomenon be explored with participants' demographics different from existing studies which covered the same phenomenon?			

case, the ultimate goal is to assess whether findings of the existing study could be expanded to participants with different characteristics (see Table 4.3).

After revising the literature and using the checklist (see Table 4.3), a scholar may end up with more than one gap. The most important thing is to clearly present a specific gap or a group of gaps to fill. It is important to note that the problem statement is not complete by simply stating the gap, but also requires presenting reasons why it is relevant to fill the gap (or address the research problem).

Purpose statement

The purpose is what a researcher wants to carry out in the study to directly or indirectly address the problem identified (Creswell, 2009). A purpose statement should have three main components: a research approach using an operative word/phrase depicting what the researcher would do, a statement portraying what will be covered in the study and information about potential participants

TABLE 4.4 Components of Research Purpose

Purpose of the Study Component	Descriptive Psychological Phenomenology (Transcendental Phenomenology)	Interpretative (Existential) Phenomenology
Research approach	Phenomenological approach informed by transcendental phenomenology	Phenomenological approach informed by interpretative phenomenology
Operative word/phrase	Capture, describe, determine, explore, discover, find out, decipher, examine, interpret, investigate, look into, analyze, make meaning, scrutinize and understand	
Focus	Nature of experience—focusing on the psychological experience of an object (phenomenon)	Meaning of being—focusing on the lived experiences of a person with something actual
Goal	Attaining the essence (meaning) of the apperceptional experience	Understanding the nature of being, selfhood and identity
Information about potential participants	Characteristics of participants who have experienced the phenomenon	

and a description about the goal stating what the researcher hopes to achieve (Adu, 2020; Creswell, 2009; see Table 4.4).

Research question(s)

There are two main types of research questions: confirmatory and exploratory. Confirmatory research questions, which are closed-ended in nature, are more likely to be used in a quantitative study. However, exploratory research questions are normally utilized in a qualitative study. Similarly, in a phenomenological study, the purpose is not about confirming the meaning of experience but rather exploring the experience to arrive at the underlying meaning of the experience (if the study is informed by transcendental phenomenology) or meaning of being (if the study is informed by interpretative phenomenology). Here are examples of research questions in a phenomenological study:

- What is it like to experience skydiving? (*Psychological research question. Informed by transcendental phenomenology*)
- What does it mean to be a skydiving instructor? (*Interpretative phenomenological research question*)

- What is the lived experience of a skydiver? (*Interpretative phenomenological research question*)
- What is the experience of skydiving for the first time? (*Psychological research question. Informed by transcendental phenomenology*)
- What is the experience of burnout among pilots? (*Psychological research question. Informed by transcendental phenomenology*)
- What does it mean to be a pilot in the midst of the COVID-19 pandemic? (*Interpretative phenomenological research question*)
- What does it mean to be a doctoral student working on a dissertation? (*Interpretative phenomenological research question*)
- What is it like to work on a dissertation for a doctoral student? (*Psychological research question. Informed by transcendental phenomenology*)
- What is it like for novice researchers to search for jobs? (*Psychological research question. Informed by transcendental phenomenology*)
- What does it mean to be a qualitative researcher in the midst of the COVID-19 pandemic? (*Interpretative phenomenological research question*)
- How do low-level employees experience bullying in their workplace? (*Psychological research question. Informed by transcendental phenomenology*)
- What is it like to experience microaggression in the workplace? (*Psychological research question. Informed by transcendental phenomenology*)
- What is it like for an African American to experience microaggression in the workplace? (*Psychological research question. Informed by transcendental phenomenology*)
- How do doctors cope with the risk of being infected as they treat COVID-19 patients? (*Psychological research question. Informed by transcendental phenomenological research question*)
- What does it mean to be a patient with a terminal illness? (*Interpretative phenomenological research question*)

As you can see from the examples of interpretative (existential) phenomenology-related research questions, the emphasis is laid on the *being*. This means that the questions drive the researcher to understand and interpret participants' experiences, leading to the discovery of the meaning of being. In other words, the researcher uses participants' experiences as a gateway to attaining the meaning of who they are or their existences as a skydiving instructor, pilot, employee, African American or patient. However, with the psychological (pure/descriptive) phenomenology-related research questions, the focus is solely on the *experience*. These questions imply that the researcher seeks to examine participants' experiences with the aim of understanding it and providing a description, depicting the essence (meaning) of the experience.

It is important to note that the research question(s) plays a huge role in determining the kind of phenomenological orientation or perspective (transcendental [psychological] or interpretative [existential]) the researcher wants to take.

Research method

Under the research method, the researcher states the approach they want to use to conduct the research inquiry. In this case, the researcher could just state "phenomenological approach." However, in explaining what the approach involves, the researcher should add whether it is driven by ideals related to transcendental or interpretative phenomenology or both. Here is where the scholar uses foundational literature on phenomenology to support their assertion on how the selected school of phenomenology informs the approach. The researcher is also expected to lay out reasons why a phenomenological approach is the best approach to help: determine the data source, recruit participants, collect data from them, analyze data and address the research question(s).

Interview questions

In order to generate rich data to help address the research question, the researcher needs to construct interview questions that are consistent with the research question(s). When conducting a study influenced by transcendental phenomenology, the researcher should ask participants questions which focus on experiences that occur in the mind (i.e., conscious acts). Some thinking acts are conceptualizing, depicting, perceiving and feeling (Churchill, 2014; Husserl, 2017). Table 4.5 shows a list of some thinking acts that could be used to help generate interview questions. Below are examples of the structure of transcendental phenomenological interview questions:

- Can you tell me what you have experienced?
- What happened at that time?
- What did you see the situation?
- How did you feel about incidence?

TABLE 4.5 List of Thinking (Conscious) Acts

Thinking (Conscious) Acts

Admiring	Discovering	Longing	Regarding
Appreciating	Dreaming	Noticing	Remembering
Assuming	Emphasizing	Noting	Sensing
Believing	Envisioning	Observing	Sighting
Conceiving	Envying	Perceiving	Speculating
Conceptualizing	Fantasizing	Picturing	Suspecting
Considering	Favoring	Pondering	Thinking
Discerning	Feeling	Projecting	Viewing
Deciding	Grasping	Realizing	Visioning
Desiring	Imaging	Recalling	Visualizing
Determining	Judging	Recognizing	Witnessing

- What do you think might have happened?
- What was going through your mind when you were experiencing this?
- How do you view this experience?
- How does it feel like experiencing this?
- What went through your mind when this happened?
- What was your perception of this?
- What do you make of this experience?

Although there may be a few overlaps between transcendental and inter-pretative phenomenological interview questions (especially questions related to perceptions), there are some differences between them. The unique aspect of interpretative phenomenological interview questions is the emphasis on captur-ing what participants did (or are doing), including their actions, intent, deci-sions and strategies (Heidegger, 2010). In other words, the questions should be centered on participants' interactions with the phenomenon (object; see Table 4.6). The goal during the interview is to ask questions that capture participants' actions such as "handling, using and taking care" of something (Heidegger, 2010, p. 67). Below are examples of the structure of interpretative phenomeno-logical interview questions:

- How did you react to the situation?
- What did you do to help address this issue?
- What was your intention?
- What did you say?
- What kind of conversations did you have?
- What do you plan to do?
- How do you see yourself as you were having that experience?
- How has the experience affected you?

TABLE 4.6 List of Actionable Experiences

Actionable Experiences

Accomplishing	Choosing	Fixing	Reacting
Acknowledging	Concerning	Guiding	Rejecting
Acting	Considering	Handling	Relating
Addressing	Consuming	Identifying	Resolving
Adopting	Coping	Influencing	Responding
Aiming	Dealing	Intending	Seeking
Allowing	Declining	Involving	Selecting
Aspiring	Directing	Operating	Trying
Attempting	Doing	Participating	Using
Building	Embracing	Performing	Waiting
Caring	Engaging	Protecting	Working
	Entertaining	Purporting	

General suggestion related to interviews

Because participants' backgrounds and their situations are relevant to help researchers better understand their experiences, it is important to collect their demographic information. Unlike the main interview questions, which are usually open-ended questions, the demographic questions can be mostly closed-ended questions. Also, the interview questions should be conversational in nature, free from abstract professional/academic concepts, jargons and ambiguous words (Turner, 2010). We suggest that researchers try as much as possible to use lay language when communicating with participants. Alternatively, if a researcher plans to use a term that may have more than one meaning and wants to avoid miscommunication, we recommend defining the term. A researcher should be sure to "ask one question at a time" and be ready to rephrase a question if a participant does not understand the initial question (Turner, 2010, p. 759). Other recommendations are as follows:

- Try to ask mainly open-ended questions with the exception of some demographic questions.
- Do not be judgmental but be empathetic when asking questions and seeking response.
- Pay attention to their response to the questions.
- Show interest in the conversation.
- Allow the interview questions to guide your conversation with participants.
- Ask follow-up questions when needed.
- Help participants to have a smooth closure of the interview. For example, ask them to share their last thoughts.

Summary

The dominant applied phenomenological research paradigms are phenomenological psychology and IPA. While the first paradigm has provenance in the foundational literature and a prescribed methodology, IPA tries to combine existential and hermeneutic phenomenology in one single approach and consequently pays a price on the methodological front due to the fact that these phenomenological orientations are so different; it is likely impossible to devise one methodology that can do justice to all of them. Consequently, IPA stands accused of not being truly phenomenological and not truly scientific. The ongoing discussions regarding the merits of IPA are largely ignored by emerging researchers who have embraced this paradigm with fewer reservations than scholars within theoretical phenomenology and phenomenological psychology.

Our perspective is that each phenomenological school, per definition, limits the scope of research. The more important question is whether phenomenology is, in fact, well suited for addressing some of the overarching social problems in a meaningful way or if it is fundamentally a paradigm that personalizes and psychologizes lived experiences with little sensitivity to social facts and cultural realities.

Instead of proclaiming fidelity to this or that school of applied phenomenological research, we encourage researchers to engage with the foundational literature in a meaningful way. Taking a non-affiliation stance gives researchers the flexibility of selecting phenomenology-related strategies that are driven by the research question(s) and purpose. We have provided minimum conditions a study should meet to be called a phenomenological study. We also discussed some of the features a phenomenological study should have, highlighting elements such as the background of the study, problem statement, purpose of the study, research question(s), research method and interview questions. In Chapters 5 and 6, we explore additional elements under a phenomenological study, such as theoretical/conceptual framework and data analysis.

Finally, we proposed to approach the epoché and phenomenological reduction in a heuristic manner. In this manner, scholars retain their knowledge of the natural world and its objects and ideas, but in the reduction, they disconnect their explanatory validities. Instead, researchers deconstruct the theories into the conceptual units and apply these for descriptive purposes. In doing so, scholars can consider the principle of parsimony and the integrity of the inductive research approach for the purpose of avoiding theoretical hegemony.

References

Adu, P. (2016). Planning an action research [PowerPoint slides]. *SlideShare*. https://www.slideshare.net/kontorphilip/planning-an-action-research

Adu, P. (2017). Writing the background of your study [PowerPoint slides]. *SlideShare*. www.slideshare.net/kontorphilip/writing-the-background-of-your-study

Adu, P. (2019). *A step-by-step guide to qualitative data coding*. Routledge. ISBN: 9781138486874

Adu, P. (2020). Differentiating theoretical and conceptual frameworks [PowerPoint slides]. *SlideShare*. www.slideshare.net/kontorphilip/differentiating-theoretical-and-conceptual-frameworks

Anderson, N. E., Slark, J., & Gott, M. (2019). Unlocking intuition and expertise: Using interpretative phenomenological analysis to explore clinical decision making. *Journal of Research in Nursing*, 24(1–2), 88–101. https://doi.org/10.1177/1744987118809528

Applebaum, M. (2012). Phenomenological psychological research as science. *Journal of Phenomenological Psychology*, 43(1), 36–72. https://doi.org/10.1163/156916212X632952

Ashworth, P. D. (2016). The lifeworld-enriching qualitative evidence. *Qualitative Research in Psychology*, 13(1), 20–32. https://doi.org/10.1080/14780887.2015.1076917

Ashworth, P. D. (2017). Interiority, exteriority and the realm of intentionality. *Journal of Phenomenological Psychology*, 48(1), 39–62. https://doi.org/10.1163/15691624-12341321

Bradbury-Jones, C., Taylor, J., & Herber, O. (2014). How theory is used and articulated in qualitative research: Development of a new typology. *Social Science & Medicine (1982)*, 120, 135–141. https://doi.org/10.1016/j.socscimed.2014.09.014

Bramer, W. M., de Jonge, G. B., Rethlefsen, M. L., Mast, F., & Kleijnen, J. (2018). A systematic approach to searching: An efficient and complete method to develop literature searches. *Journal of the Medical Library Association: JMLA*, *106*(4), 531–541. https://doi.org/10.5195/jmla.2018.283

Cairns, D. (2010). Nine fragments on psychological phenomenology. *Journal of Phenomenological Psychology*, *41*(1), 1–27. https://doi.org/10.1163/156916210X503083

Churchill, S. D. (2014). Phenomenology. In T. Teo (Ed.), *Encyclopedia of critical psychology*. Springer. https://doi.org/10.1007/978-1-4614-5583-7_219

Collins, C. S., & Stockton, C. M. (2018). The central role of theory in qualitative research. *International Journal of Qualitative Methods*. https://doi.org/10.1177/1609406918797475

Craig, D. V. (2009). *Action research essentials*. San Francisco, CA: Jossey-Bass.

Creswell, J. W. (2009). *Research design: Qualitative, quantitative, and mixed methods approaches*. Sage Publications.

Creswell, J. W., & Plano Clark, V. L. (2011). *Designing and conducting mixed methods research*. Sage Publications.

Davidsen, A. S. (2013). Phenomenological approaches in psychology and health sciences. *Qualitative Research in Psychology*, *10*(3), 318–339. https://doi.org/10.1080/14780887.2011.608466

Deep, B. (2020). Lived experience and the idea of the social in Alfred Schutz: A phenomenological study of contemporary relevance. *Journal of Indian Council of Philosophical Research*, *37*, 361–381. https://doi.org/10.1007/s40961-020-00211-9

Dreyfus, H. L. (1995). *Being-in-the-world: A complimentary on Heidegger's being and time, division 1*. The MIT Press. ISBN: 0-262-54056-8

Eatough, V., & Smith, J. A. (2017). Interpretative phenomenological analysis. In C. Willig & W. Stainton-Rogers (Eds.), *The SAGE handbook of qualitative research in psychology* (pp. 193–209). Sage Publications. ISBN: 9781473925212

Eidelson, R. J. (2003). Dangerous ideas: Five beliefs that propel groups toward conflict. *Journal of Psychology and Theology*, *31*(4), 367. https://link.gale.com/apps/doc/A112356010/AONE?u=pres1571&sid=AONE&xid=6c08a5a7

Englander, M. (2016). The phenomenological method in qualitative psychology and psychiatry. *International Journal of Qualitative Studies on Health and Well-being*, *11*(1). https://doi.org/10.3402/qhw.v11.30682

Giorgi, A. (2006). Difficulties encountered in the application of the phenomenological method in the social science. *Analise Psicologica*, *3*(24), 353–361. https://doi.org/10.1080/20797222.2008.11433956

Giorgi, A. (2010). Phenomenology and the practice of science. *Journal of the Society for Existential Analysis*, *21*(1), 3–23.

Giorgi, A. (2011). IPA science: A response to Jonathan Smith. *Journal of Phenomenological Psychology*, *42*(2), 195–216. https://doi.org/10.1163/156916211X599762

Giorgi, A. (2019). *Psychology as a human science: A phenomenological based approach*. University Professors Press. ISBN: 9781939686268

Giorgi, A., Giorgi, B., & Morley, J. (2017). The descriptive phenomenological psychological method. In C. Willig & W. Rogers (Eds.), *The SAGE handbook of qualitative research in psychology* (pp. 176–192). Sage Publications. https://doi.org/10.4135/9781526405555

Grant, C., & Osanloo, A. (2015). Understanding, selecting, and integrating a theoretical framework in dissertation research: Developing a "blueprint" for your "house". *Administrative Issues Journal*, *4*(2), 12–26. https://doi.org/10.5929/2014.4.2.9

Heidegger, M. (2010). *Being and time*. University of New York Press. ISBN-10: 1438432763

Holzman, H. R., Kudrick, T. R., & Voytek, K. P. (1996). Revisiting the relationship between crime and architectural design: An analysis of data from HUD's 1994 survey of public housing residents. *Cityscape: A Journal of Policy Development and Research*, *2*(1), 107–126. www.huduser.gov/periodicals/cityscpe/vol2num1/notes.pdf

Husserl, E. (1970). *The crisis of European sciences and transcendental phenomenology: An introduction to phenomenological philosophy.* Northwestern University Press. ISBN: 081010458X

Husserl, E. (1973). *The idea of phenomenology.* Martinius Nijhoff. ISBN: 9024701147

Husserl, E. (2001). *The shorter logical investigations.* Routledge. ISBN: 9780415241922

Husserl, E. (2017). *Ideas: General introduction to pure phenomenology.* Unwin Brothers Ltd. ISBN-10: 0415519039

Keary, E., Byrne, M., & Lawton, A. (2012). How to conduct a literature review. *The Irish Psychologist, 38*(9–10), 239–245. https://doi.org/10147/240231

Kersulov, M. (2012, September 27). *Formulating and action research question* [Video]. YouTube. https://www.youtube.com/watch?app=desktop&v=SXhOZmFID4c

Kuhn, T. S. (1996). *The structure of scientific revolutions.* The University of Chicago Press.

Lederman, N. G., & Lederman, J. S. (2015). What is a theoretical framework? A practical answer. *Journal of Science Teacher Education, 26.* https://doi.org/10.1007/s10972-015-9443-2

Maxwell, J. A. (2005). *Qualitative research design: An interactive approach.* Sage Publications. ISBN-10: 0761926089

Merleau-Ponty, M. (1978). *Phenomenology of perception.* Routledge & Kegan Paul. ISBN-10: 0710036132

Merleau-Ponty, M., Lefort, C., & Lingis, A. (1968). *The visible and the invisible followed by working notes.* Northwestern University Press. ISBN: 9780810104570

Merriam, S. B. (1995). Theory to practice: What can you tell form an N of 1?: Issues of validity and reliability in qualitative research. *Journal of Lifelong Learning, 4,* 51–60.

Miles, D. A. (2017a). A taxonomy of research gaps: Identifying and defining the seven research gaps. *Doctoral Student Workshop: Finding Research Gaps-Research Methods and Strategies,* Dallas, Texas.

Miles, D. A. (2017b). Workshop: Confessions of a dissertation chair part 1: The six mistakes doctoral students make with the dissertation. Presented at the *5th Annual 2017 Black Doctoral Network Conference,* Atlanta, GA, October 26–29.

Moran, D. (2000). *Introduction to phenomenology.* Routledge. ISBN-10: 0415183731

Moustakas, C. E. (1994). *Phenomenological research methods.* Sage Publications. ISBN: 0803957998

Müller-Bloch, C., & Kranz, J. (2014). A framework for rigorously identifying research gaps in qualitative literature reviews. *The Thirty Sixth International Conference on Information Systems,* Fort Worth 2015, pp. 1–19.

Norlyk, A., & Harder, I. (2010). What makes a phenomenological study phenomenological? An analysis of peer reviewed nursing studies. *Qualitative Health Research, 20*(3), 420–431. https://doi.org/10.1177/1049732309357435

Patton, M. Q. (2002). *Qualitative research & evaluation methods* (3rd ed.). Sage Publications. ISBN-13: 9780761919711

Pietkiewicz, I., & Smith, J. A. (2014). A practical guide to using interpretative phenomenological analysis in qualitative research psychology. *Psychological Journal, 20*(1), 7–14. https://doi.org/10.14691/CPPJ.20.1.7

Ricoeur, P. (1994). *Oneself as another.* The University of Chicago Press. ISBN: 0-226-71329-6

Sandberg, J., & Alvesson, M. (2011). Ways of constructing research questions: Gap-spotting or problematization? *Organization, 18*(23), 23–44. https://doi.org/10.1177/1350508410372151

Smith, J. A., Flowers, P., & Larkin, M. (2009). *Interpretative phenomenological analysis: Theory, method and research.* Sage Publications. ISBN: 9781412908344

Tuffour, I. (2017). A critical overview of interpretative phenomenological analysis: A contemporary qualitative research approach. *Journal of Healthcare Communication, 2*(52). https://doi.org/10.4172/2472-1654.100093

Turner, D. W. (2010). Qualitative Interview Design: A Practical Guide for Novice Investigators. *The Qualitative Report*, *15*(3), 754–760. https://doi.org/10.46743/2160-3715/2010.1178

van Manen, M. (2016). *Phenomenology of practice*. Routledge. ISBN-10: 1611329442

van Mazijk, C. (2017). Some reflections on Husserlian intentionality, intentionalism, and non-propositional content. *Canadian Journal of Philosophy*, *47*(4), 499–517. https://doi.org/10.1080/00455091.2016.1255500

Yin, X., & Zeng, L. (2020). A study on the psychological needs of nurses caring for patients with coronavirus disease 2019 from the perspective of the existence, relatedness, and growth theory. *International Journal of Nursing Sciences*, *7*, 157–160.

Zahavi, D. (2008). Phenomenology. In D. Moran (Ed.), *The Routledge companion to twentieth century philosophy* (pp. 661–692). ISBN: 0-203-87936-8 Master e-book ISBN

Zahavi, D. (2018). Intersubjectivity, sociality, community: The contribution of the early phenomenologists. In D. Zahavi (Ed.), *The Oxford handbook of the history of phenomenology* (pp. 734–752). Oxford University Press. ISBN-13: 978-0198755340

Zahavi, D. (2019a). *Phenomenology the basics*. Routledge. ISBN: 978-1-138-21670-9

Zahavi, D. (2019b). *Husserl's legacy*. Oxford University Press. ISBN: 978-0-19-885217-9

Zahavi, D. (2019c). Applied phenomenology: Why it is safe to ignore the epoché. *Continental Philosophy Review*, 1–15. https://doi.org/10.1007/s11007-019-09463-y

5

UNDERSTANDING THE RATIONALE AND ROLE OF DEVELOPING THEORETICAL/ CONCEPTUAL FRAMEWORK

Objectives

Readers will be able to

1   Understand the meanings of and differences between theory and concept.
2   Describe the rationale and role of theoretical/conceptual framework.
3   Describe how to develop a theoretical/conceptual framework within a phenomenological study.

Unpacking the meaning of theory and concept

In people's everyday lives, they make observations (such as bird, movie and sunset watching) and engage in activities (such as reading, writing, driving and eating). As time goes on, and after continuously experiencing them at different times and in different situations, people begin to form general (abstract) statements or ideas that best represent or explain these experiences. These formulated life lessons, principles and theories, which are sometimes adjusted and even rejected, may directly or indirectly regulate people's lives in terms of how they understand things (Wallis & Wright, 2020). An individual has a simple everyday theory such as, *"you are more likely to have an accident if you drive above the speed limit,"* and a more complex one as in, *"if you invest your money in the stock market, you will have a positive return on investment."* Everyday theories such as these influence how people experience phenomena and make sense of and communicate their experience.

Similarly, in the research community informed by interpretative paradigm, scholars conduct qualitative studies mainly following an inductive method of inquiry (see Adu, 2019). They perform observations through collection and analyze qualitative data to come up with findings, which are not only considered abstract in nature but also a true representation of the data. This abstract information could be referred to as a theory if it is considered to have the feature of explaining the phenomenon of study.

Meaning of a theory

So then, what is a theory? "Lexicographers trace the etymology of the word 'theory' to the late Latin noun 'theoria', and the Greek noun 'theōria' and verb 'theōrein' (usually translated as 'to look at,' 'to observe,' 'to see,' or 'to contemplate')" (Abend, 2008, p. 180). Theory is a product of a thorough and systematic examination of situations, events, experiences and/or processes (Bhattacherjee, 2012). In other words, it is a statement or a group of statements that contains concepts (themes) and relationships between them. In addition, it is capable of explaining a phenomenon (Abend, 2008). To put it differently, theories, "aid in sense-making by helping us synthesize prior empirical findings within a theoretical framework and reconcile contradictory findings by discovering contingent factors influencing the relationship between two constructs in different studies" (Bhattacherjee, 2012, p. 26).

There are different kinds of theories. Anfara and Mertz (2015) categorized them as "individual theories, organizational theories, group theories, and social theories" (p. 6). For the purpose of our discussion, we would group them into two make types: empirically based and non-empirically based theories. Let's start with non-empirically based theories, which Maxwell (2013) called conceptual theories. These theories are formed as a result of synthesizing ideas but not through analyzing empirical data when conducting research. Empirically based theories are emanated from carrying out qualitative, quantitative or mixed methods research. They are:

> "grounded" in the actual data collected, in contrast to . . . [theories that are] developed conceptually and then simply tested against empirical data. In qualitative research, both existing theory [including non-empirically based theory] and grounded theory are legitimate and valuable.
>
> *(Maxwell, 2013, p. 49)*

An empirically based theory should have five main characteristics (see Anfara & Mertz, 2015):

1 *Representation:* It should represent data that have been collected and analyzed.
2 *Inclusion of concepts:* It should contain concepts representing behaviors, events, situations or processes.
3 *Relationship:* It should show relationships between concepts.
4 *Explanation:* It should have the tendency of explaining a phenomenon or an experience.
5 *Understanding:* It should contribute to making sense of a phenomenon or an experience.

Some examples of theories are behavioral theory, systems theory, identity formation, cognitive theory and trait theory (see Grant & Osanloo, 2015). Table 5.1 shows the kinds of theories researchers should consider under their respective school of phenomenology.

In summary, the development of theory, most of the time, starts with trying to understand happenings in the world and human behavior. In the quest to make sense of occurrences and observations, research is conducted by collecting appropriate data (which is considered concrete information) and reducing them to abstract concepts (which are normally referred to as themes). Further analysis of these concepts could lead to the development of a theory, especially when using a grounded theory approach (see Charmaz, 2014). The strength or dominance of a theory depends on how well it can explain varieties of situations and experiences within the varied contexts of a particular phenomenon.

Meaning of a concept

A concept is simply an idea about something. It is normally referred to as an abstract representation of a specific situation, behavior, event or process (Adu, 2019; Green, 2014). Similarly, a concept is a product of data reduction. Data reduction is a process of systematically summarizing data (observations) with the aim of arriving at a condensed form of the data with abstraction properties (Adu, 2019). This kind of information is called theme, which can also be referred to as a concept. Imagine analyzing interview transcripts and identifying expressions related to: loss of appetite, isolation, loss of friends, loss of social contacts, little sense of happiness, little or no interest in daily activities and weight loss. These descriptors are considered concrete experiences. After examining each participant's experience and determining shared characteristics among them, you come up with *feeling depressed* or *having symptoms of depression* as a theme to represent the experiences. Continuing with abstraction, themes (concepts) generated from the data are compared to explore relationships among them, leading to the formation of a theory which best represents the data and explains the phenomenon of study (Adu, 2019; Charmaz, 2014).

Introduction to theoretical/conceptual framework

Besides meeting the purpose of a study, the end goal of conducting research is to address the research problem, contributing to the body of knowledge within a particular field (Adu, 2020). The body of knowledge includes concepts, constructs, models, and theories generated within a field of study and are at the abstract level of knowledge. Also, these components of the body of knowledge represent specific ideas and empirical data, and at the same time, depend on those ideas and data to maintain their relevance (see Table 5.2). Apart from sharing the characteristics of being abstract depictions of actual phenomena, there are differences between them (Dix, 2008). Whereas a construct houses concepts

TABLE 5.1 Schools of Phenomenology and Their Respective Kinds of Theories

School of Phenomenology	Focus of Inquiry	Methodology	Goal of Inquiry	Kinds of Theories for the Development of a Framework	Example of Theory
Transcendental phenomenology (Husserl)	Intentionality, transcendental subjectivity and subjectivity in general	Phenomenological reduction in order to turn from the phenomenon toward subjectivity	• Attain the essence of experience • Epistemological explication of experiencing	Theories related to thinking acts (see Table 4.4)	Cognitive load theory (CLT) (see Durning et al., 2013)
Phenomenological psychology (Husserl/Giorgi)	Psychological subjectivity	Reduction in order to turn from actualities toward the phenomenon	• Essential themes of apperceptional experiences	*Cognitive-oriented theories*: Cognitive-oriented theories are not about theories of phenomena but the experience of something which takes place in our minds	Learning theory (see Klein, 2002)
Existential phenomenology (Heidegger)	Dasein (i.e., mode of existence)	Attain an interpretation-mediated understanding of being through human beings' copings and dealings with the world	• Uncover the meaning of being from a horizon of temporality • Ontological explication of experiencing	Theories related to the things Dasein is engaged in such as dealing with or coping with something (see Table 4.5)	Conservation of resources (COR) theory (see Glebocka & Lisowska, 2007)
Hermeneutic phenomenology (Ricoeur)	Identity	Distanciation and suspicion Reflective interpretation of the narrative plot	• Uncovering the narrative self	Theories related to identity and selfhood	Discourse theory (see Torfing, 2005)

with common features, models illustrate the links among concepts (or constructs; Jabareen, 2009). Also, the main distinction between theory and model is that the former has more explanatory tendencies than the latter. In other words, theory can better explain a relationship between concepts than can a model (Adu, 2020; Dix, 2008). As scholars continue to conduct research within their fields of study, concepts, constructs, models and theories are developed, adopted, revised and/ or confirmed.

One of the ways of contributing to a field is to develop a framework that links what a researcher plans to do (or is doing) to what has been done. To put it differently, a framework is like a bridge connecting a concrete area of focus of a study to an abstract body of knowledge of a field (Maxwell, 2013; Sinclair, 2007). So, what is a framework? We see a framework as a presentation of theories, constructs and/or concepts in terms of their meaning, what they represent, their associated assumptions, their uses, their strengths and limitations and how they are connected to a study (Green, 2014).

You may ask, "*what makes a framework theoretical or conceptual? Is it based on the role it plays in a study or what it entails in terms of the content? Should I use theoretical framework, conceptual framework or both in a study?*" There is no clear consensus among social science researchers regarding the above questions. The answers differ depending on the book or article a reader is reviewing. There are four main assertions made by researchers about theoretical and conceptual frameworks (see Adu, 2020).

Assertion one

Some researchers have argued that both theoretical and conceptual frameworks should be used in a study (Grant & Osanloo, 2015). This is because the content of the theoretical framework is different from that of the conceptual framework (Adu, 2020). Theoretical frameworks contain a presentation of a theory or a group of relevant theories, whereas conceptual frameworks detail concepts

TABLE 5.2 Body of Knowledge

Concrete Level				*Abstract Level*
Situations, Phenomena, Behaviors And Ideas	*Concepts*	*Constructs*	*Models*	*Theories*
• *Concrete information supporting abstract knowledge*	• *Abstract labels representing concrete information*	• *Representing connections among concepts*	• *Depicting and predicting relationship among concepts*	• *Representing and explaining a phenomenon*

Note. Adopted from Adu (2020).

or constructs. However, researchers supporting this option have suggested that there should be consistency between them (Grant & Osanloo, 2015). In other words, a conceptual framework normally details concepts that are linked to the selected theory or theories discussed under a theoretical framework.

Assertion two

Other researchers argued that because a theoretical framework can play a role in a study similar to that of a conceptual framework, and vice versa, one can use either a theoretical or a conceptual framework (Parahoo, 2006). Some researchers who support this assertion have emphasized that a theoretical framework should contain a discussion of one theory, while a conceptual framework could have more than one theory, including descriptions of concepts (Adu, 2020). Other researchers have claimed the theoretical framework should consist of theories and the conceptual framework should entail concepts or constructs (Kivunja, 2018).

Assertion three

The group of researchers who hold the third assertion have claimed that researchers can use the theoretical and conceptual framework interchangeably in their research article/document because they play similar roles in a study (Jabareen, 2009). In addition, their content is alike in that both can have descriptions of concepts (Adu, 2020).

Assertion four

Another group of researchers have claimed that one is more likely to use a theoretical framework when conducting a quantitative study, but more likely to use conceptual framework when conducting a qualitative study (Imenda, 2014). This assertion brings back the notion of the deductive nature of a quantitative research, which involves collecting data to test hypotheses, which are normally derived from a theory. For this reason, a theoretical framework is frequently used in quantitative studies. On the contrary, an inductive process is aligned with a qualitative study, which involves collecting data to develop themes/concepts, leading to the generation of a theory. This explains why conceptual frameworks align better with qualitative studies than with quantitative studies.

Our thoughts about theoretical and conceptual frameworks

In terms of the content, we call a framework theoretical if it contains a discussion of a theory or group of theories. However, if it has description of concepts and/ or constructs, then we would label it a conceptual framework. Consistent with the second assertion, we believe that either theoretical or conceptual framework could be used in a phenomenological study because they can play similar roles in research (Adu, 2020). Due to the similarities in how they are used in a study, in this book, we use theoretical and conceptual frameworks interchangeably.

Rationale of having a theoretical/conceptual framework in a phenomenological study

Qualitative study is mainly informed by inductive reasoning, focusing on examining or exploring observations to ultimately develop an explanation that is in effect, leading to the generation of a theory. Researchers' descriptions of participants' experiences are informed by something (specifically, a researcher's background and the existing theories) even if we only rely on their words/ narratives (Maxwell, 2013). Similarly, participants' words are also drawn from their understanding, interpretation and theory of the lifeworld. Just imagine asking a psychotherapist how the week was. Their disclosure will be infused by their conceptual worldview. Therefore, theories or frameworks developed could help researchers better understand and conceptualize participants' experiences. However, how do scholars work within the confines of inductive reasoning and, at the same time, use theoretical/conceptual framework to inform a phenomenological study?

Let's look at this practical example: A police officer patrols an area where his theory of mind tells him that crime is rampant. He then sees a broken window and he concludes a burglary is in progress. In contrast, if his theory of mind was that it was a low-crime area and he saw the same evidence (i.e., a broken window), he may have concluded that kids in that area may have played baseball again. In both cases, the police officer has not deployed his epoché and disengaged the validity of his theory. On the contrary, in his abductive mindset and the evidence (i.e., the broken window) available, he assumes a phenomenon of crime in one case but a phenomenon of kids playing in another case.

Qualitative researchers' main goals of conducting phenomenological studies are, first, to understand participants' narratives of their experiences and, second, to describe the researcher's understanding and interpretation of their experiences, leading to the attainment of the essence of the experience or meaning of being under a transcendental phenomenology-informed study or an interpretative-informed study, respectively. Theoretical/conceptual frameworks have a place in phenomenological studies, but they should be put in check so as to prevent them from fully dominating the research process, especially when it comes to making sense of a participant's experience. Further, employing transparent and feasible epoché is consistent with the use of theory or framework in phenomenology. In other words, the explanatory features of the framework (including its associated theories) are set aside when analyzing the experiences of participants. The practice of epoché encourages the use of the descriptive features of a theory or framework to inform the inquiry process while bracketing its explanatory characteristics from being used to validate findings, thereby avoiding overlooking unique but relevant aspects of the data during analysis (Husserl, 2017; Maxwell, 2013). Additionally, when discussing the problem, an unrestricted theory could be posed in a study; Maxwell (2013) argued that it leads to "shoehorning questions, methods, and data into preconceived categories and preventing the researcher from seeing events and relationships that don't fit the theory" (p. 53). Back to the example about the police officer, he would have arrived at the true understanding of the incident if he had suspended the validity or explanatory element of his theory.

Theoretical/conceptual framework could be used as a perspective while gaining understanding of participants' experience. Under hermeneutic phenomenology, Ricoeur (2019) suggested the use of faith and suspicion when interpreting what participants said. The two theoretical perspectives that could assist this process are Freudian psychoanalysis and Marxist theories (Davey, 2008). Therefore, theories can be used to initially learn participants' narratives and then take a critical look at what has been taken for granted, questioning researchers' assumptions of reality (Itao, 2010)

Besides the main reason discussed earlier, below are additional and general rationales for having theoretical/conceptual frameworks in a phenomenological study. These rationales are based on Adu's (2020) presentation, *Differentiating theoretical and conceptual frameworks.*

Connecting to existing knowledge

Studies should not be done in isolation. They should be anchored to an existing body of knowledge in a particular field. A study and existing knowledge can be appropriately connected using a theoretical/conceptual framework. For instance, imagine a researcher wants to conduct a phenomenological study on doctoral students' experiences of preparing for and taking a comprehensive exam. This type of exam is normally taken by doctoral students after they have completed their course work, transitioning into the start of their dissertations. Using existing theory and/or concepts that explain and/or represent aspects of their experiences would help in developing a framework.

Contributing to existing knowledge

As indicated earlier, the main goal of conducting a research is to address a gap in existing studies to contribute to the field of knowledge or to address a problem in one's professional practice (Adu, 2020). There are numerous ways in which theoretical/conceptual framework can facilitate this process. One way is using existing theory or concepts to help explain a problem/focus of study, transforming the everyday experience and its lay language into abstract terms used within a particular field or profession. Moreover, concepts discussed in the framework can be used to generate themes, which are then used to analyze qualitative data. In addition, a framework can serve as a repository of terminologies used among consumers of research, making it easier to communicate findings with shared scholarly language. Last, findings can be compared with the framework, leading to the appropriate contribution to the body of knowledge.

Delimiting the study

Delimiting a study involves drawing boundaries for a phenomenological study, contributing to the likelihood the study can be successfully carried out (i.e., feasibility), appropriately put into context (i.e., contextualization) and properly transferred to similar contexts (i.e., transferability). A theoretical/conceptual framework could help in narrowing the focus of the study to an aspect that is researchable and doable.

Informing the study

Having a theoretical/conceptual framework could inform areas of a topic a researcher should focus on. For a phenomenological approach, a framework could direct a researcher to areas that need to be explored, thereby filling the gap identified. It could also help develop the research questions and the kinds of questions to ask during interviews, making sure all aspects of the research focus have been exhausted. Additionally, it could inform the type of data analysis (whether content analysis or thematic analysis) suitable to extensively analyze the data (see Vaismoradi et al., 2013). With content analysis, codes/themes are generated from the framework and used to label relevant excerpts extracted from the data, while with thematic analysis, codes/themes are generated based on the relevant information selected from the data.

Justifying the study

When conducting research, a researcher may be asked, why do you think it is important to carry out the study? The reason could be there is an unexplored area that needs to be studied to better bring to light or understand the issue (Sandberg & Alvesson, 2011). Another reason could be there are methodology-related issues with a previous study, and the researcher plans to use their study to address the flaws (Sandberg & Alvesson, 2011). Besides these rationales, as scholars present the theories/concepts and their respective meaning and representation when working on the framework, they could argue for the need to conduct a study to fill a gap or address limitations.

Understanding the study

Sometimes, the topic of interest may not be clear in terms of what the phenomenon of the study constitutes, what the problem is and what the purpose should be. This is where having a framework comes in handy. A researcher could examine and synthesize appropriate theories or concepts, helping to better understand the study. One example is using chaos and complexity theory as part of a theoretical framework to understand the experience of workplace bullying (see Amos, 2020). Maxwell (2013) cautioned researchers against using or applying a theory without critically examining its strengths, "limitations, distortions, and blind spots" (p. 52).

Role of a theoretical/conceptual framework in a study

In order to successfully use a framework in a phenomenological study, a researcher needs to determine the specific role(s) it can play in the study. According to Adu (2020), there are mainly six roles a theoretical/conceptual framework could perform. A framework can be viewed as a connector, converter, decipherer, gap spotter, guide and/or standpoint (Adu, 2020; Maxwell, 2013; Sinclair, 2007). A researcher does not have to focus on all six when developing a framework. A scholar could select one, two or three roles for the framework.

Connector

As a connector, theory or concepts within the framework are "operationalized," indicating what they mean or represent. The aim is to match them to the description of what one wants to study or the problem they want to address. It also involves critically examining each theory or concept in terms of its assumptions, strengths and limitations before making an appropriate connection between them and the aspects of the study.

Converter

As a converter, the role of the framework is to use the theory and/or concepts to transform ideas or concrete information about the study (which is written in layman's terms; Adu, 2020). This role is similar to a content analysis approach, in that it involves selecting an appropriate theory and/or concepts from the literature, creating themes/codes from them and using the themes/codes to represent relevant excerpts in the description of the study. At the end, the researcher presents the phenomenon of interest, purpose of study and/or research question(s) in a language mainly used in their field of study. The converter role is also a consistent aspect of phenomenological epoché, where a researcher is encouraged to suspend the explanatory power of a selected theory but utilize its descriptors to help generate codes/themes during data analysis.

Decipherer

A theoretical/conceptual framework could be used to make sense of the problem to be studied (Adu, 2020). Theories and/or concepts discussed under the framework focus on explaining the problem—facilitating coming up with the best way it should be addressed in the study. Sometimes, you may have limited information about the problem you want to study. A framework could help in connecting the dots in terms of the causes, extent and implications of the problem of the study.

Gap spotter

To adequately contribute to the field of knowledge, researchers should first identify a gap in the existing literature (Sandberg & Alvesson, 2011). Some of the gaps which could be spotted when reviewing literature are: lack of adequate research on an area, inappropriate use of methodology, inconclusive findings, contradictory findings and unexplored topics in different contexts and/or populations (see Sandberg & Alvesson, 2011). Besides this, utilizing a theoretical/conceptual framework can help a researcher identify a gap. As a gap spotter, a researcher critically examines theories and/or concepts in a framework, exploring how much they explain the phenomenon or problem of study (Adu, 2020). In effect, an unexplained area could be a gap a study could fill. Further, after critically evaluating the selected theories/concepts, the limitation the researcher arrived at (such as their inability to accurately represent or help understand all the aspects of the problem of the study) could be the gap the researcher could address (Dix, 2008, p. 18). This limitation could inform the purpose of the study and, consequently, the researcher could use the study to address it.

Guide

Theoretical/conceptual frameworks could be used to guide the construction of the purpose of the study, research questions and codes/themes. A framework informs the focus of a study using concepts discussed to conceptualize and clarify specific areas or aspects of the phenomenon a researcher plans to study. It also guides in framing the research questions and what concepts or terms to use in the questions. Last, it could be used to inform the kinds of codes or themes needed to represent relevant information obtained from the data.

Standpoint

As a standpoint, a theoretical/conceptual framework is used as a lens for viewing research from a particular perspective. To help the audience better understand the researcher's viewpoint, the researcher needs to extensively explain the theory or concepts that form the framework and how the study will include its components. If a researcher plans to conduct a study using feminist theory within the framework, it is expected that the researcher will present their understanding of feminism and share ideas they have about the study, addressing questions like: What is feminist theory? What does it mean to have a feminist perspective? What are the strengths, limitations and assumptions related to the theory? How does the researcher see the phenomenon or problem of the study?

Roadmap to developing theoretical/conceptual framework

The roadmap to the development of a theoretical/conceptual framework is (most of the time) not linear (Adu, 2020). It is mostly an open and unrestricted process, going back and forth between selecting potentially appropriate theories or concepts and developing the framework. At the end, the researcher arrives at a well-designed framework, comprehensively depicting its role in the study and detailing the meaning and representation of theories and concepts. The actions1 a researcher could take to come up with a framework are given in the next section.

Search for potential theories and/or concepts

Researchers could start the framework development process by thinking about and taking note of potential theories and concepts that may have connections to the phenomenon (issue) of study and/or the problem they plan to address. Researchers should extensively review each of them, searching for information about them in terms of what researchers have written about, how they have been used in studies, their suggested strengths, limitations and assumptions. Another strategy for getting access to theories and concepts that have a shared relationship with a topic is to search for literature about the focus of the study.

It is possible that there are limited theories and concepts within your field that have connection with what the researcher intends to study. In this situation, the researcher could explore other disciplines, looking for appropriate theories and concepts and adopting them for the study. At the end of the search, the researcher should have potential theories and/or concepts to work with. Alternatively, a researcher could use a unique type of literature review, called a scoping review, to help come up with an appropriate theory or a group of theories for the development of a framework (see Chapter 6).

Determine potential use of the theories and/or concepts

After identifying potential theories and/or concepts, the question researchers should think about is: What is the potential use of the theories and concepts selected? There are five main ways they can be used (see Table 5.3). They can be used to explain aspects of the study, such as topic, problem and purpose of the study. Besides explaining, concepts identified in the literature (or derived from theories) can serve as a label representing "lay" description, depicting relevant aspects of the study. Also, researchers can use theories and concepts to justify the importance of conducting the study. Another way is to use them to inform certain aspects of the study. For instance, they can inform the development of

TABLE 5.3 Theories and Concept Use and Their Respective Goals and Framework Roles

Use	Goal	Corresponding Framework Role
Explaining the study	To make meaning of the topic or problem of study	Decipherer
Representing the study	To label relevant ideas in the study	Connector and converter
Justifying the study	To establish the reason why it is important to conduct the study	Gap spotter
Informing the study	To guide the conceptualization of the problem of study, development of the research purpose and questions, selection of an approach research approach, data collection techniques and data analysis strategies and/or interpretation of findings	Guide
Viewing the study	To carry out research inquiry from a particular perspective	Standpoint

the research problem and research questions, decisions about research approach, data collection strategies, data analysis techniques and interpretation of the findings. Last, they can be used as a lens to conduct a study. At this point, it would be valuable to document the researchers' thought process while determining how potential theories and concepts could assist the yet-to-be-developed framework in playing a role in the study. These initial thoughts will be useful when writing about the framework.

Choose appropriate theories and/or concepts

Once a researcher has potential theories and/or concepts with their respective use, the next step is to match their use to their corresponding framework role (see Table 5.2). The researcher then selects the theory, theories or a group of concepts that meet the following two criteria suggested by Dix (2008; see Adu, 2020):

- *Correct match:* Under this criterion, a researcher selects a theory/concept that, as Dix (2008) put it, "accurately represent[s]" or matches the role (or set of role) you want your framework to play in the study (p. 193). At this point, do not worry about the number of theories or concepts you arrived at. The most important thing is that they meet the first condition.
- *Complete match:* Dix (2008) referred to the criterion "completeness" with a question, "does it cover all the relevant phenomena and issues?" (p. 18). Similarly, this question could be put as *does the theory or group of concepts completely match the assigned role(s) of the framework?* In an ideal situation, it is the hope

that a researcher finds a theory or group of concepts that has the potential of totally assisting the framework to fulfill its role(s). However, the researcher may encounter a situation where the theory or concept covers a portion of the obligations of the framework. In this case, additional theories or concepts are needed to complement the ones initially selected.

Write about the framework

Writing a framework could be a daunting task. The quality of a written framework partly depends on the initial effort taken to gather and select appropriate theories/constructs/concepts for the development of the framework. According to Adu (2020), a good theoretical/conceptual framework should have the following components:

- *Meaning* of the selected theory and/or concepts;
- *Representation* of the selected theory and/or concepts;
- *Connection* of the selected theory and/or concepts to the study;
- *Utilization* of the framework in the study;
- *Contribution* of the selected theory and/or concepts.

Meaning of the selected theory and/or concepts

Presentation of a framework (most of the time) starts with a description of the theory/concepts selected. At this point, it is assumed that the researcher has adequate knowledge about theory or concepts of interest. The researcher has digested all the relevant information and is ready to share their understanding of them. The readers may want answers to the following questions when reading a framework to know what the theory or a group of theories or concepts is about:

- What is the theory (a group of theories) and/or concepts the researcher has chosen?
- Who is/are the proponent(s) of the theory (a group of theories) and/or concepts?
- Based on what the researcher has learned, what is their understanding of them?
- What are the views of researchers/scholars about them?
- Thinking about how to use them, what are their strengths, limitations and assumptions?
- Which literature supports the researcher's assertions?

A researcher does not have to address all these questions, but the most important thing is to make sure they meet these conditions: First, a researcher thoughtfully builds a well-structured theoretical/conceptual framework; second, they communicate the meaning of theory (or a group of theories) and/or concepts in a way the reader can easily understand.

Representation of the selected theory and/or concepts

Here is where a researcher describes what the theory or concepts constitute or cover (Adu, 2020). This could overlap the description of their meaning, but writing about their representation entails detailing specific behaviors, situations or processes they characterize. This is similar to operationally defining a variable/ concept in a quantitative study. It also involves presenting relevant concepts and subconcepts and how they are connected to the theory of interest.

Connection of the selected theory and/or concepts to the study

At this stage, it is assumed that the selected theory and/or concepts have some connection with the study. When writing about a framework, it is important to show how it is linked to a specific aspect of the study, such as the phenomenon or experience of the phenomenon being explored, practical problem, research problem, delimitation of the study, purpose statement, research question, research method, data collection process and/or data analysis. There is flexibility here: A researcher does not have to explicitly state how they are linked to parts of the study. However, they creatively and implicitly present the relationship.

Utilization of the framework in the study

With this component, a researcher is expected to state the specific role(s) they want the framework to play in the study. As indicated earlier, there are six roles to choose from: connector, converter, decipherer, gap spotter, guide and standpoint. The researcher should articulate the role(s) in such a way that readers understand what it looks like for a theoretical/conceptual framework to play a certain function in a phenomenological study. How the framework will be used (in relation to their roles) could be written in a direct (explicit) or an indirect (implicit) way. The most important thing is to make sure readers know about the framework's role(s).

Contribution of the selected theory and/or concepts

As pillars support the structure of a house, theories and concepts help in supporting the role(s) of the framework (see Grant & Osanloo, 2015). Without theories and/or concepts, there will be no theoretical/conceptual framework. Theories and/or concepts help in building the structure of the framework – facilitating how the framework carries out its obligation(s). In the end, the writing under this component should address these questions: "*How do you plan to use the theories and/or concepts?" "Considering their use, how do they contribute to the role(s) of the framework?"*

Making a visual representation of a framework

The final, but optional, task in relation to developing a theoretical/conceptual framework is to create visual representation (Adu, 2020). This is about translating the written framework into a visual image with the aim of helping readers get more understanding of the theoretical/conceptual framework. The illustration is not done just to "check off the box," but to develop an esthetic but simple depiction of what the framework is, communicating its main elements to readers. There are a lot of tools available that help researchers to creatively represent a framework. Pertaining to Microsoft Word, authors can use either *Shapes* or *SmartArt* functions to help illustrate the theoretical/conceptual framework (see Figures 5.1 and 5.2). Alternatively, Cmap is a good option when it comes to creating a concept map (https://cmap.ihmc.us/) to represent the framework (Figure 5.3). To learn about how to use this free software, see page 171 of Adu's (2019) book, *A Step-by-Step Guide to Qualitative Data Coding*. Another free software program that provides many options and flexibility in designing a visual

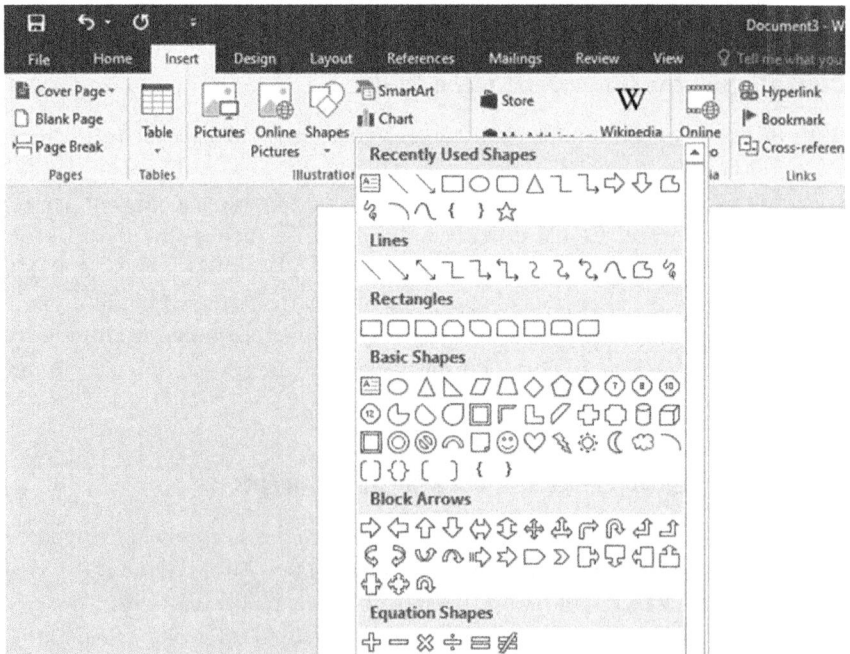

FIGURE 5.1 A Display of the "*Shapes*" Function on the Microsoft Word Document

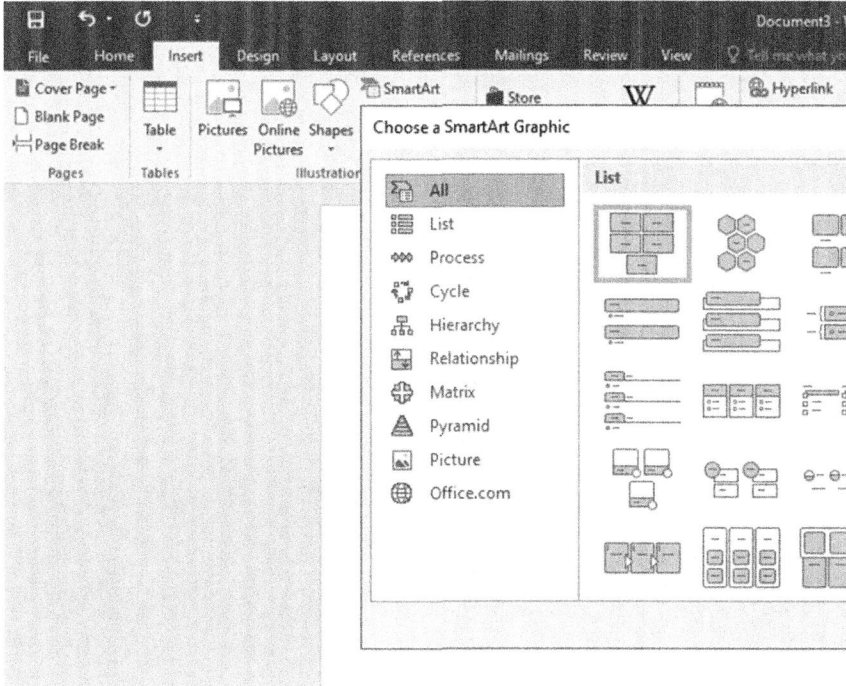

FIGURE 5.2 A Display of the "*SmartArt*" Function on the Microsoft Word Document

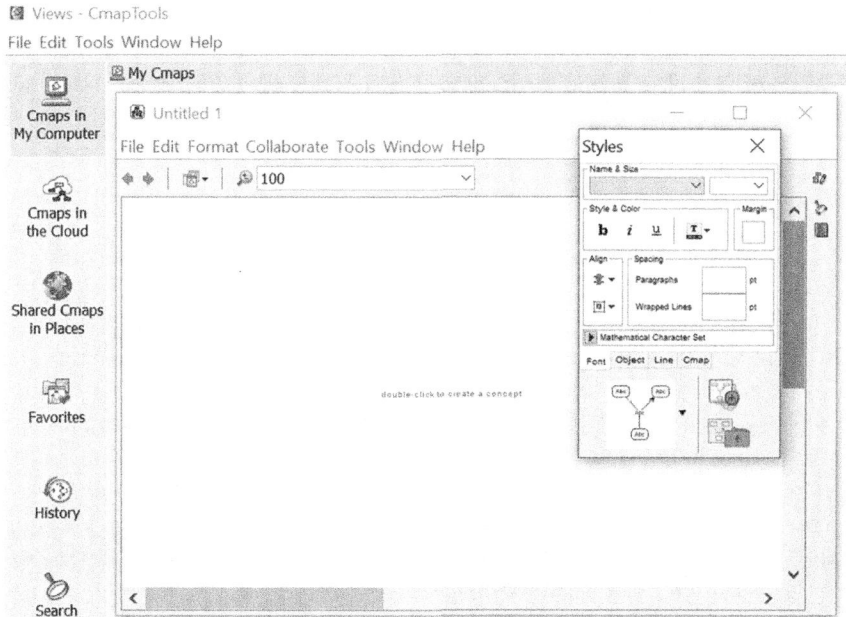

FIGURE 5.3 A Display of "*Cmap*" Interface

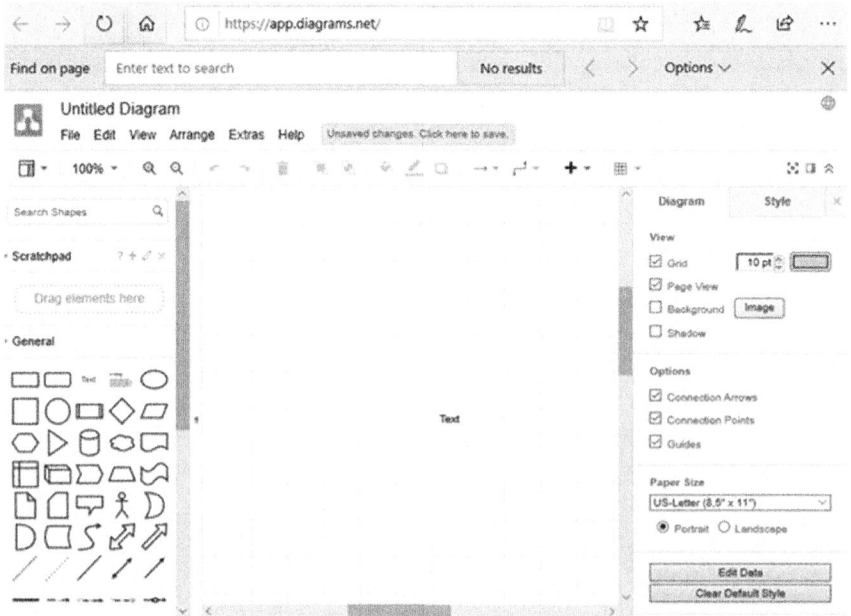

FIGURE 5.4   A Display of "*draw.io*" Interface

representation of a framework is draw.io (https://app.diagrams.net/). With this diagramming software, a researcher can turn an imaginative framework into an informative illustration (Figure 5.4). For beginners, Figure 5.5 shows the shapes researchers could start with. To access their instructional videos, go to: www. youtube.com/c/drawioapp/videos.

Summary

Theoretical/conceptual framework development is an art. It takes dedication and a considerable amount of time to master this craft. To help you get the foundational knowledge of a framework, we mainly discussed general information on the definition, features, rationale, role and development process of theoretical/ conceptual frameworks within a qualitative study. We also shared the reasons why it is relevant to have a theoretical/conceptual framework in a phenomenological study. We believe that as phenomenological researchers, a framework (including its associate theory) could influence the data we collect from participants, analysis of data and presentation of findings. In order to prevent a theory from influencing the understanding and explanation of participants' experiences, we put a hold on its explanatory nature. However, we use the theory's descriptive power, taking notes of its associated concepts and using them to help inform the creation of codes and themes. Chapter 6 details practical illustrations of what has been discussed in this chapter.

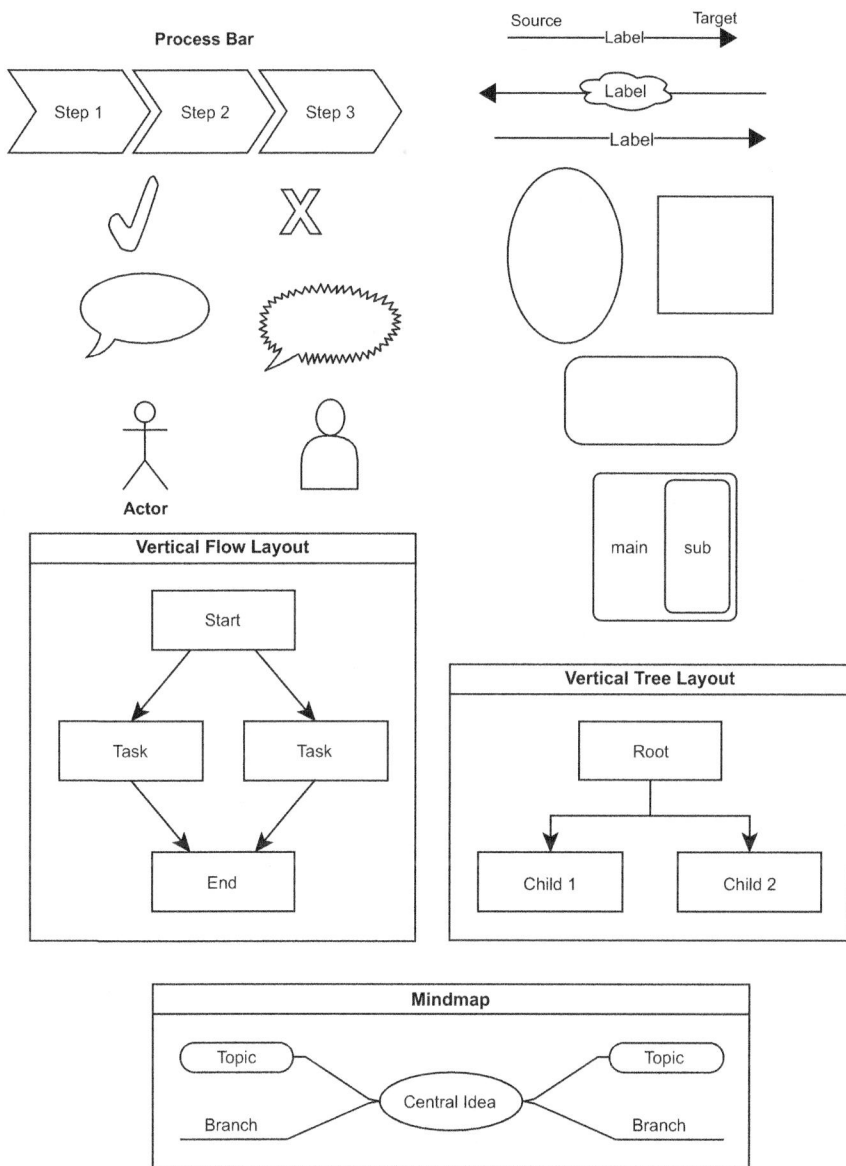

FIGURE 5.5 A Display of Illustration Templates From "*draw.io*"

References

Abend, G. (2008). The meaning of "theory". *Sociological Theory*, 26(2), 173–199. www.jstor. org/stable/20453103

Adu, P. (2019). *A step-by-step guide to qualitative data coding.* Routledge.

Adu, P. (2020). Differentiating theoretical and conceptual frameworks [PowerPoint slides]. *SlideShare.* www.slideshare.net/kontorphilip/differentiating-theoretical-and-conceptual-frameworks

Amos, N. M. (2020). *Chaos and complexity theory applied to bullying at work*. The National Career Development Association. www.ncda.org/aws/NCDA/pt/sd/news_article/148 442/_PARENT/CC_layout_details/false

Anfara, V. A., & Mertz, N. T. (2015). Setting the stage. In V. A. Anfara & N. T. Mertz (Eds.), *Theoretical frameworks in qualitative research*. Sage Publications.

Bhattacherjee, A. (2012). *Social science research: Principles, methods, and practices*. Textbooks Collection. Scholar Commons, University of South Florida.

Charmaz, K. (2014). *Constructing grounded theory*. Sage Publications.

Davey, N. (2008). Twentieth century hermeneutics. In D. Moran (Ed.), *The Routledge companion to twentieth century philosophy* (pp. 693–735). ISBN: 0-203-87936-8 Master e-book ISBN

Dix, A. (2008). Theoretical analysis and theory creation. In P. Cairns & A. L. Cox (Eds.), *Research methods in human-computer interaction* (pp. 175–195). Cambridge University Press.

Durning, S. J., Costanzo, M., Artino, A. R., Jr., Dyrbye, L. N., Beckman, T. J., Schuwirth, L., Holmboe, E., Roy, M. J., Wittich, C. M., Lipner, R. S., & van der Vleuten, C. (2013). Functional neuroimaging correlates of burnout among internal medicine residents and faculty members. *Frontiers in Psychiatry*, *4*, 131. https://doi.org/10.3389/fpsyt.2013.00131

Głębocka, A., & Lisowska, E. (2007). Professional burnout and stress among polish physicians explained by the Hobfoll resources theory. *Journal of Physiology and Pharmacology: An Official Journal of the Polish Physiological Society*, *58*(Suppl. 5, 1), 243–252.

Grant, C., & Osanloo, A. (2015). Understanding, selecting, and integrating a theoretical framework in dissertation research: Developing a "blueprint" for your "house". *Administrative Issues Journal*, *4*. https://doi.org/10.5929/2014.4.2.9

Green, H. E. (2014). Use of theoretical and conceptual frameworks in qualitative research. *Nurse Researcher*, *21*(6), 34–38. https://doi.org/10.7748/nr.21.6.34.e1252

Husserl, E. (2017). *Ideas: General introduction to pure phenomenology*. Unwin Brothers Ltd. ISBN-10: 0415519039

Imenda, S. (2014). Is there a conceptual difference between theoretical and conceptual frameworks? *Journal of Social Science*, *38*(2), 185–195. https://doi.org/10.1080/097189 23.2014.11893249

Itao, A. D. S. (2010). Poaul Ricoeur's hermeneutics of symbols: A critical dialectic of suspicion and faith. *Kritike an Online Journal of Philosophy*, *4*(2), 1–17. https://doi.org/10.25138/4.2.a.1

Jabareen, Y. (2009). Building a conceptual framework: Philosophy, definitions, and procedure. *International Journal of Qualitative Methods*, 49–62. https://doi.org/10.1177/160940690900800406

Kivunja, C. (2018). Distinguishing between theory, theoretical framework, and conceptual framework: A systematic review of lessons from the field. *International Journal of Higher Education*, *7*(6), 44. https://doi.org/10.5430/ijhe.v7n6p44

Klein, D. F. (2002). Historical aspects of anxiety. *Dialogues in Clinical Neuroscience*, *4*(3), 295–304.

Maxwell, J. A. (2013). *Qualitative research design: An interactive approach*. Sage Publications.

Parahoo, K. (2006). *Nursing research: Principles, process and issues*. Palgrave Macmillan.

Ricoeur, P. (2019). *Hermeneutics and the human sciences*. Cambridge University Press. ISBN-10: 0521280028

Sandberg, J., & Alvesson, M. (2011). Ways of constructing research questions: Gap-spotting or problematization? *Organization*, *18*(23), 23–44. https://doi.org/10.1177/1350508410372151

Sinclair, M. (2007). A guide to understanding theoretical and conceptual frameworks. *Evidence-Based Midwifery*, *5*(2), 39.

Torfing, J. (2005). Discourse theory: Achievements, arguments, and challenges. In D. Howarth & J. Torfing (Eds.), *Discourse theory in European politics*. Palgrave Macmillan. https://doi.org/10.1057/9780230523364_1

Vaismoradi, M., Turunen, H., & Bondas, T. (2013). Content analysis and thematic analysis: Implications for conducting a qualitative descriptive study. *Nursing & Health Sciences, 15*(3), 398–405. https://doi.org/10.1111/nhs.12048

Wallis, E. S., & Wright, B. (2020). Basics of theory: A brief, plain language, introduction. *MethodSpace*. www.methodspace.com/basics-of-theory-a-brief-plain-language-introduction/

6

DEVELOPING THEORETICAL/ CONCEPTUAL FRAMEWORK

Objectives

Readers will be able to:

1 Conduct scoping literature review;
2 Identify appropriate theories/concepts;
3 Use theories/concepts to create theoretical/conceptual framework;
4 Develop visual representation of their framework.

Conducting scoping review

Determining the theories, models, constructs and/or concepts (i.e., elements of a framework) is among the initial steps scholars take to help in the development of theoretical/conceptual frameworks. Some researchers use the theories and concepts they are familiar with to facilitate the building of the framework. Others may be lucky to accidentally come across a promising theory or a group of concepts perceived as useful in the construction of the framework. However, there is a systematic way of searching for an appropriate theory and associated concepts, making sure that the chosen theory is consistent with the philosophical features of the selected school of phenomenology and in line with the principle of parsimony. According to Epstein (1984), the principle of parsimony indicates

> where we have no reason to do otherwise and where two theories account
> for the same facts, we should prefer the one which is briefer, which makes
> assumptions with which we can easily dispense, which refers to observables, and which has the greatest possible generality.

(p. 119)

Conducting literature scoping is one of the ways of accessing theories/concepts related to the phenomenon of study. Before we expound on this literature review strategy, let us briefly discuss how this type of literature review is different from traditional literature review and systematic literature review (see Munn et al., 2018). Traditional literature review involves strategically looking for and writing about research done and/or information written about the topic of interest (Yale Library, 2020). So, what is the essence of conducting this type of literature review? Here is a list of reasons for conducting a traditional literature review:

- Documenting what is known about the research problem;
- Identifying a gap in the literature (i.e., what further needs to be known about the problem or what needs to be addressed);
- Educating the audience about the topic;
- Helping to develop research questions;
- Using the existing studies to justify the focus of the study;
- Situating the study in the body of knowledge of the field.

However, systematic literature review goes beyond just looking for what is out there (in relation to the phenomenon of study), examining what the author found and reporting the outcome (Munn et al., 2018). It involves methodologically setting criteria for the selection of literature, carefully determining the sources of the literature, extensively searching for the right literature, critically analyzing them, and developing categories/themes to help add to the research question (Tricco et al., 2016). With this type of literature review, the literature is viewed as data that need to be analyzed in a systematic and transparent manner to help address the research question.

Scoping review is considered a type of literature review that falls in between a traditional and a systematic literature review (Munn et al., 2018). This is because it is more thorough and structured in searching for literature than the traditional review but less comprehensive and critical than the systematic literature review (Sucharew & Macaluso, 2019). So, what is scoping review? According to Munn et al. (2018):

> True to their name, scoping reviews are an ideal tool to determine the scope or coverage of a body of literature on a given topic and give clear indication of the volume of literature and studies available as well as an overview (broad or detailed) of its focus.
>
> *(p. 2)*

In other words, it is the process of searching for information about a phenomenon of interest, organizing and analyzing what the researcher found, and providing a summary of the outcome of the review. The scoping review process is normally driven by a broad and descriptive question set by the researcher (Arksey & O'Malley, 2005; Sucharew & Macaluso, 2019). The process is about transparently looking for information from the literature and reporting the outcome of the literature search without doing a critical and extensive analysis of the results of the search (Munn et al., 2018). In other words, it involves researchers preventing themselves from interpreting what they found but limiting themselves to understanding and describing the outcome of the literature search process (Sucharew & Macaluso, 2019). Scoping review procedures can be grouped into seven main steps (see Arksey & O'Malley, 2005; Schaink et al., 2012; Sucharew & Macaluso, 2019; Tricco et al., 2016). These are: developing a research question, determining the appropriate database to search, setting criteria for literature selection, searching for literature, selecting the right literature, analyzing the selected literature and reporting the findings.

Because this chapter is more of a demonstration of how to search for theories or concepts related to the phenomenon of study, let us assume that we are conducting a research project, *Burnout among primary care physicians in the United States*. At this point, our goal is to come up with a theory or a group of theories about burnout that can be used to help develop our theoretical/conceptual framework. Using the scoping review strategy, the following list shows the stages using a modification of the original steps listed above:

1   Creating a scoping review question
2   Determining sources of literature
3   Searching for literature that has theories of interest
4   Selecting appropriate literature for further analysis
5   Extracting theories and their characteristics from the selected literature
6   Deciding on an appropriate theory for the development of the framework

Step 1. Creating a scoping review question

A scoping review question is the question a researcher plans to address after analyzing relevant literature that has information about the theory of interest (Arksey & O'Malley, 2005; Schaink et al., 2012; Sucharew & Macaluso, 2019; Tricco et al., 2016). The essence of having such a question is to help guide where to look for theories and what literature to select for the analysis. In other words, it is not a research question for a study, but a question designed to help look for the right theory for the development of the theoretical/conceptual framework. The question should be open-ended and exploratory in nature.

Demonstration 6.1

Phenomenological study informed by transcendental phenomenology

Because this type of study aims at arriving at the meaning of physicians' experience of burnout, the focus of the scoping review is to find theories that explain not the burnout itself but the experience of it. Therefore, the scoping review question we can pose is, *"what theories explain the mental experience of burnout, particularly among physicians?"* Close attention should be paid to theories of burnout that emphasize the thought process, consciousness and perception of people experiencing burnout. This is because, with transcendental phenomenology, an experience occurs in one's thoughts (Husserl, 2017).

Phenomenological study informed by interpretative phenomenology

Using the lens of interpretative phenomenology, actions, including intent associated with a phenomenon (e.g., burnout), is the lived experience (Heidegger, 2010). By analyzing participants' actions and intentions, a scholar will be able to understand what it means to be who they are. Based on this assertion, the theories should be capable of explaining actions and strategies related to participants' burnout. Therefore, the scoping review question could be, *"what theories explain the actions, intentions and coping behaviors associated with the experience of burnout, particularly among physicians?"*

Step 2. Determining sources of literature

At this point, the hope is to get access to theories that have been discussed within a research community and have empirically been developed and/or validated by researchers. This is not to imply that theories that have not been conceptually developed cannot be considered when developing a theoretical/conceptual framework. The literature of interest includes, but is not limited to, peer-reviewed articles, dissertations, books, theses, unpublished research and/or evaluation reports (Peters et al., 2015; Sucharew & Macaluso, 2019). So how can you get access to some of the literature? Using "relevant [electronic] databases (MEDLINE, EMBASE, Social Work Abstracts, PsycINFO, Scholars Portal, PubMed, Google Scholar) . . ." would help (Schaink et al., 2012, p. 2). Also, other databases such as EBSCOhost and ProQuest can be appropriate sources of articles and dissertations. Moreover, many open-access journals are available to explore online and provide access to relevant literature (see https://doaj.org/). In addition, Arksey and O'Malley (2005) recommended manually reviewing reference lists of literature to select relevant cited references for a scoping review.

Demonstration 6.2

Phenomenological study

There are three main terms/concepts we want to see in a piece of literature before reviewing it. These are: physicians, burnout and theory/theories. So, databases that are more likely to have literature about *physicians* or *medical doctors* are MEDLINE and PubMed. Also, because *burnout* can be considered as a psychological term, "coined in the 1970s by the American psychologist

Herbert Freudenberger," studies about it are more likely to be found in the PsycINFO database (IQWiG, 2020, para. 1). Therefore, we will initially access articles from the three databases mentioned above. We may also look for literature through Google Scholar and may review the reference lists of articles when need be.

Step 3. Searching for literature which has theories of interest

At this stage, scholars should think about the kinds of words and/or phrases they want to use to search for relevant literature. It is important to take note of key search words and any synonyms that are more likely to be used in literature (Bramer et al., 2018; Cooper et al., 2018). To efficiently and effectively use the selected database(s), a researcher needs to familiarize themself with the appropriate way of using syntax in conducting the search. "Common syntax components include the use of parentheses and Boolean operators such as 'AND,' 'OR,' and 'NOT,' which are available in all major interfaces" (Bramer et al., 2018, p. 536). Bramer et al. (2018) provided rich information about databases and their respective syntaxes (see, p. 535).

- **Searching based on relationship between words.** Researchers normally use Boolean operators to create syntax showing relationship between words and how they should appear in literature for it to be retrieved from the database (see UOW Library, 2020).

  - If you want the database system to extract articles containing the words *book* and *pen*, the syntax would be "*book* AND *pen*."
  - If you want the database system to extract articles containing either the word *book* or *pen*, the syntax would be, "*book* OR *pen*."
  - If you want the database system to extract articles containing the word *book* but not *pen*, the syntax would be, "*book* NOT *pen*."

- **Searching a group of words or phrases.** Researchers normally use quotation marks to search for literature with a particular group of words or phrases (see, UOW Library, 2020). Also, parenthesis can be used in syntax to search for literature which has a combination of phrases.

  - If a researcher wants the database system to select articles containing a group of words (a phrase), such as *interesting book*, the syntax would be, "*interesting book*."
  - If a researcher wants the database system to select articles containing a group of phrases such as *interesting book* and *red pen*, the syntax would be, "*interesting book*" AND "*red pen*."
  - If a researcher wants the database system to select articles containing either one phrase (i.e., *interesting book*) or the other phrase (i.e., *red pen*), the syntax would be, "*interesting book*" OR "*red pen*."

- If a researcher wants the database system to select articles containing one phrase (i.e., *interesting book*) but not the other phrase (i.e., *red pen*), the syntax would be, "*interesting book*" NOT "*red pen*."
- If a researcher wants the database system to select articles containing two phrases (i.e., *interesting book* and *blue pen*) but not the other phrase (i.e., *red pen*), the syntax would be, "*interesting book*" AND "*blue pen*" NOT "*red pen*."

- **Searching words with a share stem word.** This involves adding an asterisk to a stem or root word, commanding the database to display articles that have that stem word with any suffix (NPS Dudley Knox Library, 2020). For instance, if you indicate "use★" as the search syntax, the articles extracted from the database should have at least one of the following—use, uses, using, useful, usefulness, usefully, usability, useable and the like.

Demonstration 6.3

Phenomenological study

Informed by literature search strategies discussed above, we went to MED-LINE, PubMed and PsycINFO databases to search for literature that was about physicians' burnout and had information on a theory about burnout. We used the following search syntax; "Burnout AND theory★ AND (physicians or doctors)." This means that we wanted literature that contained "burnout," theory★" (or words with the stem "theory" plus a suffix) and, in addition, had either the term "physicians" or "doctors." In all, the search of three databases produced an output of 263 citations. Eighty-four (32 percent) of the citations were extracted from MEDLINE, while 101 (38 percent) and 78 (30 percent) citations were obtained from PubMed and PsycINFO, respectively.

Commentary 6.2 You can see that we used one type of search syntax (i.e., "Burnout AND theory★ AND [physicians or doctors]"), and it produced very promising results. However, this may not be case in other situations. So, it is very important to be flexible at this stage, creating and trying out more than one type of search syntax to see which one elicits a good number of valuable citations. Similarly, researchers can explore other databases to see what they have if the initial literature sources do not generate substantial outcomes. Searching for literature can be a daunting task. Nevertheless, being strategic by applying best practices in literature search under a scoping review could yield fruitful results (see Arksey & O'Malley, 2005; Schaink et al., 2012; Sucharew & Macaluso, 2019; Tricco et al., 2016).

Step 4. Selecting the appropriate literature for further analysis

The next step is to skim through the list of literature extracted as a product of the literature search and select the ones that meet the set criteria. So, in coming up with criteria, the question you could ask is "*what conditions should a literature meet to be selected for further analysis?*" At this stage, you could be faced with reviewing hundreds or even thousands of citations. Due to this, it is important to create criteria that are clear, straightforward and easy to use to quickly determine which of the literature should be selected (see Subramanyam, 2013). You could set the criteria related to the date of publication, terms of interest, research location and/or participants and even the type of study.

Demonstration 6.4

Phenomenological study

Before starting the literature selection process, we developed the criteria a piece of literature should meet to be part of the review. First, the title of the article should have the term *burnout*. Second, the article or study should be about physicians. With the second criterion, we reviewed the abstracts, looking for terms such as *physicians* or *doctors*, referring to them as participants in the study. Third, the abstract should contain *theory* and/or *theories*. The rationale for these requirements was to make sure we were selecting articles that had information about a theory or group of theories that explains the burnout or physicians' experiences of burnout.

Out of the 84 citations extracted from the MEDLINE database, 15 were selected based on the set criteria (see Figure 6.1). Also, seven were selected from 101 citations we extracted from PubMed. Last, five out of 78 citations searched from PsycINFO were selected for further analysis. Looking at the selected articles under the MEDLINE database, two of them were also chosen under PubMed and PsycINFO (see Figure 6.2). Besides this, three of the MEDLINE articles were also part of the list of PubMed selected articles. One of the MEDLINE articles was part of the PsycINFO articles. Overall, 19 articles met the selection criteria with the publication year ranging from 1994 to 2020 (see Table 6.1). Most of them were research articles about quantitative studies.

Commentary 6.3 We focused on two parts of the articles to decide whether to select them or not. For each article, we quickly looked at the title to find out whether there was any mention of *burnout* and skimmed the abstract to see whether reference was made on theory/theories in relation to burnout and if the study was about physicians. When we were not sure about the selection, we quickly went through the article, looking at the introduction and literature review section, to help us make an informed decision.

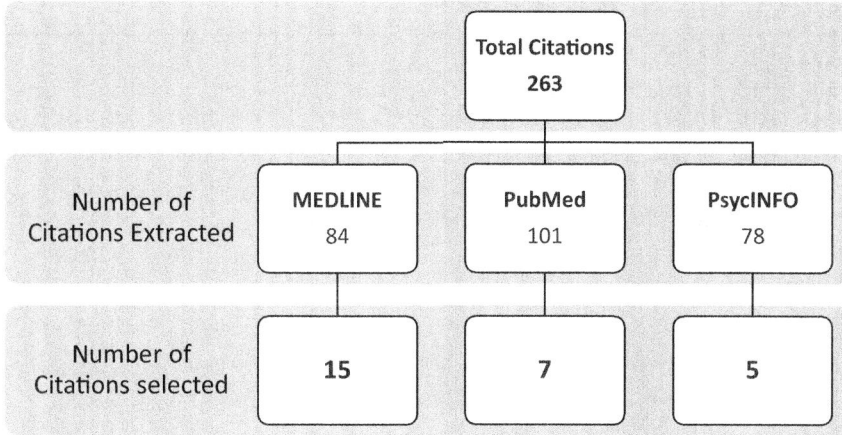

FIGURE 6.1 Number of Citations Extracted and Selected Under Their Respective Database

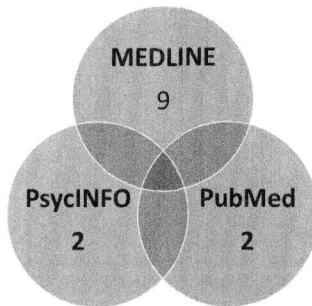

FIGURE 6.2 Number of Selected Citations Under Their Respective Database Including Articles Found in More Than One Database

It is always advisable to use bibliographic software to save and organize selected citations/articles. We used RefWorks to save our citations. As we were exporting the citations to the reference management software, we looked for the full articles and downloaded them. You may not have full access to some articles in one database. You could explore other databases to see whether they are available. One of the strategies we used was to search for the articles on Google Scholar. Occasionally, the search led us to the ResearchGate website to access the articles.

Researchers could be faced with a situation where there is no theory or are limited theories related to the phenomenon of interest. A researcher could search and select literature that has models, propositions and concepts related to the focus of interest. These explanatory elements could be further analyzed, leading to the development of a conceptual framework.

TABLE 6.1 Articles and Their Characteristics

Authors	Type Of Article	Type Of Research
Brady et al. (2020)	Research article	Quantitative research
Dall'Ora et al. (2020)	Research article	Systematic literature review
De Maeyer and Schoenmakers (2019)	Research article	Quantitative research
de Wit et al. (2020)	Research article	Mixed methods study
Durning et al. (2013)	Research article	Quantitative research
Gazelle et al. (2014)	Research article	Qualitative research
Głębock and Lisowska (2007)	Research article	Quantitative research
Gregory and Menser (2015)	Research article	Quantitative research
Gregory et al. (2018)	Research article	Quantitative research
Innstrand et al. (2008)	Research article	Quantitative research
Jackson-Koku and Grime (2019)	Research article	Systematic review
Koh et al. (2020)	Research article	Qualitative research
Lu et al. (2020)	Research article	Qualitative research
Teoh et al. (2020)	Research article	Quantitative research
Tucker et al. (2017)	Evaluation research article	Program Evaluation
Van Dierendonck et al. (1994)	Research article	Quantitative research
Williams et al. (2019)	Research article	Systematic review
Winning (2020)	Perspective article	N/A
Zwack and Schweitzer (2013)	Research article	Qualitative research

Step 5. Extracting theories and their characteristics from the selected literature

At this point, the goal is to review the selected articles and extract all theories that have explanatory characteristics in relation the experience of a phenomenon. However, if the study is informed by transcendental phenomenology, the ultimate goal (under this step) is to find a theory or group of theories that explains the mental side of the experience of a phenomenon through thought process (consciousness). Similarly, researchers informed by interpretative phenomenology seek to identify a theory or group of theories that explains the lived experience of a phenomenon through actions and intentions.

Demonstration 6.5

Phenomenological study

We used NVivo 12 (Version 12.6.959; QSR International Pty Ltd, 2019) to help organize the theories and their concepts and characteristics. NVivo 12 is a qualitative data analysis software program used for creating and organizing codes/categories/themes to help address qualitative research questions (Adu, 2019). The steps for theory extraction could be followed irrespective of what school forms a researcher's phenomenological research. Here are the steps we followed to arrive at nine theories which could potentially explain the experience of burnout among physicians:

1   *Uploading the articles into a qualitative data analysis software program (i.e., NVivo):* We loaded all the 19 articles into NVivo to start the theory selection process.

    a   After loading the articles, a case was created for each article. A case (in NVivo) is a folder the researcher/analyst creates to house an article and their characteristics. It can also be viewed as a connector, linking characteristics of the articles to their respective files, which have been uploaded into the software.

2   *Creating an Excel spreadsheet to house literature characteristics:* We created an Excel spreadsheet to document characteristics of the 19 selected articles (see Figure 6.3). The spreadsheet contained authors' names, year of publication, title of the articles, type of article and type of research.

    a   The essence of creating this spreadsheet was to help connect the features of the articles to the theories extracted using NVivo.

3   *Uploading the spreadsheet containing literature characteristics:* We then uploaded the spreadsheet into NVivo and linked the features of each article to their respective case

4   *Reviewing each article fishing for theories:* Consistent with the scoping review technique, we went through each article and coded theories identified by:

    a   Creating a code for any theory about burnout identified;
    b   Using the theory name to label the code created;
    c   Dropping any relevant description about the theory into the code.

       (i)   We saw codes as storages accommodating statements about the selected theories.
      (ii)   At this stage, our goal was not to evaluate the theories but to gather them for further analysis.

At the end of the theory selection process, we found seven theories with explanatory tendencies in relation to experiencing the phenomenon of burnout. They are cognitive load theory (CLT), conservation of resources (COR) theory, emotional intelligence, equity theory and object relations theory (see Table 6.2).

Commentary 6.4   We were able to get information about the theories from the following sections of the articles: introduction, theoretical/conceptual framework and literature review. However, there was at least one article in which we

Authors	Year of Publication	Title	Type of article	Type of research
Brady et al. (2020)	2020	Describing the emotional exhaustion, depersonalization...	Research article	Quantitative research
Dall'Ora et al. (2020)	2020	Burnout in nursing; A theoretical review	Research article	Systematic literature review
De Maeyer and Schoenmakers (2019)	2019	Exploring intergenerational differences in burnout...	Research article	Quantitative research
de Wit et al. (2020)	2020	Canadian emergency physician psychological distress...	Research article	Mixed methods study
Durning et al. (2013)	2013	Functional neuroimaging correlates of burnout...	Research article	Quantitative research
Gazelle et al. (2014)	2014	Physician burnout: Coaching a way out	Research article	Qualitative research
Glebock and Lisowska (2007)	2007	Professional burnout and stress among polish physicians...	Research article	Quantitative research
Gregory and Menser (2015)	2015	Burnout among primary care physicians: A test of the areas of worklife model	Research article	Quantitative research
Gregory et al. (2018)	2018	An organizational intervention to reduce physician burnout	Research article	Quantitative research
Innstrand et al. (2008)	2008	Positive and negative work-family interaction...	Research article	Quantitative research
Jackson-Koku and Grime (2019)	2019	Emotion regulation and burnout in doctors: A systematic review	Research article	Systematic review
Koh et al. (2020)	2020	Burnout and resilience after a decade in palliative care:...	Research article	Qualitative research
Lu et al. (2020)	2020	Gender differences in surgeon burnout...	Research article	Qualitative research
Teoh et al. (2020)	2020	Individual and organizational psychosocial predictors of hospital doctors...	Research article	Quantitative research
Tucker et al. (2017)	2017	Finding the sweet spot: Developing, implementing...	Evaluation research article	Program Evaluation
Van Dierendonck et al. (1994)	1994	Burnout among general practitioners: A perspective from equity theory	Research article	Quantitative research
Williams et al. (2019)	2019	The personal and professional consequences of physician burnout...	Research article	Systematic review
Winning (2020)	2020	The use of an object: Exploring physician burnout...	Perspective article	N/A
Zwack and Schweitzer (2013)	2013	If every fifth physician is affected by burnout...	Research article	Qualitative research

FIGURE 6.3 Literature Characteristics

got a useful description of one of the theories selected under the discussion section. When scoping the literature for theories, it is important (but not required) to document/code some of the concepts related to the selected theories. They could be useful tools when critically examining the theories. As shown in Figure 6.4, burnout-related concepts, such as depersonalization, emotional exhaustion, feeling of inequity and the like, were coded for further examination and use when needed. Moreover, we also created codes to house information about the definition, history and effects of burnout (see Figure 6.4). Creating these codes was not the main goal of conducting a scoping review (which was to extract theories), but they may be helpful if we want to learn more about burnout.

It is also important not to overlook models, especially if they can explain an experience of the phenomenon of study, although the main focus is to look for theories. They may be valuable in adding further clarification or explanation to what a particular theory represents. For example, we initially coded *job resources– demands model* due to its ability to explain the causes of burnout. This model was finally brought under *job demands–resources theory*. Last, after the initial extraction of theories, a researcher should review them to make sure theories with different names are consolidated. For instance, Hobfoll's theory was brought under the *COR theory* because it posited that the main factors that lead to burnout among physicians are limited resources to match work demand and dwindling resources without the means of replenishing them. In the end, the *COR theory* emerged as the theory with most articles connected to it (see Figure 6.2).

Step 6. Deciding on an appropriate theory for the development of the framework

This is the stage where a researcher chooses an appropriate theory, addressing the scoping review question. There are three factors a researcher could consider

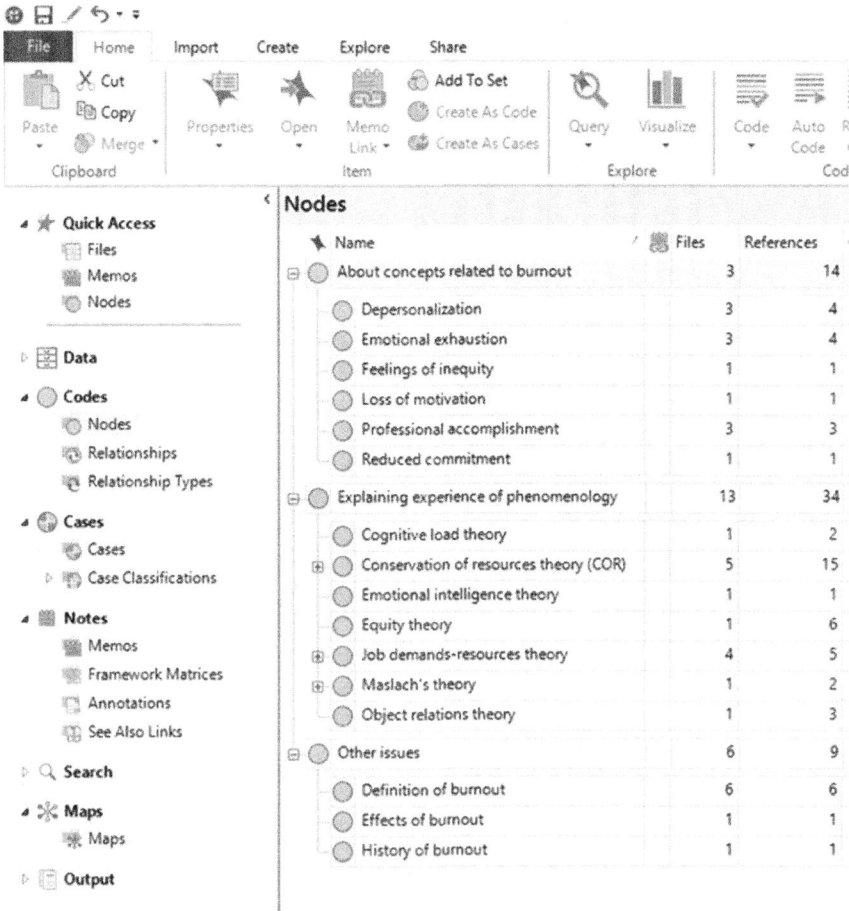

FIGURE 6.4   Display of Theories Extracted and Their Concepts and Characteristics in NVivo

when selecting the right theory. They need to make sure the selected theory fits the features of the chosen school of phenomenology, has met the principle of parsimony and has concepts and terms useful when analyzing data. We came up with a rating tool that will be helpful for choosing the right theory or theories (see Table 6.3). It contains five items with five-point Likert scale.

Theory and school of phenomenology match

With these criteria, researchers are expected to critically examine the theories in terms of what they mean, represent and explain and review how consistent they are with the chosen school of phenomenology. For instance, because transcendental phenomenology emphasizes consciousness and intentionality with

TABLE 6.2 Theories Selected and Their Sampled Statements

Theory	Number Of Articles	Number Of Relevant Information Gathered	Sampled Statement	Meaning
CLT	1	2	"CLT would postulate that the impact of emotional exhaustion would further exacerbate limited processing space through inefficient activation, like a computer processing unit whose function is slowed in performing a desired task by too many simultaneous processes" (Durning et al., 2013, p. 5).	This explains the *effect of burnout*. When physicians are emotionally tired, it takes a toll on their "cognitive resources"—leading to limited function of their cognitive abilities and, in effect, negatively impacting their clinical work (Durning et al., 2013, p. 5).
COR theory	5	15	"Hobfoll's conservation of resources theory, the burnout syndrome is defined as a process of expenditure, loss and run-down developing gradually over time. It occurs when the restoration of the resources in the form of cognitive, emotional, and physical abilities does not appear" (Glebocka & Lisowska, 2007).	This explains the *causes of burnout*. When resources needed to complete a task is not sufficient or there is a continuous dwindling of resources, burnout is experienced.
Emotional intelligence theory	1	1	"Emotional intelligence theory suggests that emotion regulation skills facilitate the maintenance of appropriate emotions, reducing or adapting undesirable emotions in oneself and others. Emotion regulation is usually automatic but can be controlled through learnt strategies" (Jackson-Koku & Grime, 2019, p. 1).	This explains the *management of burnout*. Burnout will dissipate if physicians are capable of effectively regulating their emotions (i.e., having emotional intelligence).
Equity theory	1	6	"Equity theory predicts that when people experience inequity, for example, when GPs meet harassment by patients, they will try to reduce this tension in order to restore equity" (Van Dierendonck et al., 1994, p. 89).	This explains the *cause and solution of burnout*. In the quest for maintaining equity in the physicians' unhealthy relationship with patients, they devise strategies that are more likely to lead to burnout.

(Continued)

TABLE 6.2 (Continued)

Theory	Number Of Articles	Number Of Relevant Information Gathered	Sampled Statement	Meaning
Job demands-resources theory	4	5	"The job demands-resources theory suggests that burnout results from increased physical or psychological work demands and reduced resources" (de Wit et al., 2020, p. 2).	This explains the *causes of burnout*. The two main factors contributing to physicians' burnout are: high job demands and inadequate resources to match work demands.
Maslach's theory	1	2	"Maslach theorised that burnout is a state, which occurs as a result of a prolonged mismatch between a person and at least one of the . . . six dimensions of work" (Dall'Ora et al., 2020, p. 2).	This explains the *causes of burnout*. The causes include physicians' unmet expectations, worked demands and compensations.
Object relations theory	1	3	". . . the clinician's body is made into an object, both in the individual, intimate dispensation of care to another human body and within the wider structures of the institutionalisation and regulation of healthcare systems" (Winning, 2020, p. 5). "It provides a critical understanding of the genesis and enactment of blame and retribution in the face of medical error, both within and outwith the medical profession" (Winning, 2020, p. 5).	This explains the *causes of burnout*. Objectifying, projecting and blaming physicians lead to burnout.

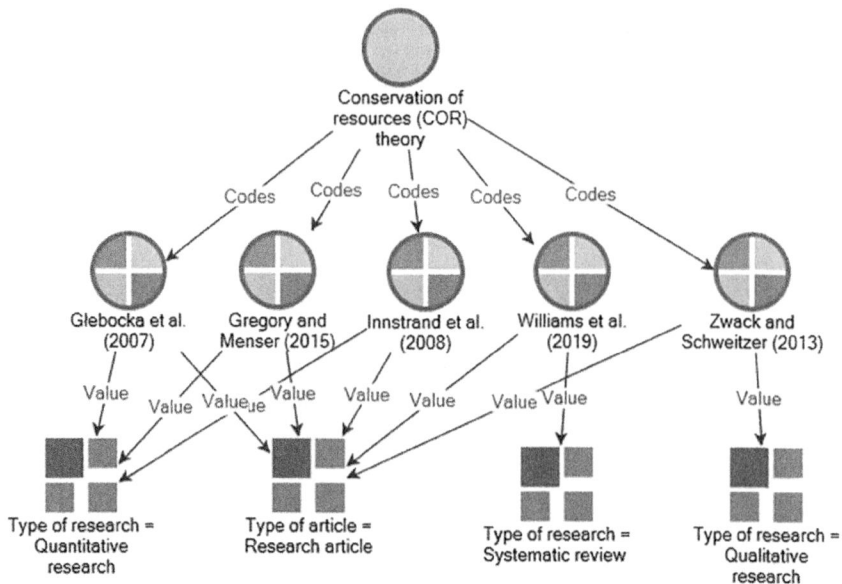

FIGURE 6.5 Project Map Displaying a Theory and Its Connections

Note: This figure was created in NVivo 12 (Version 12.6.959; QSR International Pty Ltd, 2019).

TABLE 6.3 Theory Selection Rating Tool

	Extremely Unlikely	Unlikely	Neutral	Likely	Extremely Likely	Comments
1. *Theory and school of phenomenology match*						
2. *Adherence to the principle of parsimony*						
• *Brevity*						
• *Few assumptions*						
• *Extent of theory coverage*						
3. *Useful for descriptive purpose*						

respect to the experience of a phenomenon, the theory to be considered should have explanatory elements of cognitive process. On the contrary, interpretative phenomenology tends to focus on actions as a source of making meaning of an experience, leading to the selection of a theory with explanatory elements of doing something, acting and/or reacting in a certain way and interacting with the objects in the world (Heidegger, 2010).

Adherence to the principle of parsimony

This principle promotes the need to have a theory that is concise, that has a small number of assumptions and that covers almost all aspects of the topic/phenomenon of study (Epstein, 1984).

- **Brevity:** In terms of the theory being concise, Epstein (1984) noted that "where two theories account for the same facts and where we have no other reason to prefer one over the other, we should probably prefer the briefer" (p. 120).
- **Assumptions:** With respect to assumption, having a theory with fewer assumptions is better than having one with a lot of assumptions, provided both theories adequately explain the same phenomenon or its experience (Epstein, 1984). Assumptions are assertions that are not based on empirical evidence but need to exist for a theory to be true (Adu, 2016; Epstein, 1984).
- **Theory coverage:** Concerning the extent of a phenomenon a theory covers, making sure to consider the one that "account[s] for" more aspects of the phenomenon or its experience is preferred (Epstein, 1984, p. 123). If a researcher has too much left over in terms of what the theory covers, they leave a lot of room for criticism and confusion.

Useful for descriptive purpose

As discussed in Chapter 4, in a phenomenological study, researchers use theories for descriptive purposes when analyzing data. Normalizing the practice of epoché, which was suggested by Husserl (2017), researchers suspend the explanatory validity of a theory and use its concepts and terminologies to help describe the relevant information captured from the data. In other words, when using theories in a phenomenological study, researchers retain their descriptive perspective as they suspend their explanatory power. At this point, the theory is reduced to become part of the phenomenon, moving from an explanatory to a descriptive (heuristic) tool. When a scholar reduces the theory to a phenomenon, it becomes part of a depository of descriptors needed to be used to code the data. Therefore, a good theory should have descriptors that could be used during the data analysis stage.

Demonstration 6.6

Phenomenological study informed by transcendental phenomenology

The scoping review question we addressed was "*what theories explain the mental experience of burnout, particularly among physicians?*" Looking at the statements for each theory and our understanding of them, we selected CLT and COR theory as two main theories that are aligned with the features of transcendental subjectivity (i.e., universal meaning of consciousness) and psychological subjectivity (i.e., personal meaning of cognition; see Table 6.2). The next step was to use the *theory rating selecting tool* to help critically assess and rate the two theories, preparing the way to making the final decision. The results showed that both theories had the same ratings (see Tables 6.4 and 6.5). In the end, we decided to choose both because neither of them covered all aspects of the experience of burnout. While CLT covers the effect of burnout, COR theory explains the causes of burnout.

Phenomenological study informed by interpretative phenomenology

With our interpretative phenomenology-informed study, our focus at the scoping review stage was to select theories that explain actions in relation to the experience of burnout. The theories that were consistent with interpretative phenomenology and addressed the scoping review question (*"what theories explain the actions, intentions and coping behaviors associated with the experience of burnout, particularly among physicians?"*) were emotional intelligence theory and equity theory. In order to make sure we were making the right decision, we used the *theory rating selecting tool* to assess their consistency, parsimony and coverage (see Tables 6.6 and 6.7). In effect, we chose equity theory as a better theory with extensive coverage compared to emotional intelligence theory, which mainly accounts for the management and solution of burnout. As shown in Table 6.2, the equity theory accounts for both the cause and solution of burnout.

Commentary 6.5 The *theory selection rating tool* is used not only to assess the appropriateness of a theory but also to aid in understanding its characteristics, which will be useful when developing theoretical/conceptual framework. In the theory assessment tables, the last column (i.e., *Comment* column) is dedicated to writing reflections and documenting anything that a researcher thinks is important to take note of. Importantly, a researcher does not have to have only one theory for the development of the framework. Sometimes, having a single theory may not be adequate, hence the need to have additional theory or theories to complement the main one. There may be times when a researcher may not arrive at a perfect theory. One strategy is to use it but highlight the limitations when developing the framework. One may ask what if there is no theory that best fits my study? The researcher could use models, constructs and/or concepts to help build a theoretical/conceptual framework. A researcher could also adapt and utilize some of the theory selection strategies discussed in this chapter to come up with viable pieces of the framework puzzle.

TABLE 6.4 Theory Selection Rating for Cognitive Load Theory (CLT) Under a Transcendental Phenomenology-Informed Study

	Extremely Unlikely	Unlikely	Neutral	Likely	Extremely Likely	Comments
Theory and school of phenomenology match				CLT		Both CLT and transcendental phenomenology are based on thinking acts.
Adherence to the principle of parsimony						
• **Brevity**				CLT		There are three main components with clear description of the relationship between them. It shows "*emotional exhaustion*" leading to "*cognitive load*" and then having an adverse effect on "*work performance*".
• **Few assumptions**				CLT		One could assume that this theory is true if a physician has not developed strategy to effectively deal with the burnout.
• **Extent of theory coverage**			CLT			This accounts for the effect of burnout.
• **Useful for descriptive purpose**			CLT			It does not have a lot of descriptors, but they will be helpful during data analysis.

Building a theoretical/conceptual framework

At this point, a researcher has selected the theory/theories needed to draft your theoretical framework. In Chapter 5, we discussed specific steps researchers could follow to create a framework. We also provided five elements a well-constructed framework should have. It should contain: the meaning of the theory/theories, what they represent, the connection they have with the phenomenon of the study (or experience of the phenomenon), the use of the framework and the contribution of the theory/theories.

TABLE 6.5 Theory Selection Rating for Conservation of Resources (COR) Theory Under a Transcendental Phenomenology-Informed Study

	Extremely Unlikely	Unlikely	Neutral	Likely	Extremely Likely	Comments
Theory and school of phenomenology match					COR theory	With COR theory, loss of cognitive abilities is part of burnout experience.
Adherence to the principle of parsimony						
• **Brevity**					COR theory	COR theory is concise—depicting that continuous reduction of resources without reciprocal replenishment leads to burnout.
• **Few assumptions**					COR theory	
• **Extent of theory coverage**				COR theory		This theory covers the causes of burnout.
Useful for descriptive purpose				COR theory		It does not have a lot of descriptors, but they will be helpful during data analysis.

Demonstration 6.7

Theoretical framework under a phenomenological study informed by transcendental phenomenology

There are two main theories that best account for physicians' experiences of burnout. They are COR theory and CLT. According to Durning et al. (2013), "CLT would postulate that the impact of emotional exhaustion would further exacerbate limited processing space through inefficient activation, like a computer processing unit whose function is slowed in performing a desired task by too many simultaneous processes" (p. 5). Besides,

> Hobfoll's conservation of resources theory, the burnout syndrome is defined as a process of expenditure, loss and run-down developing gradually over time. It occurs when the restoration of the resources in the form of cognitive, emotional, and physical abilities does not appear.
>
> *(Głebocka & Lisowska, 2007, p. 246)*

TABLE 6.6 Theory Selection Rating for Emotional Intelligence Theory Under an Interpretative Phenomenology-Informed Study

	Extremely Unlikely	Unlikely	Neutral	Likely	Extremely Likely	Comments
Theory and school of phenomenology match				Emotional intelligence theory		This theory is consistent with the act of dealing with things in the world (Heidegger, 2010).
Adherence to the principle of parsimony						
• **Brevity**				Emotional intelligence theory		
• **Few assumptions**					Emotional intelligence theory	It has three assumptions (see Carthy & Jameson, 2016).
• **Extent of theory coverage**				Emotional intelligence theory		It covers the management aspect of burnout but cannot be used to account for the cause of burnout.
Useful for descriptive purpose			Emotional intelligence theory			It does not have sufficient descriptors to facilitate the development of codes/themes at the data analysis stage.

TABLE 6.7 Theory Selection Rating for Equity Theory Under an Interpretative Phenomenology-Informed Study

	Extremely Unlikely	*Unlikely*	*Neutral*	*Likely*	*Extremely Likely*	*Comments*
Theory and school of phenomenology match					Equity theory	This is consistent with interpretative phenomenology due its emphasis of taking action to address the inequity experienced by physicians.
Adherence to the principle of parsimony						
• **Brevity**					Equity theory	The theory is brief—clearly depicting the concepts in play.
• **Few assumptions**					Equity theory	There is no known assumption.
• **Extent of theory coverage**					Equity theory	The theory accounts for the cause and management of burnout.
Useful for descriptive purpose					Equity theory	It has a good number of descriptors needed to facilitate the generation of codes/themes at the data analysis stage.

Neither COR theory nor CLT accounts for all aspects of physicians' experiences of burnout. While COR theory covers the causes of burnout, CLT explains the effects of burnout. Under the COR theory, there are mainly four concepts involved: depletion of resources, insufficient resources, completion of work-related task and experience of burnout. Resources are anything that help physicians to carry out their work-related duties. Some examples of resources include time with patients, conducive working environment, cognitive abilities, quality work tools and the like. Under the CLT, there are five components in play (Durning et al., 2013). They are:

- *Cognitive resources:* They are supplies needed to process cognitive tasks such as diagnosing patients and deciding on the right drug for them.
- *Cognitive tasks:* They are duties that require cognitive resources to be carried out.

- *Cognitive loads:* They are tasks sent into the physicians' working memory to be processed and completed.
- *Exhaustion:* This is a state of being physically, emotionally and/or psychological drained. It can also be referred to as burnout.
- *Work performance:* This is concerned with how well a task is done.

Informed by transcendental phenomenology, we combined the two theories to explain physicians' mental experiences of burnout (Husserl, 2017). However, Husserl's (2017) notion of experience of a phenomenon as a mental act was challenged by Merleau-Ponty (1978), emphasizing the mediating role the body plays in an experience. To Merleau-Ponty (1978), the body and consciousness are inseparable, the same way the subject (which consists of the body and mind) is connected to the world. Applying his assertion of body–mind coexistence to the experience of a burnout, physicians' body interaction with the environment of insufficient resources leads to the mental experience of stress and cognitive exhaustion. Physicians' mentally drained experiences could then manifest in their bodies, affecting their physical health, which could reciprocally exacerbate the mental condition of stress and exhaustion (Engebretsen & Bjorbækmo, 2020).

Similarly, based on the combination of the two theories, burnout (i.e., feeling of cognitive exhaustion) occurs when there are dwindling and insufficient resources with no success in replenishing them (Głebocka & Lisowska, 2007). Also, continuous experience of burnout tends to put burden on the cognitive resources, limiting the resources needed to complete cognitive tasks (Durning et al., 2013). These unchecked cognitive overloads adversely contribute to physicians' work performance. As shown in Figure 6.6, when physicians are faced with exhaustion (especially burnout), they to resolve it using existing cognitive resources. A part of the resources is also allocated to performing work-related cognitive tasks, exerting unsustainable pressure on the working memory dedicated to processing information. This cognitive overload adversely impacts work performance.

Implementing the phenomenology technique of epoché, we suspended the validity of the theories used in this framework, but we applied concepts described under these theories to help analyze the data (Husserl, 2017). Suspending validity of the theories means not using the data to validate the theories or mold the data to take the shape of the theories. However, some of the concepts were used to inform the codes/themes created when needed.

This framework played two roles in this study. In the role as a converter, concepts under this framework were used to inform the transformation of participants' narratives into abstract terms. Also, it played the role of a standpoint (i.e., lens), viewing participants' interview responses as a manifestation of their experience, which occurred in their consciousness or cognition.

In implementing these roles, the concepts related to the theories were subtly used to label relevant information selected in the data. However, this strategy is different from content analysis; the codes/themes are first developed and connected to the relevant excerpts in the data (see Erlingsson & Brysiewicz, 2017;

Vaismoradi et al., 2013; Zhang & Wildemuth, 2005). In this study, the concepts did not dictate the construction of codes/themes but aided their development, which supports the notion that an experience is what happens in the consciousness.

Demonstration 6.8

Theoretical framework under a phenomenological study informed by interpretative phenomenology

Equity theory states that people invest their time and resources into an entity or a group of entities with the expectation of reaping equivalent reward. When they realize that the reward is disproportionally lower than what they have invested, they become discomfited and sometimes disappointed, which could then lead to burnout. In other words, "equity theory postulates that the experience of inequity will lead to emotional discomfort (Adams, 1963, 1965; Walster

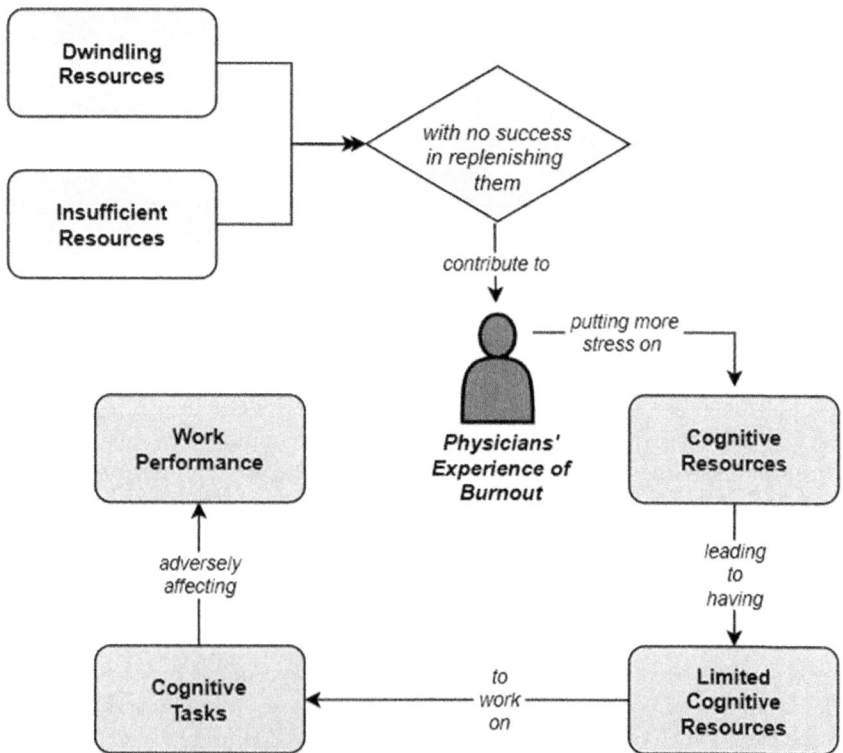

FIGURE 6.6 Framework Showing the Combination of Conservation of Resources (COR) Theory and Cognitive Load Theory (CLT)

Note: This figure was created in draw.io (Version 13.9.5; draw.io, 2020).

et al., 1978). In the work setting, persistent feelings of inequity may lead to burnout as a manifestation thereof" (Smets et al., 2004, p. 1901). Also, in the quest for addressing this inequity, physicians can develop negative attitudes, leading to burnout if they are not able to achieve the state of equity (Van Dierendonck et al., 1994). As Van Dierendonck et al. (1994) put it, "equity theory predicts that when people experience inequity, for example when GPs [general physicians] meet harassment by patients, they will try to reduce this tension in order to restore equity" (p. 89). There are four main concepts under this theory. They are:

- *Equity:* It is a perceived balance between what a physician invests and what he/she got in return.
- *Inequity:* It is a perceived imbalance between what a physician invests and what he/she got in return.
- *Investment:* It is the commitment put into something or someone with the expectation of gaining comparable desired outcomes.
- *Returns:* They are outcomes emerged as the results of an investment made.

Consistent with the interpretative (existential) phenomenology, which emphasizes reviewing people's actions to get to the meaning of their being, the equity theory mainly accounts for the actions taken leading to their experience of burnout. Similarly, Sartre's (2017) notion under existentialism portrays an experience of subjects as taking actions that are in line with how they see themselves in the future. In other words, subjects make sure their actions match their projections of self, achieving equity in the end.

To expand the equity theory's coverage, it could also be used to explain how physicians address burnout and dismantle the cycle of experiencing inequality. The cycle of inequity occurs when physicians who are experiencing burnout (which emanated from loss of investment) fail to make adequate investment to offset the initial loss. We assert that for physicians to break from the cycle of experiencing inequity leading to burnout, they need to come up with new strategies of investment which are more likely to yield a positive outcome (see Figure 6.7).

Heidegger (2010) started his proposition on phenomenology by discussing the concept of being, which he referred to as Dasein. His definition of Dasein is portrayed as a being brought into this world, inseparably integrated into things and other beings of the world. As Heidegger (2010) stated, "'being together with' . . . the world, in the sense of being absorbed in the world, which must be further interpreted, is an existential which is grounded in being-in" (p. 55). He frequently referred to Dasein as "being-in-the-world" and used the term "thrownness" to depict the state of being "thrown" into the world of restrictions and "possibilities" (p. 140). Therefore, we could see the physicians' situation as being thrown into the cycle of inequality with seemingly limited choice at the initial stage, but they are in a quest for knowing and understanding themselves as they explore strategies

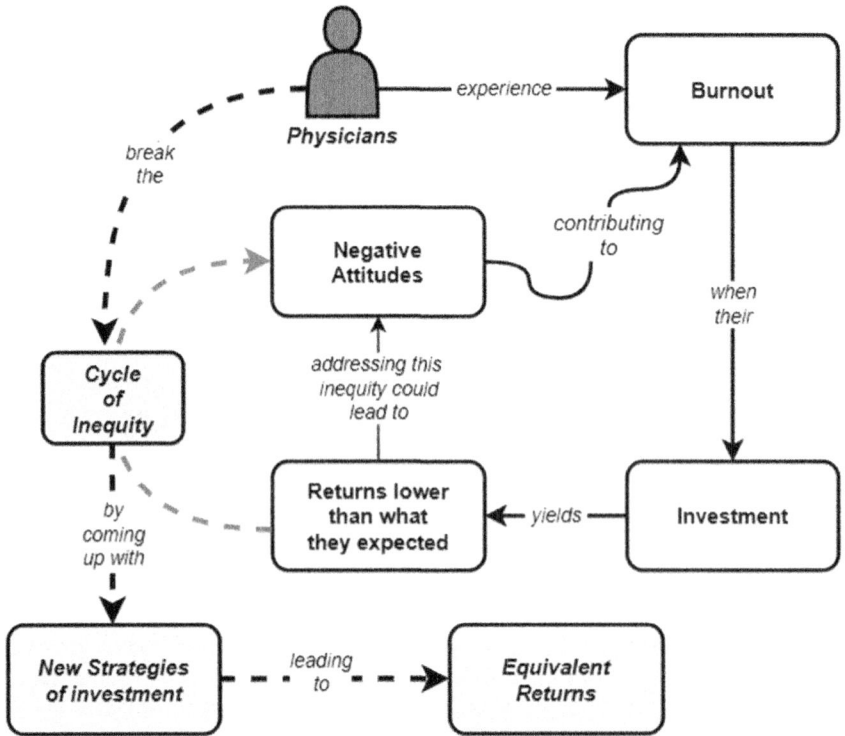

FIGURE 6.7 Framework with Equity Theory Depicting the Cause of and Solution for Burnout

Note: This figure was created in draw.io (Version 13.9.5; draw.io, 2020).

to break the cycle (Heidegger, 2010). This implies that one of the natures of our being is the ability to examine opportunities and make decisions.

Applying epoché, we did not use the equity theory to mold the data or to validate them with the results. However, we used the concepts within the theory to help generate codes/themes at the data analysis phase (Husserl, 2017). This is consistent with Heidegger's (2010) suggestion of dismantling conceptualizations and theories when making sense of participants' experiences. We see this framework as a decipherer, helping to understand not only the cause of but the solution for burnout. However, when analyzing the data, we used only its concepts as an interpretative tool to assist in interpreting the data. Also, we used it as a converter, aiding with the transformation of relevant information in the data into codes/themes.

Commentary 6.6   Before writing about a theoretical/conceptual framework, researchers need to first make sure they have all relevant knowledge about the selected theory/theories. Without fully understanding the theories, it will be difficult to communicate them well to the readers. To learn more about our selected theories, we checked reference lists of some of the initially selected articles to see whether there was additional relevant literature. Alternatively, another systematic strategy is to conduct what Turner et al. (2018) called *theoretical literature review*. This involves searching, selecting and reviewing literature about the theory of interest.

We started the drafting process by writing about each of the five components of a good framework (see Chapter 5 for discussion of the components). We then brought the written components together and creatively arranged them and refined the framework into a finished piece. Last, we created an illustration to represent the framework. We suggest that researchers try as much as possible to use illustrations not to complicate their frameworks but to provide additional understanding of what they have written.

When writing, make conscious effort not to throw concepts and constructs to your readers. However, authors should ensure that they and the readers are on the same page with respect to what they mean. If possible, try to creatively incorporate definitions of terms in a framework, making the information easy to digest. Last, there is nothing like a "perfect" theoretical or conceptual framework. At the initial stage of research, a framework can be considered a work-in-progress. Therefore, be flexible and ready to make changes to it when needed.

Summary

As demonstrated earlier, scoping review is a feasible strategy to access the right theories, models and/or concepts for the development of a theoretical/conceptual framework under a phenomenological study. After gathering potential theories, we suggest researchers subject them to critical examination, assessing their brevity, assumptions and coverage (Epstein, 1984). We have created a theory selection rating tool to help determine the right theory for a phenomenological study. The final step of the framework development is to write about the theory. This final process is an art, meticulously crafting the framework in such a way that readers understand what the theory associated with the framework represents, what its roles are, what the related concepts mean, what their relationships are and the like. Always be ready to revise a framework when needed.

References

Adams, J. S. (1963). Towards an understanding of equity. *Journal of Abnormal and Social Psychology, 67,* 422–436.

Adams, J. S. (1965). Inequity in social exchange. *Advances in Experimental Social Psychology, 2,* 267–299.

Adu, P. (2016). Writing the methodology chapter of your dissertation [PowerPoint slides]. *SlideShare.* www2.slideshare.net/kontorphilip/writing-the-methodology-chapter-of-your-dissertation

Adu, P. (2019). *A step-by-step guide to qualitative data coding.* Routledge.

Arksey, H., & O'Malley, L. (2005). Scoping studies: Towards a methodological framework. *International Journal of Social Research Methodology: Theory & Practice, 8*(1), 19–32. https://doi.org/10.1080/1364557032000119616

Brady, K. J. S., Ni, P., Sheldrick, R. C., Trockel, M. T., Shanafelt, T. D., Rowe, S. G., Schneider, J. I., & Kazis, L. E. (2020). Describing the emotional exhaustion, depersonalization, and low personal accomplishment symptoms associated with Maslach burnout inventory subscale scores in US physicians: An item response theory analysis. *Journal of Patient-Reported Outcomes, 4*(1), 42. https://doi.org/10.1186/s41687-020-00204-x

Bramer, W., Jonge, G. B., Rethlefsen, M., Mast, F., & Kleijnen, J. (2018). A systematic approach to searching: An efficient and complete method to develop literature searches. *Journal of the Medical Library Association: JMLA, 106,* 531–541.

Carthy, A., & Jameson, A. (2016). *The emotionally intelligent college: Transforming third level education to help students and educators reach their maximum potential.* Cambridge Scholar.

Cooper, C., Booth, A., Varley-Campbell, J., Britten, N., & Garside, R. (2018). Defining the process to literature searching in systematic reviews: A literature review of guidance and supporting studies. *BMC Medical Research Methodology, 18*(1), 85. https://doi.org/10.1186/s12874-018-0545-3

Dall'Ora, C., Ball, J., Reinius, M., & Griffiths, P. (2020). Burnout in nursing: A theoretical review. *Human Resources for Health, 18*(1), 41. https://doi.org/10.1186/s12960-020-00469-9

De Maeyer, C., & Schoenmakers, B. (2019). Exploring intergenerational differences in burnout and how they relate to work engagement, norms, and values: A mixed-methods study. *BJGP Open, 3*(2). https://doi.org/10.3399/bjgpopen18X101637

de Wit, K., Mercuri, M., Wallner, C., Clayton, N., Archambault, P., Ritchie, K., Gérin-Lajoie, C., Gray, S., Schwartz, L., & Chan, T. (2020). Canadian emergency physician psychological distress and burnout during the first 10 weeks of COVID-19: A mixed-methods study. *Journal of the American College of Emergency Physicians Open.* https://doi.org/10.1002/emp2.12225

Durning, S. J., Costanzo, M., Artino, A. R., Jr., Dyrbye, L. N., Beckman, T. J., Schuwirth, L., Holmboe, E., Roy, M. J., Wittich, C. M., Lipner, R. S., & van der Vleuten, C. (2013). Functional neuroimaging correlates of burnout among internal medicine residents and faculty members. *Frontiers in Psychiatry, 4,* 131. https://doi.org/10.3389/fpsyt.2013.00131

Engebretsen, K. M., & Bjorbækmo, W. S. (2020). Out of chaos-meaning arises: The lived experience of re-habituating the habitual body when suffering from burnout. *Qualitative Health Research, 30*(10), 1468–1479. https://doi.org/10.1177/1049732320914584

Epstein, R. (1984). The principle of parsimony and some applications in psychology. *The Journal of Mind and Behavior, 5*(2), 119–130. www.jstor.org/stable/43853318

Erlingsson, C., & Brysiewicz, P. (2017). A hands-on guide to doing content analysis. *African Journal of Emergency Medicine: Revue Africaine de la Medecine D'urgence, 7*(3), 93–99. https://doi.org/10.1016/j.afjem.2017.08.001

Gazelle, G., Liebschutz, J. M., & Riess, H. (2014). Physician burnout: Coaching a way out. *Journal of General Internal Medicine, 30*(4), 508–513. https://doi.org/10.1007/s11606-014-3144-y

Głebocka, A., & Lisowska, E. (2007). Professional burnout and stress among polish physicians explained by the Hobfoll resources theory. *Journal of Physiology and Pharmacology: An Official Journal of the Polish Physiological Society, 58*(Suppl. 5), 243–252. https://tcsedsystem.idm.oclc.org/login?url=http://search.ebscohost.com/login.aspx?direct=true&db=cmedm&AN=18204134&site=ehost-live

Gregory, S. T., & Menser, T. (2015). Burnout among primary care physicians: A test of the areas of worklife model. *Journal of Healthcare Management/American College of Healthcare Executives, 60*(2), 133–148.

Gregory, S. T., Menser, T., & Gregory, B. T. (2018). An organizational intervention to reduce physician burnout. *Journal of Healthcare Management/American College of Healthcare Executives, 63*(5), 338–352. https://doi.org/10.1097/JHM-D-16-00037

Heidegger, M. (2010). *Being and time.* University of New York Press. ISBN-10: 1438432763

Husserl, E. (2017). *Ideas: General introduction to pure phenomenology.* Unwin Brothers Ltd. ISBN-10: 0415519039

Innstrand, S. T., Langballe, E. M., Espnes, G. A., Falkum, E., & Aasland, O. G. (2008). Positive and negative work-family interaction and burnout: A longitudinal study of reciprocal relations. *Work & Stress, 22*(1), 1–15. https://doi.org/10.1080/02678370801975842

IQWiG. (2020, June 18). *Depression: What is burnout?* October 24. www.ncbi.nlm.nih.gov/books/NBK279286/

Jackson-Koku, G., & Grime, P. (2019). Emotion regulation and burnout in doctors: A systematic review. *Occupational Medicine (Oxford, England), 69*(1), 9–21. https://doi.org/10.1093/occmed/kqz004

Koh, M. Y. H., Hum, A. Y. M., Khoo, H. S., Ho, A. H. Y., Chong, P. H., Ong, W. Y., Ong, J., Neo, P. S. H., & Yong, W. C. (2020). Burnout and resilience after a decade in palliative care: What survivors have to teach us: A qualitative study of palliative care clinicians with more than 10 years of experience. *Journal of Pain and Symptom Management, 59*(1), 105–115. https://doi.org/10.1016/j.jpainsymman.2019.08.008

Lu, P. W., Columbus, A. B., Fields, A. C., Melnitchouk, N., & Cho, N. L. (2020). Gender differences in surgeon burnout and barriers to career satisfaction: A qualitative exploration. *The Journal of Surgical Research, 247,* 28–33. https://doi.org/10.1016/j.jss.2019.10.045

Merleau-Ponty, M. (1978). *Phenomenology of perception.* Routledge & Kegan Paul. ISBN-10: 0710036132

Munn, Z., Peters, M. D., Stern, C., Tufănaru, C., Mcarthur, A., & Aromataris, E. (2018). Systematic review or scoping review? Guidance for authors when choosing between a systematic or scoping review approach. *BMC Medical Research Methodology, 18.*

NPS Dudley Knox Library. (2020, October 24). *Search basics: Search tip sheets.* https://libguides.nps.edu/search/tips

Peters, M. D., Godfrey, C. M., Khalil, H., McInerney, P., Parker, D., & Soares, C. B. (2015). Guidance for conducting systematic scoping reviews. *International Journal of Evidence-Based Healthcare, 13*(3), 141–146. https://doi.org/10.1097/XEB.0000000000000050

QSR International Pty Ltd. (2019). *NVivo 12.* Version 12.6.959 [Computer software]. www.qsrinternational.com/nvivo/nvivo-products

Sartre, J. P. (2017). *Being and nothingness: An essay on phenomenological ontology.* AST Publishing House.

Schaink, A. K., Kuluski, K., Lyons, R. F., Fortin, M., Jadad, A. R., Upshur, R., & Wodchis, W. P. (2012). A scoping review and thematic classification of patient complexity: Offering a unifying framework. *Journal of Comorbidity, 2,* 1–9. https://doi.org/10.15256/joc.2012.2.15

Smets, E. M. A., Visser, M. R. M., Oort, F. J., Schaufeli, W. B., & De Haes, H. J. C. J. M. (2004). Perceived inequity: Does it explain burnout among medical specialists? *Journal of Applied Social Psychology, 34*(9), 1900–1918.

Subramanyam, R. (2013). Art of reading a journal article: Methodically and effectively. *Journal of Oral and Maxillofacial Pathology: JOMFP, 17*(1), 65–70. https://doi.org/10.4103/0973-029X.110733

Sucharew, H., & Macaluso, M. (2019). Methods for research evidence synthesis: The scoping review approach. *J. Hosp. Med.* (7), 416–418. https://doi.org/10.12788/jhm.3248

Teoh, K. R. H., Hassard, J., & Cox, T. (2020). Individual and organizational psychosocial predictors of hospital doctors' work-related well-being: A multilevel and moderation perspective. *Health Care Management Review, 45*(2), 162–172. https://doi.org/10.1097/HMR.0000000000000207

Tricco, A. C., Lillie, E., Zarin, W., O'Brien, K., Colquhoun, H., Kastner, M., Levac, D., Ng, C., Sharpe, J. P., Wilson, K., Kenny, M., Warren, R., Wilson, C., Stelfox, H. T., & Straus, S. E. (2016). A scoping review on the conduct and reporting of scoping reviews. *BMC Medical Research Methodology, 16*, 15. https://doi.org/10.1186/s12874-016-0116-4

Tucker, T., Bouvette, M., Daly, S., & Grassau, P. (2017). Finding the sweet spot: Developing, implementing and evaluating a burn out and compassion fatigue intervention for third year medical trainees. *Evaluation and Program Planning, 65*, 106–112. https://doi.org/10.1016/j.evalprogplan.2017.07.006

Turner, J. R., Baker, R., & Kellner, F. (2018). Theoretical literature review: Tracing the life cycle of a theory and its verified and falsified statements. *Human Resource Development Review, 17*(1), 34–61. https://doi.org/10.1177/1534484317749680

UOW Library. (2020, October 24). *Literature review: How to search effectively.* https://uow.libguides.com/literaturereview/how

Vaismoradi, M., Turunen, H., & Bondas, T. (2013). Content analysis and thematic analysis: Implications for conducting a qualitative descriptive study. *Nursing & Health Sciences, 15*(3), 398–405. https://doi.org/10.1111/nhs.12048

Van Dierendonck, D., Schaufeli, W. B., & Sixma, H. J. (1994). Burnout among general practitioners: A perspective from equity theory. *Journal of Social and Clinical Psychology, 13*(1), 86–100. http://dx.doi.org.tcsedsystem.idm.oclc.org/10.1521/jscp.1994.13.1.86

Walster, E., Walster, G. W., & Berscheid, E. (1978). *Equity theory and research.* Allyn and Bacon.

Williams, E. S., Rathert, C., & Buttigieg, S. C. (2019). The personal and professional consequences of physician burnout: A systematic review of the literature. *Medical Care Research and Review: MCRR, 77*(5), 371–386. https://doi.org/10.1177/1077558719856787

Winning, J. (2020). The use of an object: Exploring physician burnout through object relations theory. *Medical Humanities.* https://doi.org/10.1136/medhum-2019-011752

Yale Library. (2020, December 20). *Systematic reviews and evidence synthesis: Review types.* https://guides.library.yale.edu/searching/review-types

Zhang, Y., & Wildemuth, B. M. (2005). Qualitative analysis of content. *Human Brain Mapping, 30*(7), 2197–2206. www.ischool.utexas.edu/~yanz/Content_analysis.pdf

Zwack, J., & Schweitzer, J. (2013). If every fifth physician is affected by burnout, what about the other four? Resilience strategies of experienced physicians. *Academic Medicine: Journal of the Association of American Medical Colleges, 88*(3), 382–389. https://doi.org/10.1097/ACM.0b013e318281696b

7

APPLYING THEORETICAL/ CONCEPTUAL FRAMEWORK (AT THE DATA ANALYSIS PHASE)

Objectives

Readers will be able to:

1   Conduct qualitative data analysis informed by transcendental phenomenology.
2   Conduct qualitative data analysis informed by interpretative phenomenology.
3   Distinguish between codes/themes generated from the perspective of transcendental phenomenology from ones developed from the standpoint of interpretative phenomenology.

Getting started with a phenomenological study

This chapter is mainly a demonstration of how to analyze data collected under a phenomenological study. The data used to do this demonstration are about *burnout among primary care physicians in the United States*. We want to emphasize that these are not real data. They were developed for teaching purpose and first used in the presentation "Coding Qualitative Data: A Practical Guide to Completing Qualitative Data Analysis" (Adu, 2019b).

Let us assume that this is a short, structured interview conducted with five physicians who shared about their experiences, thoughts and mitigating strategies for burnout. In terms of their demographics, the average age was 52 years (SD =16.49), with the youngest physician being 33 years old and the oldest being 70 years old (see Table 7.1). Most of them were women and their work experience ranged from 2 to 35 years. With respect to their ethnicity, two were African American, two were European Americans and one was Asian American.

Also, let us assume that the hypothetical researcher wanted to examine the experience of burnout among primary care physicians. What will the purpose statement and research question look like? It depends on whether the study is

TABLE 7.1 Demographics of Participants (Primary Care Physician)

Participant's ID	Age	Gender	Years of Experience	Ethnicity
P1	37	Female	12	African American
P2	55	Male	25	Caucasian
P3	70	Male	35	Caucasian
P4	33	Female	2	African American
P5	65	Female	30	Asian

TABLE 7.2 Research Purpose and Question and Their Respective Schools of Phenomenology

	Informed by Transcendental Phenomenology	Informed by Interpretative Phenomenology
Purpose Statement	The purpose of this transcendental phenomenology-informed phenomenological study is to examine the experience of primary care physicians' experience of burnout with the goal of attaining the essence of their experience.	The purpose of this interpretative phenomenology-informed phenomenological study is to examine the lived experience of primary care physicians' experience of burnout with the goal of attaining the meaning of their being.
Research Question	What does it mean for primary care physicians to experience burnout?	What does it mean to be a primary care physician experiencing burnout?
Focus	Phenomenology of thoughts or thinking acts	Phenomenology of being
Ultimate Goal	To attain universal meaning of experience	To attain the meaning of being

informed by transcendental or interpretative phenomenology. Table 7.2 shows the research purpose and question under their respective schools.

Commentary 7.1: You may ask: *Why are the research purpose and question informed by transcendental phenomenology completely different from those informed by interpretative phenomenology?* This is because there are differences between them in terms of their philosophical assertions. With transcendental phenomenology, experience occurs through consciousness (Husserl, 2017). Therefore, understanding of the physicians' experiences of burnout starts with critically examining their thoughts, giving way to the realization of the universal meaning of the experience of burnout. On the contrary, looking at interpretative phenomenology, experience goes beyond a passive conceptualization of a phenomenon but includes active interaction with the object of focus (Heidegger, 2010). Hence, to get to the understanding of what it is like to be a physician experiencing burnout, a researcher needs to examine their actions, mitigating strategies and intentions related to this phenomenon. Table 7.2 shows that research purpose and question, focus and ultimate goals should be informed by their respective schools and there should be consistency between them.

Applying theoretical/conceptual framework

There are many ways of applying a theoretical/conceptual framework in a phenomenological study. It can be used to inform the development of the interview questions, as mentioned in Chapter 5. Also, the concepts linked to the framework could be used to transform research findings, having the kinds of terms used in a research community to help facilitate the comparison between the findings and existing knowledge. Another way is to apply theoretical/conceptual framework within data analysis process using its concepts to inform the development of codes/themes.

Qualitative analysis is simply reviewing data and generating meanings in the form of codes, themes and/or their connections with the aim of answering the research question(s) (Adu, 2019a). With an interpretative phenomenology-informed study, the data will be participants' disclosures (i.e., attestations) of their experience, which are called *speech-acts* (Ricoeur, 1994). Similarly, under a study informed by transcendental phenomenology, participants' manifestation of thoughts through their experiences of the phenomenon could be referred to as *thinking acts* (Husserl, 2017). These kinds of data are analyzed to help arrive at the essence of experience or meaning of being (i.e., existence) depending on whether the study is informed by transcendental or interpretative phenomenology. Implementing the minimum form of epoché at the data analysis level, a researcher could suspend the explanatory power of the theoretical/conceptual framework and use its concepts as descriptive and interpretative tools in a transcendental and an interpretative phenomenology-inspired study, respectively. Therefore, a framework can play a role as a convertor, using some of the terms in its reservoir of concepts to represent relevant information selected from the data, thereby helping to uncover the meaning of experience, or make meaning of being.

Demonstration 7.1: Conducting data analysis in a phenomenological research informed by transcendental phenomenology

With a transcendental phenomenology-informed study, our concern is not about the phenomenon (which is burnout) but participants' conscious acts (i.e., their experience of burnout). From a transcendental phenomenological perspective, through intentionality, burnout was presented to physicians' cognition, making it possible for thinking acts to occur (Husserl, 2017). As researchers, our role here is to review, understand and describe the thinking acts presented to us by participants. By doing so, we should be able to get to the meaning of their experience of burnout. The data analysis involved practicing epoché and phenomenological reduction, using description-focused coding strategy to generate codes, using an individual-based sorting strategy to create emerging themes, applying imaginative variation to arrive at essential themes and further examining the essential themes to come up with the universality of the thinking acts (which is the essence of the experience; Adu, 2019a; Giorgi, 2010; Husserl, 2017).

Practicing epoché and phenomenological reduction

Epoché and reduction under the transcendental phenomenology revolves around Husserl's (2017) assertion of suspending natural attitude and embracing phenomenological attitude. Naturalizing this assertion at the data analysis stage, we performed the following tasks:

- *Suspending the validity of theories and framework:* Theories and frameworks have both explanatory and descriptive powers to help make sense of what people experience. However, looking from the transcendental phenomenological perspective, to uncover the meaning of an experience, a researcher needs to set aside the explanatory features (i.e., ability to establish the cause–effect relationship) of theories and framework. Rather, researchers could use them as descriptive tools, using their associated concepts to code the data and/or develop themes when needed. For example, concepts under the framework showing the combination of COR theory and CLT could be used to represent some of the relevant excerpts found in the data (see Chapter 6).
- *Depersonalizing participants' experience:* With this strategy, the researcher's role is to detach participants' characteristic and context from their experience with the goal of attaining universal meaning of the experience. As Churchill (2014) indicated, "the phenomenologist shifts the attention away from the individual experience grasped for its own sake and towards the 'category' or class of experiences of which the individual experience is now taken as merely an example" (p. 4). Therefore, the researcher's aim is to move from having experience with ideographic features to a depersonalized experience with nomothetic characteristics, getting to the universal meaning of the experience (which is the essence of the experience; Churchill, 2014).

Using description-focused coding strategy to generate codes

The initial stage of the qualitative analysis process is to look for relevant information in participants' transcripts and label them. A label (which is normally a phrase between two and five words) is called a code (Adu, 2019a). At this point, because the plan is to understand and describe participants' experience (without making interpretation or inference), description-focused coding strategy is appropriate (Adu, 2019a). Description-focused coding is a type of coding method used in "describing relevant excerpt selected [from the data and] creating a code that reflects the description of the excerpt" (Adu, 2019b, slide 6). The researcher's role is to look for thinking acts, such as appreciating, conceptualizing, desiring, emphasizing, fantasizing, feeling, imagining, judging, perceiving, recognizing, remembering, sensing and the like, in relation to the experience of burnout (Churchill, 2014; Husserl, 2017).

Coding steps taken (developing initial codes) (see Exhibits 7.1–7.5)

1   With the research question in mind (which was *what does it mean for primary care physicians to experience burnout?*), we went through the data and selected the relevant excerpts.
2   Using a description-focused coding strategy, we created codes (which were descriptive phrases) representing participants' thinking acts in relation to their experiences of burnout.

  • We performed the analysis using qualitative data analysis software called NVivo 12 (Version 12.6.959; QSR International Pty Ltd, 2019) (see Figure 7.1).
  • We also used Microsoft Word to manually code the data for demonstration purposes (see Exhibits 7.1–7.5).

Outcome (developing initial codes)

•   In all, 28 codes were created with *Feeling overwhelmed with work* (which has four case counts and eight code counts), which emerged as a dominant code (see Table 7.3).

Commentary 7.2: We see codes as containers created to house relevant excerpts selected from the data (Adu, 2019a). So, we went through participants' responses, searching conscious (thinking) acts that have something to do with physicians' experiences of burnout. As shown in the list of codes generated, most of them have characteristics of cognitive-related experience (see Table 7.3). The dominant code, *Feeling overwhelmed with work*, has eight relevant extracts in its container (i.e., eight code counts) and four participants connected to this container (i.e., four case counts). All the codes are products of the thoughtful implementation of the description-focus coding strategy. We tried to first understand what participants said and create codes portraying what they said they experienced but not what we thought their experience was. That was also the moment we started the journey of moving from the ideographic to the nomothetic stage (Churchill, 2014).

Using individual-based sorting strategy to create emerging themes

One of the code categorization strategies that could help in the journey to the attainment of the essence of the experience is an individual-based sorting strategy (Adu, 2019a). Sorting involves reviewing the features of each code and putting codes into clusters based on their shared relationships. There are two main sorting strategies. The main difference is that for the group-based sorting, the categorization process is done by groups of not less than 10 but for the

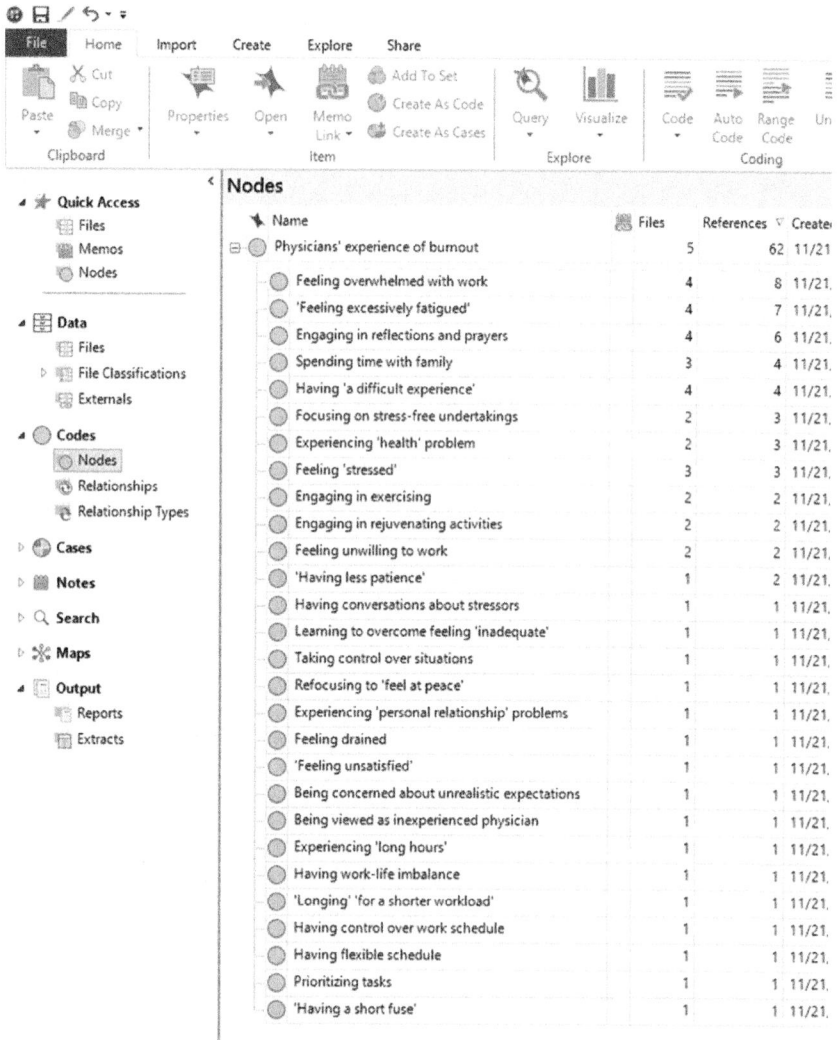

Nodes

Name	Files	References	Create
Physicians' experience of burnout	5	62	11/21
Feeling overwhelmed with work	4	8	11/21,
'Feeling excessively fatigued'	4	7	11/21,
Engaging in reflections and prayers	4	6	11/21,
Spending time with family	3	4	11/21,
Having 'a difficult experience'	4	4	11/21,
Focusing on stress-free undertakings	2	3	11/21,
Experiencing 'health' problem	2	3	11/21,
Feeling 'stressed'	3	3	11/21,
Engaging in exercising	2	2	11/21,
Engaging in rejuvenating activities	2	2	11/21,
Feeling unwilling to work	2	2	11/21,
'Having less patience'	1	2	11/21,
Having conversations about stressors	1	1	11/21,
Learning to overcome feeling 'inadequate'	1	1	11/21,
Taking control over situations	1	1	11/21,
Refocusing to 'feel at peace'	1	1	11/21,
Experiencing 'personal relationship' problems	1	1	11/21,
Feeling drained	1	1	11/21,
'Feeling unsatisfied'	1	1	11/21,
Being concerned about unrealistic expectations	1	1	11/21,
Being viewed as inexperienced physician	1	1	11/21,
Experiencing 'long hours'	1	1	11/21,
Having work-life imbalance	1	1	11/21,
'Longing' 'for a shorter workload'	1	1	11/21,
Having control over work schedule	1	1	11/21,
Having flexible schedule	1	1	11/21,
Prioritizing tasks	1	1	11/21,
'Having a short fuse'	1	1	11/21,

FIGURE 7.1 Display of the Codes Created in NVivo 12

Source: (Version 12.6.959; QSR International Pty Ltd, 2019)

Note: This figure captures manual coding done using Microsoft Word document.

individual-based sorting, one person (who is normally the researcher) does the sorting (see Adu, 2019a).

Sorting steps taken (developing emerging themes) (see Tables 7.4–7.5)

1 Created a table on a Microsoft Word document with two *Rows* and at least seven *Columns*.

2 Labeled the first *Column* as *Cluster* 1 through to the last *Column* as *Cluster* 7.

Participant 1

1. **How old are you?** 37
2. **How long have you been in in this profession?** 12 years
3. **What is your gender?** Female
4. **What is your ethnicity?** African American
5. **How did you become interested in medicine?** Growing up with a parent in healthcare; my mom was a nurse assistant, and she would take me to work with her to take care of elderly patients. She took care of them just as if they were here family, and I loved seeing the difference she made in their lives.
6. **Do you experience burnout/stress at work?** Yes, and many physician's do as well.
7. **How do you experience burnout?** Long hours, numerous clinical and administrative tasks
8. **What do you think are the causes of the burnout?** A lack of balance with work, and home life will often cause physicians to feel stressed and burned out. It is difficult to give your all at work, as well as do the same at home, just due to fatigue. However, for those that are working parents, and especially those with a hectic schedule, we must find a way to make it work, so that we can be effective for our patient's and family.
9. **What do you do to reduce your burnout?** Spend time in prayer and reflection, time with family, and exercising. All these things help to refocus my mind and help me feel at peace again.
10. **How do you see the effects of burnout on your life?** The effects of burnout can be far reaching in personal relationships, and in personal health.
11. **How do you experience burnout?** Feeling excessively fatigued and having less patience with those in my life.
12. **What do you see in your life that makes you conclude that you are experiencing burnout?** Feeling tired, and having a short fuse, and impatience in life and in work.
13. **What is it like to experience burnout?** It is a difficult experience, because you would rather have more balance in life, but sometimes, it is difficult to strike a balance.
14. **What do you do to cope with burnout?** Self-reflection, and prayer to help gain peace, and wisdom.

Experiencing 'long hours'

Feeling overwhelmed with work

Feeling 'stressed'

Having work-life imbalance

Feeling overwhelmed with work

Engaging in reflections and prayers

Refocusing to 'feel at peace'

Spending time with family

Engaging in exercising

Experiencing 'personal relationships' problems

Experiencing 'health' problem

'Feeling excessively fatigued'

'Having less patience'

'Feeling excessively fatigued'

'Having a short fuse'

'Having less patience'

Engaging in reflections and prayers

EXHIBIT 7.1   Coded Transcript From Participant "P1" Using Description-Focused Coding Strategy

Note: This figure captures manual coding done using Microsoft Word document.

3   Reviewed each code and dropped codes with shared relationship into one *Cluster*.
4   Created more clusters as needed.
5   With the research question in mind, reviewed codes in each *Cluster*.
6   Labeled each *Cluster* based on the features of the codes in it.

Outcome (developing emerging themes)

• In all, seven emerging themes were developed with *Being determined to resolve burnout stressors* (which has five case counts and 18 code counts), which emerged as the dominant theme (see Table 7.6).

Commentary 7.3: Always be flexible when conducting sorting. There were times when we changed the cluster membership of codes due to a new insight we had. Sometimes, researchers will be tempted to bring their own understanding into the analysis, implying and interpreting what participants said. Researchers should always remind themselves about their role in this process. They are to allow the data to speak to them, focusing on describing what they directly hear from participants. At this stage, researchers should make sure the labels of

Participant 2

1. **How old are you?** 55
2. **How long have you been in this profession?** 25 years
3. **What is your gender?** Male
4. **What is your ethnicity?** Caucasian
5. **How did you become interested in medicine?** Feeling drawn to helping sick people feel better
6. **Do you experience burnout/stress at work?** Occasionally, I do. Things have changed in the workplace as compared to when I first began my profession in healthcare. Now we have many more administrative tasks to complete, and much of our records, have become electronic based, which is sometimes difficult to get the hang of, when you are used to paper charting.　　　　　Feeling overwhelmed with work
7. **How do you experience burnout?** A hectic work schedule including hospital rounds and office work will often take of much of my week and cause me to feel a bit tired and burned out.　　　Feeling overwhelmed with work / 'Feeling excessively fatigued'
8. **What do you think are the causes of the burnout?** Multiple patients, clinical, and administrative tasks to accomplish in a short period of time.　　　Feeling overwhelmed with work
9. **What do you do to reduce your burnout?** Any moment I can get, I take vacation with my wife, and spend time with my 2 grandchildren.　　　Spending time with family
10. **How do you see the effects of burnout on your life?** The affects are minimized when I focus on the things in my life that make me happy.　　　Focusing on stress-free undertakings
11. **How do you experience burnout?** Longing sometimes for a shorter workload.　　　'Longing' 'for a shorter workload'
12. **What do you see in your life that makes you conclude that you are experiencing burnout?** Feeling tired, and less willing to get work tasks done.　　　'Feeling excessively fatigued' / Feeling unwilling to work
13. **What is it like to experience burnout?** It is difficult but manageable if you learn to prioritize.　　　Having 'a difficult experience' / Prioritizing tasks
14. **What do you do to cope with burnout?** Taking time out to remember why I chose my profession, and to enjoy my family.　　　Engaging in reflections and prayers / Spending time with family

EXHIBIT 7.2　Coded Transcript From Participant "P2" Using Description-Focused Coding Strategy

Note: This figure captures manual coding done using Microsoft Word document.

the emerging themes do not only depict participants' experience but also reflect their thinking acts. Researchers may notice that they have not yet directly used some of the concepts under the framework of this study. This shows that, at this point, the researcher only used the concepts when needed.

Applying imaginative variation to arrive at essential themes

The original intent of imaginative variation was to be used by philosophers/ phenomenologists who have experienced or are experiencing a phenomenon. This involves engaging in thinking acts, experiencing the phenomenon in different ways (i.e., from varied perspectives) with the hope of arriving at the

Participant 3

1. **How old are you?** 70
2. **How long have you been in this profession?** 35 + years
3. **What is your gender?** Male
4. **What is your ethnicity?** Caucasian
5. **How did you become interested in medicine?** My Dad was also a
   physician, and he would take me to work with him ever since I was a little
   boy. I would go around and do house calls with him to help deliver a baby, or
   see a sick child, or adult that needed care. My Dad was the town physician.
6. **Do you experience burnout/stress at work?** Rarely, because I work on a
   part time and per-diem basis, so I can choose my hours, and time for
   working. | Having flexible schedule
7. **How do you experience burnout?** I don't have much of the stressors at
   work that many of my younger counterparts do because I am essentially
   retired, but I don't know what it would be like to not work, and take care of
   people, I love what I do, and this is what I've known for so long.
8. **What do you think are the causes of the burnout?** For many of the
   younger physician's it is probably not being able to take much time out for
   themselves and their families if they have one, because the practice of
   medicine can be grueling and if you are not of the right mindset, you can
   easily fall.   Spending time with family
9. **What do you do to reduce your burnout?** I spend time with my family as
   much as I can, and I control the hours I would like to work. | Having control over work schedule
10. **How do you see the effects of burnout on your life?** The effects are
    minimal because my schedule is not very strenuous.
11. **How do you experience burnout?** I don't experience it too much, but
    occasionally if I have a challenge with a patient or colleague, I take it one   Taking control over situations
    step at a time, and try to bring peace to my situation. |
12. **What do you see in your life that makes you conclude that you are**
    experiencing burnout? At the moment, I don't experience burnout
    regularly. However, when I was younger, I would often feel very fatigued   'Feeling excessively fatigued'
    when burned out due to long hours of work. |
13. **What is it like to experience burnout?** It is draining to the body, and mind. |
14. **What do you do to cope with burnout?** When, I did experience it, I would   Feeling drained
    talk about my stressors quite a bit, with my wife. |

     Having conservations about stressors

EXHIBIT 7.3 Coded Transcript From Participant "P3" Using Description-Focused
Coding Strategy

Note: This figure captures manual coding done using Microsoft Word document.

overarching meaning of their own experience. However, in phenomenological
research, the focus of the study is not the researcher's experience (i.e., having
a first-person perspective) but the experience of the participants (i.e., having a
third-person perspective). This makes application of imaginative variation challenging if a researcher examines how each participant experienced a phenomenon from varied perspectives. Addressing this problem, Giorgi (2006) suggested
that to appropriately naturalize imaginative variation, researchers need to acquire
a variation of an experience. In other words, proper application of imaginative
variation in a phenomenological research starts at the participants' recruitment
stage, involving selecting those who have a varied range of experience. This is
similar to positioning people at different angles to observe an object (such as a
tree or a table) and giving an account of their experiences from their assigned
perspectives. At the end, a researcher comes up with an account that is common
across all participants' narratives about their observation.

Participant 4

1. **How old are you?** 33
2. **How long have you been in this profession?** 2 years
3. **What is your gender?** Female
4. **What is your ethnicity?** African American
5. **How did you become interested in medicine?** I always loved teaching, and at the same time I loved the sciences, and biology as a child, so my passions always pointed to something in the health care field. I would volunteer at my local hospital to serve snacks, books, and deliver gifts to sick patients, and I just loved the joy I could bring just by being present, and listening to their concerns. So, I naturally fell in love with medicine, and when I had the chance to apply to medical school, I jumped at it, and here I am today as a Pediatric Hospitalist.
6. **Do you experience burnout/stress at work?** Yes, usually on a day to day basis.
7. **How do you experience burnout?** As a new physician, you have to build the trust of your patients. This is especially so since I appear so young to many of my parents. They can't believe I am the physician that will be taking care of their child's needs. Because of this, I often have to work a lot harder than some of my older counterparts, and this is what can cause me to feel stressed and burned out at times. | *Feeling overwhelmed with work* / *Feeling 'stressed'*
8. **What do you think are the causes of the burnout?** It all depends on what level you are in your career. If you are a young physician like me, it's all about proving your worth, and learning how to navigate the ropes of this new and exciting profession. | *Being viewed as inexperienced physician*
9. **What do you do to reduce your burnout?** I read a lot, and learn as much as I can, because the more you know, the less likely you are going to feel inadequate if ever a situation arises. | *Learning to overcome feeling 'inadequate'*
10. **How do you see the effects of burnout on your life?** It affects my health I'm sure, because constant stress can often lead to harmful health consequences, i.e. Constant headaches, chronic illness, difficulty feeling rested, even when I'm not working. | *Experiencing 'health' problem* / *Feeling unwilling to work*
11. **How do you experience burnout?** Within my health, and then in my daily life, especially if I am not able to do the tasks I want to do if I am not up to it. | *Experiencing 'health' problem*
12. **What do you see in your life that makes you conclude that you are experiencing burnout?** Frequent illness, Excessive fatigue. | *'Feeling excessively fatigued'*
13. **What is it like to experience burnout?** It is very difficult especially when you are still young, to feel so tired all the time. | *Having 'a difficult experience'* / *'Feeling excessively fatigued'*
14. **What do you do to cope with burnout?** I try if possible, to take walks, and get alone time for myself and read a book I really enjoy. | *Engaging in exercising* / *Engaging in reflections and prayers* / *Engaging in rejuvenating activities*

EXHIBIT 7.4 Coded Transcript From Participant "P4" Using Description-Focused Coding Strategy

Note: This figure captures manual coding done using Microsoft Word document.

Similarly, with the case of the experience of burnout among primary care physicians, assuming that it was an actual research, we would have considered sampling doctors from various primary care specialties such as internal medicine, pediatrics and family medicine. We then would have analyzed the stories about their experience of burnout and attain themes shared across these participants with varied primary care specialties. These themes are referred to as essential themes (Husserl, 2001), and out of these themes, the essence of the experience is derived.

Imagination variation steps taken (arriving at essential themes) (see table 7.7)

1 Reviewed the characteristics of the emerging themes in terms of what they represent;
2 Compared them to see whether there was the possibility to merge some of them;

Participant 5

1. **How old are you?** 65
2. **How long have you been in this profession?** 30 years
3. **What is your gender?** Female
4. **What is your ethnicity?** Asian — *Feeling overwhelmed with work*
5. **How did you become interested in medicine?** I come from a long line of medical doctors, nurses, therapist, and it was just natural for me to want to do something with healthcare.
6. **Do you experience burnout/stress at work?** Not usually — *Feeling 'stressed'*
7. **How do you experience burnout?** If and when, I did experience burnout it was in my earlier years when I first started out in my career. I was young, and new at the practice of medicine, and much was expected of me, and if I had trouble delivering, it would just cause so much stress for me. However, as I grew to be as seasoned physician, that stress became less and less, and now that I own my own private practice, those stressors don't really come up anymore. If anything, the stress is more so in ensuring my business is successful. — *Being concerned about unrealistic expectations* / *Engaging in reflections and prayers*
8. **What do you think are the causes of the burnout?** Causes of burnout for many physicians, are the expectations that many of our families, patients, and society place on us: i.e. We are expected to know the answers for all medical problems, even when at times, there may not be a definitive answer. — *Engaging in rejuvenating activities*
9. **What do you do to reduce your burnout?** I practice positive thinking, I attend church, and volunteer at the local women's shelter in my neighborhood with my children. — *Focusing on stress-free undertakings*
10. **How do you see the effects of burnout on your life?** It is minimal, when I focus on the things I can change, and less on the negative things.
11. **How do you experience burnout?** In my day to day work life, trying to accomplish, tasks that are expected of me at work. — *'Feeling unsatisfied'*
12. **What do you see in your life that makes you conclude that you are experiencing burnout?** Feeling unsatisfied with the way some of my days end. They often feel overwhelming unless I find a way to take control of my work life. — *Feeling overwhelmed with work*
13. **What is it like to experience burnout?** It is difficult, especially if you don't have a good handle on your work-life balance. — *Having 'a difficult experience'*
14. **What do you do to cope with burnout?** Focusing on ways to help others and thinking on the things of God that are peaceful, and hopeful. — *Focusing on stress-free undertakings* / *Engaging in reflections and prayers*

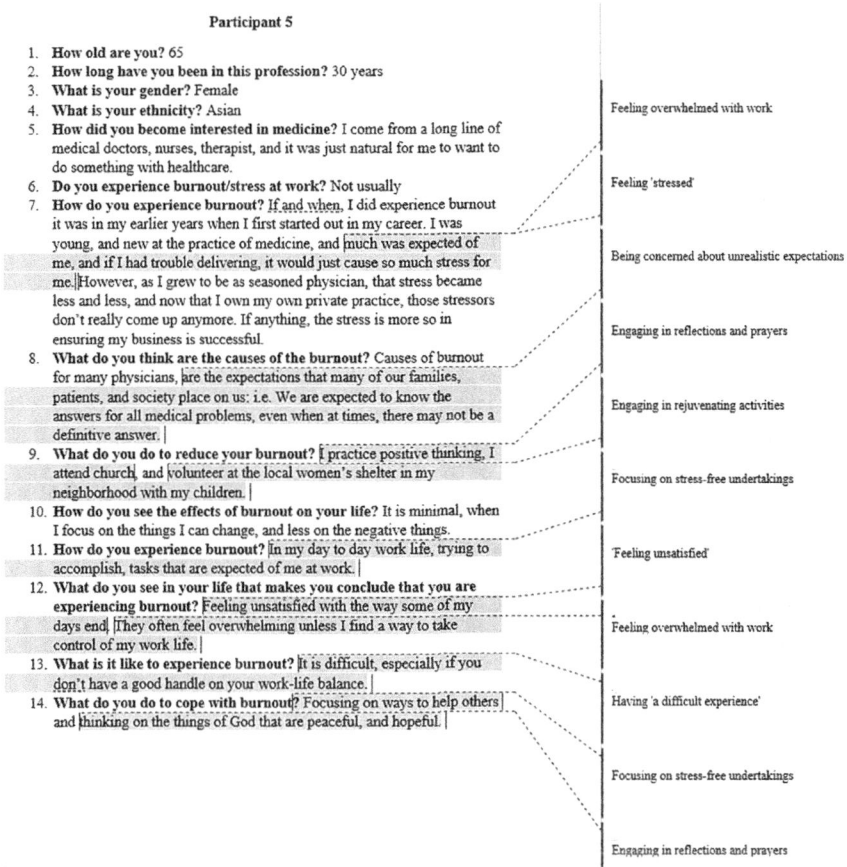

EXHIBIT 7.5 Coded Transcript From Participant "P5" Using Description-Focused Coding Strategy

3   Reviewed the case counts of each of the themes;
4   Selected the themes with majority of participants connected to them;
5   Labeled the selected themes as emerging themes.

Outcome (arriving at essential themes)

- Two of the emerging themes (i.e., "*Being determined to resolve burnout stressors*" and "*Having a favorable work schedule*") were merged to form *Being proactive in addressing burnout stressors* as an essential theme (see Figure 7.2).
- We eliminated the emerging theme *Experiencing health and personal issues* from being part of the essential themes because it had only two participants associated with it. At the end, we came up with five essential themes (see Table 7.7).

Commentary 7.4: Engaging in the process of arriving at the essential themes is an art. It is about carefully reviewing all the emerging themes, exploring potential

TABLE 7.3 Initial Codes Generated Using Description-Focused Coding Strategy (From a Transcendental Phenomenological Perspective)

Initial Code	Case Count (Number of Participants)	Code Count (Number of Relevant Excerpts)
1. Feeling overwhelmed with work	4	8
2. 'Feeling excessively fatigued'	4	7
3. Engaging in reflections and prayers	4	6
4. Spending time with family	3	4
5. Having 'a difficult experience'	4	4
6. Focusing on stress-free undertakings	2	3
7. Experiencing 'health' problem	2	3
8. Feeling 'stressed'	3	3
9. Engaging in exercising	2	2
10. Engaging in rejuvenating activities	2	2
11. Feeling unwilling to work	2	2
12. 'Having less patience'	1	2
13. Having conversations about stressors	1	1
14. Learning to overcome feeling 'inadequate'	1	1
15. Taking control over situations	1	1
16. Refocusing to 'feel at peace'	1	1
17. Experiencing 'personal relationship' problems	1	1
18. Feeling drained	1	1
19. 'Feeling unsatisfied'	1	1
20. Being concerned about unrealistic expectations	1	1
21. Being viewed as an inexperienced physician	1	1
22. Experiencing 'long hours'	1	1
23. Having work1–life imbalance	1	1
24. 'Longing' 'for a shorter workload'	1	1
25. Having control over work schedule	1	1
26. Having flexible schedule	1	1
27. Prioritizing tasks	1	1
28. 'Having a short fuse'	1	1

TABLE 7.4 Sorted Codes (About Primary Care Physicians' Experience of Burnout) Under Their Respective Clusters (From a Transcendental Phenomenological Perspective)

Cluster 1	Cluster 2	Cluster 3	Cluster 4	Cluster 5	Cluster 6	Cluster 7
• Engaging in reflections and prayers • Spending time with family • Engaging in exercising • Engaging in rejuvenating activities • Focusing on stress-free undertakings • Refocusing to 'feel at peace'	• 'Feeling excessively fatigued' • Having 'a difficult experience' • Feeling drained • 'Feeling unsatisfied'	• Feeling overwhelmed with work • Feeling 'stressed' • Being concerned about unrealistic expectations • Being viewed as an inexperienced physician • Experiencing 'long hours' • Having work–life imbalance • 'Longing' 'for a shorter workload'	• Experiencing 'health' problem • Experiencing 'personal relationship' problems	• Feeling unwilling to work • 'Having a short fuse' • 'Having less patience'	• Having conversations about stressors • Taking control over situations • Learning to overcome feeling 'inadequate'	• Having control over work schedule • Having flexible schedule • Prioritizing tasks

TABLE 7.5 Sorted Codes (About Primary Care Physicians' Experience of Burnout) Under Their Respective Labeled Clusters (From a Transcendental Phenomenological Perspective)

Cluster 1: Engaging in rejuvenating activities	Cluster 2: Feeling exhausted	Cluster 3: Feeling overwhelmed with work	Cluster 4: Experiencing health and personal issues	Cluster 5: Having a negative attitude toward work	Cluster 6: Being determined to resolve burnout stressors	Cluster 7: Having a favorable work schedule
• Engaging in reflections and prayers • Spending time with family • Engaging in exercising • Engaging in rejuvenating activities • Focusing on stress-free undertakings • Refocusing to 'feel at peace'	• 'Feeling excessively fatigued' • Having 'a difficult experience' • Feeling drained • 'Feeling unsatisfied'	• Feeling overwhelmed with work • Feeling 'stressed' • Being concerned about unrealistic expectations • Being viewed as an inexperienced physician • Experiencing 'long hours' • Having work-life imbalance • 'Longing' 'for a shorter workload'	• Experiencing 'health' problem • Experiencing 'personal relationship' problems	• Feeling unwilling to work • 'Having a short fuse' • 'Having less patience'	• Having conversations about stressors • Taking control over situations • Learning to overcome feeling 'inadequate'	• Having control over work schedule • Having flexible schedule • Prioritizing tasks

TABLE 7.6 Emerging Themes Reflecting Primary Care Physicians' Experience of Burnout (From a Transcendental Phenomenological Perspective)

Emerging Theme	Case Count (Number of Participants)	Code Count (Number of Relevant Excerpts)
1. Being determined to resolve burnout stressors	5	18
2. Engaging in rejuvenating activities	4	16
3. Experiencing health and personal issues	5	13
4. Feeling exhausted	3	5
5. Feeling overwhelmed with work	2	4
6. Having a favorable work schedule	2	3
7. Having a negative attitude toward work	2	3

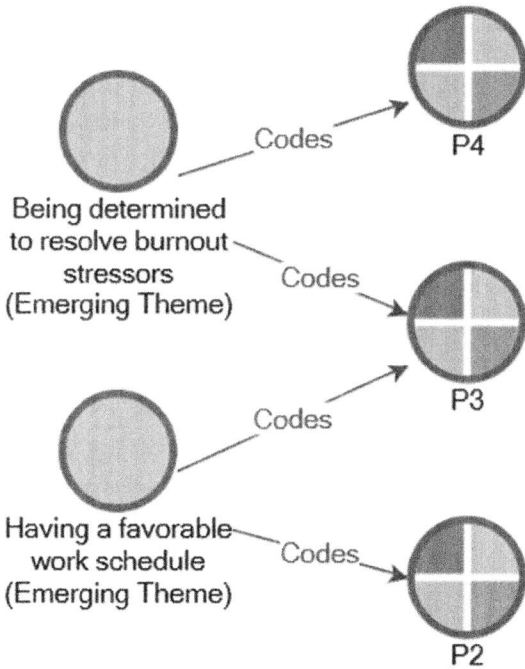

FIGURE 7.2 Two Emerging Themes and Their Respective Participants

Note: This figure was created in NVivo 12 (Version 12.6.959; QSR International Pty Ltd, 2019).

mergers of some of the themes and deciding which of them qualify to be labeled as commonly shared themes (i.e., essential themes). Although this is a part of the process of depersonalizing the themes to help reach findings with monothetic features, the case counts connected to each theme could play a significant role

TABLE 7.7 Essential Themes Reflecting Primary Care Physicians' Experience of Burnout (From a Transcendental Phenomenological Perspective)

Essential Theme (Not Informed By The Framework Concepts)	Essential Theme (Informed By The Framework Concepts)	Case Count	Code Count
1. **Engaging in rejuvenating activities**	1. Engaging in restoration of resources	5	18
2. **Feeling exhausted**	2. Suffering dwindling cognitive resources	5	13
3. **Feeling overwhelmed with work**	3. Having limited cognitive resources	4	16
4. **Being proactive in addressing burnout stressors**	4. Being proactive in addressing dwindling resources	3	6
5. **Having a negative attitude toward work**	5. Having a negative attitude toward work	3	5

in determining the themes that are essential. A theme is likely to be referred to as a common theme if most of the participants are connected to it. At this stage, be ready to set aside any theme which does not have a threshold of 50 percent of the case count.

In Table 7.7, there are two columns for the display of the essential themes: one for themes not informed by the theoretical/conceptual framework and the other informed by the framework concepts. This is just to demonstrate that this is the appropriate stage to transform the essential themes into themes informed by the concepts connected to the framework. Chapter 6 has the description and illustration of the theoretical/conceptual framework (see Figure 6.6). The transformation is needed only if a researcher plans to use their framework concepts as a descriptive tool in a phenomenological study. When conducting the transformation, make sure the transformed themes are not changing the meaning of the original essential themes. Also, it is important to avoid the risk of converting the original themes to strictly fit the terms used in the framework. By doing so, it could change the meaning of the themes. At this point, researchers should still practice epoché, thus preventing the temptation of molding the themes to fit the framework. Last, it is acceptable to maintain the original essential themes if no term in the framework can be used to replace it. For instance, the theme *Having a negative attitude toward work* was not changed.

If a researcher were to present (in writing) about the original essential themes (or a revised version), they could describe the following (see Adu, 2019a):

• The meaning of the essential themes;
• The kind of experience (thinking acts) they represent;
• The excerpts from the data to support the themes and their assertions.

Uncovering the essence of the experience

Here is where the attainment of the universal meaning of experience, free from ideographic features, is completed. This stage is still at the descriptive level of qualitative analysis because from the transcendental phenomenological perspective, the goal of the analysis is to uncover the transcending meaning of experience. However, making interpretation or inference will not lead to the true essence of the experience. Practically, unearthing the universal meaning of the experience of burnout starts with examining the meaning and features of the essential themes and the relationships between them.

Sorting steps taken (uncovering the essence of the experience)

1   Reviewed the characteristics of the essential themes in terms of their meaning and what they represent;
2   Compared them to see whether there were relationships among them.
3   Determined the type of relationships they have;
4   Drafted a statement depicting the relationship and reflecting shared experience of burnout.

Outcome (uncovering the essence of the experience)

Here is the essence of the primary care physicians' experience of burnout:

Option 1: Based on original essential themes
Burnout often manifests in a primary care physician as a feeling of exhaustion as a result of being overwhelmed with work, coupled with having a negative attitude toward work. The experience of burnout could be addressed by putting in check its stressors and experiencing stress-free engagements.
Option 2: Based on essential themes informed by the framework concepts
Burnout often manifests among primary care physicians in the midst of experiencing dwindling cognitive resources and carrying out cognitive tasks with limited cognitive resources. The experience of burnout is also coupled with having a negative attitude toward work. The experience could be addressed by being proactive in solving declining resources and engaging in restoration of the resources.
Below are definitions of some of the concepts used in the above essence of experience:

- *Cognitive resources:* They are supplies needed to process cognitive tasks such as diagnosing patients and deciding on the right drug for them.
- *Cognitive tasks:* They are duties that require cognitive resources to be carried out.
- *Exhaustion:* It is a state of being physically, emotionally and/or psychologically drained. It can also be referred to as burnout.

Commentary 7.5: Uncovering the essence of the experience was a challenging task but rewarding when finished. It involves learning more of the essential themes, including looking into relevant excerpts in the data connected to each of them. To move to the universality of the results, the essence should revolve around the experience of burnout but not the physicians who experienced it. The essence assists in expanding knowledge about the experience more so than of the population. As researchers carry out this exercise, they should be sure to document their reflections and understanding of the themes and their relationships. Being familiar with the types of relationship would be helpful in this process. Adu (2019a) discussed concurrent, chronological, overlapping, embedded, exploratory and causal relationships (see pp. 168–171). Similarly, Casagrande and Hale (1967) deliberated on 13 types of relationships, namely antonymy, attributive, circularity, class inclusion, comparison, contingency, exemplification, function, grading, operational, provenience, spatial and synonymy (see p. 168). A useful technique we used was to create a table and write about our understanding of the themes, considering the relevant data extracts the themes were representing (see Table 7.8). It helped us determine relationships among the themes.

As shown in the outcome above, there is an essence statement based on the original essential themes (i.e., *Option 1*) and another that is an essence statement

TABLE 7.8 Essential Themes and Reflections (From a Transcendental Phenomenological Perspective)

Original Essential Themes	Essential Theme (Informed by The Framework Concepts)	Reflections
Feeling overwhelmed with work	Engaging in restoration of resources	*This could mean that the resources available cannot keep up with the tasks needed to be accomplished.*
Being proactive in addressing burnout stressors	Suffering dwindling cognitive resources	*If the factors contributing to burnout are addressed, there is more likely burnout will dissipate.*
Feeling exhausted	Having limited cognitive resources	*Working in an environment with limited resources with no plans to replenish them could have a toll on physicians' physical and psychological wellbeing.*
Having a negative attitude toward work	Being proactive in addressing dwindling resources	*Being unsuccessful in restoring the depleted resources leads to having a negative attitude toward work and anyone connected to it.*
Engaging in rejuvenating activities	Having a negative attitude toward work	*Primary care physicians seem to engage in recreational, family and community activities—giving them rejuvenation to help deal with limited or depleting resources needed to complete tasks.*

based on essential themes informed by the framework concepts (i.e., *Option 2*). A researcher does not have to do both. However, we used the strategy of first drafting the essence based on the original essential themes and, second, transforming it into a new essence statement utilizing essential themes inspired by the framework concepts. With this strategy, we were able to compare *Option 1* with *Option 2*. This was to ensure that the meaning of the essence statement had not changed after the transformation.

In terms of drafting the essence statement, a researcher may not get a "perfect" outcome at the initial stage. Researchers should be ready to revise the statement when needed. When we were working on the essence, we ended up writing several drafts. Here are some of them:

Draft 1

Feeling exhausted is not avoidable when burnout stressors are not addressed. Burnout is experienced when its stressors are not addressed. It could lead to negative attitude toward work. One strategy used to curtail burnout is to engage in rejuvenating activities.

Draft 2

When the factors contributing to burnout stressors are not addressed, primary care physicians become overwhelmed, leading to the feeling of physical and psychological exhaustion (i.e., burnout). In effect, those with unresolved burnout experiences develop negative attitudes toward work, but, in most cases, they engage in rejuvenating activities—helping them to cope with burnout.

Demonstration 7.2: conducting data analysis in a phenomenological research informed by interpretative (existential) phenomenology

A phenomenological study with an interpretative (existential) phenomenology is concerned with not only interpreting participants' experiences but also attaining meaning of their being (existence). In addition, it is possible for a researcher informed by interpretative phenomenology to focus on uncovering the meaning of being of the phenomenon (object) participants have experienced. According to Heidegger (2010), human beings are part of the world engaging in acts such as dealing, interacting with, consuming, producing, relating to, "handling, using, taking care of" something (p. 67). So, in order to get to the meaning of participants' being, researchers need to access their dealings in the world. They could get access to such rich information by interviewing them. Participants' disclosures, which are also called attestations, are viewed as "speech-acts" (Heidegger, 2010, p. 162). Their attestations may include evaluative assertions (or "reference[s]") about the phenomenon they have experienced (Heidegger, 2010, p. 74). Evaluative assertions are statements made by participants about what the phenomenon they have experienced means to them. These kinds of assertions are helpful to researchers who plan to discover the being of the phenomenon of interest (see Table 7.9).

Let us zoom in to the data we analyzed. The research question we addressed was *what does it mean to be a primary care physician experiencing burnout?* Based on this

TABLE 7.9 Focus of Study and Their Respective Primary Source of Data

Focus of Study	Example of Research Question	Primary Source of Data
Being of participants	What does it mean to be a primary care physician experiencing burnout?	Attestations (i.e., participants' account of their experience)
Being of phenomenon	What is the meaning of being of burnout?	Evaluative assertations (i.e., participants' account of what the phenomenon means to them or their views on the phenomenon they have experienced)

question, we sought for participants' actions, intentions and reactions with respect to their experience of burnout. We made meaning of their relevant speech-acts, developing meaningful themes. We further analyzed the themes to help create a narrative of being which informed the uncovering of the meaning of being of a primary care physician experiencing burnout (Heidegger, 2010; Ricoeur, 1994). The data analysis involved practicing epoché and reduction, using interpretation-focused coding strategies to generate codes, using individual-based sorting strategies to create emerging themes, transforming emerging themes into meaningful themes, creating a narrative of being and uncovering the meaning of being (Adu, 2019a; Heidegger, 2010; Ricoeur, 1994).

Practicing epoché and reduction

Heidegger (2010) suggested three strategies of interpretative (existential) phenomenology that have some elements of epoché and reduction. They are "reduction, construction and destruction" (Heidegger, 2010, p. 35). Another epoché and reduction technique Heidegger recommended was to adhere to the notion of temporality, which involves the reduction of natural time associated with participants' disclosures.

- *Reduction:* This is about moving the focus from people who experienced a phenomenon to making sense of their experience with the goal of discovering the meaning of their being (Heidegger, 2010). Similarly, with our data analysis, our focus was to interpret participants' attestations to get closer to unearthing the meaning of their existence of being faced with burnout.
- *Construction:* Under this phenomenological strategy, the operative word is *interpretation*. Making sense of participants' attestations and evaluative assertations is the key to detecting the meaning of their existence (Heidegger, 2010; Ricoeur, 1994). In the analysis, we strictly followed interpretative phenomenology-inspired steps to help reach the essence of being in a working environment experiencing burnout.
- *Destruction:* Unchecked assumptions and frameworks including theories could adversely affect the interpretation of speech-acts. In response, Heidegger

(2010) suggested the need to dismantle existing conceptualizations and assumptions when engaging in interpreting participants' disclosures. This is similar to Husserl's (2017) recommendation of setting aside the explanatory feature of a theory or framework and using its concepts, in this case, as an interpretative tool to help make meaning of the speech-acts.

- *Temporality adherence:* According Heidegger (2010), this strategy involves not looking at participants' disclosures of lived experience as a narrative situated within their subjective time. Instead, the task is to view the recall of their experience as a current memory belief, collapsing the natural (subjective) time of the past, present and future into now (present). In effect, participants' disclosures are reduced to speech-acts, ready to be analyzed using interpretation-focused coding strategy.

Using interpretation-focused coding strategy to generate codes

Interpretation-focused coding involves making meaning of participants' attestations and developing codes to reflect the meanings researchers come up with (Adu, 2019a). Because participants are inseparably linked to the world and the things in it, who they are and the situation they are in influence how they experience a phenomenon (Heidegger, 2010). So, researchers are more likely not to arrive at an unsubstantiated and incomplete interpretation if they only focus on what participants said without considering the context within which it was said. The researcher's role is not to investigate what truly happened (in terms of their experience) but to make sense of what they said happened (Dennett, 1991). When searching for relevant information from the data to interpret, focus more on their actions, intentions and reactions in terms of their experience with the phenomenon. To put it differently, the researcher's focus is more on understanding and interpreting participants' actions and less on their thought process (i.e., thinking acts).

Coding steps taken (developing initial codes) (see Exhibits 7.6–7.10)

1 With the research question in mind (which was: *What does it mean to be a primary care physician experiencing burnout?*), we went through the data (i.e., speech-acts) and selected relevant excerpts.

2 Using interpretation-focused coding strategy, we created codes, which were interpretative phrases representing the meaning of participants' actions, intentions and reactions:

   a Examining what they mean (considering who said them and the context within which they were said);

   b Generating codes that reflect the meaning of the selected portions of the speech-acts

      i We did the analysis using free qualitative data analysis software called QDA Miner Lite (Version 2.0.8; Provalis Research, 2020) (see Figure 7.3).

Outcome (developing initial codes)

- In all, 38 codes were created with *Feeling excessively fatigued* (which had four case counts and five code counts), which emerged as a dominant code (see Table 7.10).

Project   Cases   Variables   Codes   Document   Retrieve   Analyze   Help

CASES:
- ▶ P1
- P2
- P3
- P4
- P5

VARIABLES
- FILE P1
- DOCUMENT [DOCUMENT]

CODES
- 🔍 ▾
- ⊟ 👥 Physicians' experience of burnout
  - ● 'Having less patience'
  - ● 'Feeling excessively fatigued'
  - ● 'Having a short fuse'
  - ● Attending church
  - ● Being incapable of completing tasks
  - ● Being ready dealing with burnout
  - ● Being young and inexperienced
  - ● Difficulty experiencing burnout
  - ● Engaging in exercising
  - ● Engaging in 'prayer and reflection'
  - ● Engaging in volunteering
  - ● Experiencing unwillingness to work
  - ● Feeling mentally and physically drained
  - ● Feeling unsatisfied with day's work
  - ● Focusing on helping others
  - ● Focusing on source of happiness
  - ● Getting things done at work
  - ● Having 'long hours'
  - ● Having 'personal health' issues
  - ● Having 'personal relationship' issues
  - ● Having a conversation about stressors
  - ● Having a demanding workload
  - ● Having a flexible schedule
  - ● Having control over working hours
  - ● Having long working hours
  - ● Having relatively high workload
  - ● Having time with self
  - ● Lacking work-life balance
  - ● Learning as much as possible
  - ● Practicing positive thinking
  - ● Pressured to meet unrealistic expectations
  - ● Spending time with family
  - ● Things get better with experience
  - ● Wishing for 'shorter workload'
  - ● Working harder than normal
  - ● Working under limited time
  - ● Work-life imbalance
  - ● Work-life imbalance resulting in fatigue

DOCUMENTS:

DOCUMENT

Times New Roman   12   **B** *I* U

CODE: Work-life imbalance resulting in fatigue

Participant 1

1. How old are you? 37

2. How long have you been in in this profession? 12 years

3. What is your gender? Female

4. What is your ethnicity? African American

5. How did you become interested in medicine? Growing up with a parent in health care; my mom was a nurse assistant, and she would take me to work with her to take care of elderly patients. She took care of them just as if they were her family, and I loved seeing the difference she made in their lives.

6. Do you experience burnout/stress at work? Yes, and many physicians do as well.

7. How do you experience burnout? Long hours, numerous clinical and administrative tasks

8. What do you think are the causes of the burnout? A lack of balance with work, and home life will often cause physicians to feel stressed, and burned out. It is difficult to give your all at work, as well as do the same at home, just due to fatigue. However, for those that are working parents, and especially those with a hectic schedule, we must find a way to make it work, so that we can be effective for our patient's and family.

9. What do you do to reduce your burnout? Spend time in prayer and reflection, time with family, and exercising. All these things help to refocus my mind, and help me feel at peace again.

FIGURE 7.3   Display of the Codes Created in QDA Miner Lite

Note: This figure captures the coding done using QDA Miner Lite (Version 2.0.8; Provalis Research, 2020).

Participant 1

1. **How old are you?** 37

2. **How long have you been in in this profession?** 12 years

3. **What is your gender?** Female

4. **What is your ethnicity?** African American

5. **How did you become interested in medicine?** Growing up with a parent in healthcare; my mom was a nurse assistant, and she would take me to work with her to take care of elderly patients. She took care of them just as if they were here family, and I loved seeing the difference she made in their lives.

6. **Do you experience burnout/stress at work?** Yes, and many physician's do as well.

7. **How do you experience burnout?** Long hours, numerous clinical and administrative tasks
    ] Having 'long hours'
    Having relatively high workload

8. **What do you think are the causes of the burnout?** A lack of balance with work, and home life will often cause physicians to feel stressed, and burned out. It is difficult to give your all at work, as well as do the same at home, just due to fatigue. However, for those that are working parents, and especially those with a hectic schedule, we must find a way to make it work, so that we can be effective for our patient's and family.
    Lacking work-life balance
    Work-life imbalance resulting to fatigue

9. **What do you do to reduce your burnout?** Spend time in prayer and reflection, time with family, and exercising. All these things help to refocus my mind, and help me feel at peace again.
    ] Engaging in 'prayer and reflection'
    ] Engaging in exercising
    Spending time with family

10. **How do you see the effects of burnout on your life?** The effects of burnout can be far reaching in personal relationships, and in personal health.
    Having 'personal relationships' issues
    Having 'personal health' issues

11. **How do you experience burnout?** Feeling excessively fatigued and having less patience with those in my life.
    'Feeling excessively fatigued'
    'Having less patience'

12. **What do you see in your life that makes you conclude that you are experiencing burnout?** Feeling tired, and having a short fuse, and impatience in life and in work.
    'Having a short fuse'
    'Feeling excessively fatigued'
    'Having less patience'

13. **What is it like to experience burnout?** It is a difficult experience, because you would rather have more balance in life, but sometimes, it is difficult to strike a balance.
    Difficulty experiencing burnout
    Work-life imbalance

14. **What do you do to cope with burnout?** Self-reflection, and prayer to help gain peace, and wisdom.
    Engaging in 'prayer and reflection'

EXHIBIT 7.6   Coded Transcript From Participant "P1" Using Interpretation-Focused Coding Strategy

Note: This figure captures the coding done using QDA Miner Lite (Version 2.0.8; Provalis Research, 2020).

Commentary 7.6.: Our focus was to look for expressions of what primary care physicians did, were doing or intended to do in relation to their experience with burnout, make sense of relevant attestations and generate codes to represent them. Also, if our interpretation of an excerpt had a relationship with an existing code, we connected that code to it. As shown in Table 7.10, almost all the codes generated start with a gerund (i.e., verb + "ing"). This technique is adopted from grounded theory analysis, where a code is generated starting with a gerund that best captures a behavior or process (Adu, 2017; Charmaz, 2014). This helped in capturing the art of "handling, using and taking care of" something and the like (Heidegger, 2010, p. 67). It is important to note that the meaning of participants' being is determined by what they do. So, generating gerund-led codes could facilitate in unearthing the essence of their being.

Participant 2

1. **How old are you?** 55

2. **How long have you been in this profession?** 25 years

3. **What is your gender?** Male

4. **What is your ethnicity?** Caucasian

5. **How did you become interested in medicine?** Feeling drawn to helping sick people feel better

6. **Do you experience burnout/stress at work?** Occasionally, I do. Things have changed in the workplace as compared to when I first began my profession in healthcare. Now we have many more administrative tasks to complete, and much of our records, have become electronic based, which is sometimes difficult to get the hang of, when you are used to paper charting. | Having relatively high workload

7. **How do you experience burnout?** A hectic work schedule including hospital rounds and office work will often take of much of my week, and cause me to feel a bit tired and burned out. | Having relatively high workload

8. **What do you think are the causes of the burnout?** Multiple patients, clinical, and administrative tasks to accomplish in a short period of time. | Working under limited time

9. **What do you do to reduce your burnout?** Any moment I can get, I take vacation with my wife, and spend time with my 2 grandchildren. | Spending time with family

10. **How do you see the effects of burnout on your life?** The effects are minimized when I focus on the things in my life that make me happy. | Focusing on source of happiness

11. **How do you experience burnout?** Longing sometimes for a shorter workload. | Wishing for 'shorter workload'

12. **What do you see in your life that makes you conclude that you are experiencing burnout?** Feeling tired, and less willing to get work tasks done. | Experiencing unwillingness to work / 'Feeling excessively fatigued'

13. **What is it like to experience burnout?** It is difficult but manageable if you learn to prioritize. | Difficulty experiencing burnout / Being ready dealing with burnout

14. **What do you do to cope with burnout?** Taking time out to remember why I chose my profession, and to enjoy my family. | Engaging in 'prayer and reflection' / Spending time with family

EXHIBIT 7.7   Coded Transcript From Participant "P2" Using Interpretation-Focused Coding Strategy

Note: This figure captures the coding done using QDA Miner Lite (Version 2.0.8; Provalis Research, 2020).

Using individual-based sorting strategy to create emerging themes

At this stage, what needs to be done is grouping codes based on their shared relationships and come up with themes representing and further interpreting the group of codes (Adu, 2019a).

Sorting steps taken (developing emerging themes) (see Tables 7.11–7.13)

1. Created a table on a Microsoft Word document with two *Rows* and at least seven *Columns*;
2. Labeled the first *Column* as *Cluster* 1 through to the last *Column* as *Cluster* 7;
3. Reviewed each code and drop codes with shared relationship into one *Cluster*;
4. Created more clusters as needed;

Participant 3

1. **How old are you?** 70

2. **How long have you been in this profession?** 35 + years

3. **What is your gender?** Male

4. **What is your ethnicity?** Caucasian

5. **How did you become interested in medicine?** My Dad was also a physician, and he would take me to work with him ever since I was a little boy. I would go around and do house calls with him to help deliver a baby, or see a sick child, or adult that needed care. My Dad was the town physician.

6. **Do you experience burnout/stress at work?** Rarely, because I work on a part time and per-diem basis, so I can choose my hours, and time for working.

7. **How do you experience burnout?** I don't have much of the stressors at work that many of my younger counterparts do because I am essentially retired, but I don't know what it would be like to not work, and take care of people, I love what I do, and this is what I've known for so long.

8. **What do you think are the causes of the burnout?** For many of the younger physician's it is probably not being able to take much time out for themselves and their families if they have one, because the practice of medicine can be grueling and if you are not of the right mindset, you can easily fall. — Having a demanding workload

9. **What do you do to reduce your burnout?** I spend time with my family as much as I can, and I control the hours I would like to work. — Spending time with family / Having control over working hours

10. **How do you see the effects of burnout on your life?** The effects are minimal because my schedule is not very strenuous. — Having a flexible schedule

11. **How do you experience burnout?** I don't experience it too much, but occasionally if I have a challenge with a patient or colleague, I take it one step at a time, and try to bring peace to my situation.

12. **What do you see in your life that makes you conclude that you are experiencing burnout?** At the moment, I don't experience burnout regularly. However, when I was younger, I would often feel very fatigued when burned out due to long hours of work. — 'Feeling excessively fatigued' / Having long working hours

13. **What is it like to experience burnout?** It is draining to the body, and mind. — Feeling mentally and physically drained

14. **What do you do to cope with burnout?** When, I did experience it, I would talk about my stressors quite a bit, with my wife. — Having a conversation about stressors

EXHIBIT 7.8 Coded Transcript From Participant "P3" Using Interpretation-Focused Coding Strategy

Note: This figure captures the coding done using QDA Miner Lite (Version 2.0.8; Provalis Research, 2020).

5.   Reviewed codes in each *Cluster*;
6.   Labeled each *Cluster* based on the features of the codes grouped.

Outcome (developing emerging themes)

•   In all, eight emerging themes were developed with *Having symptoms of exhaustion* (which has five case counts and 13 code counts), which emerged as the dominant theme (see Table 6.13).

Commentary 7.7: As researchers extensively engage in the sorting process, they should keep in mind its rationale, which is to create themes needed to determine

Participant 4

1. **How old are you?** 33

2. **How long have you been in this profession?** 2 years

3. **What is your gender?** Female

4. **What is your ethnicity?** African American

5. **How did you become interested in medicine?** I always loved teaching, and at the same time I loved the sciences, and biology as a child, so my passions always pointed to something in the health care field. I would volunteer at my local hospital to serve snacks, books, and deliver gifts to sick patients, and I just loved the joy I could bring just by being present, and listening to their concerns. So, I naturally fell in love with medicine, and when I had the chance to apply to medical school, I jumped at it, and here I am today as a Pediatric Hospitalist.

6. **Do you experience burnout/stress at work?** Yes, usually on a day to day basis.

7. **How do you experience burnout?** As a new physician, you have to build the trust of your patients. This is especially so since I appear so young to many of my parents. They can't believe I am the physician that will be taking care of their child's needs. Because of this, I often have to work a lot harder than some of my older counterparts, and this is what can cause me to feel stressed and burnout at times. | Working harder than normal

8. **What do you think are the causes of the burnout?** It all depends on what level you are in your career. If you are a young physician like me, it's all about proving your worth, and learning how to navigate the ropes of this new and exciting profession. | Being young and inexperienced

9. **What do you do to reduce your burnout?** I read a lot, and learn as much as I can, because the more you know, the less likely you are going to feel inadequate if ever a situation arises. | Learning as much as possible

10. **How do you see the effects of burnout on your life?** It affects my health I'm sure, because constant stress can often lead to harmful health consequences, ie. Constant headaches, chronic illness, difficulty feeling rested, even when I'm not working. | Having 'personal health' issues

11. **How do you experience burnout?** Within my health, and then in my daily life, especially if I am not able to do the tasks I want to do if I am not up to it. | Being incapable to complete tasks

12. **What do you see in your life that makes you conclude that you are experiencing burnout?** Frequent illness, Excessive fatigue. | Having 'personal health' issues

13. **What is it like to experience burnout?** It is very difficult especially when you are still young, to feel so tired all the time. | Difficulty experiencing burnout / 'Feeling excessively fatigued'

14. **What do you do to cope with burnout?** I try if possible to take walks, and get alone time for myself and read a book I really enjoy. | Engaging in exercising / Having time with self / Focusing on source of happiness

EXHIBIT 7.9 Coded Transcript From Participant "P4" Using Interpretation-Focused Coding Strategy

Note: This figure captures the coding done using QDA Miner Lite (Version 2.0.8; Provalis Research, 2020).

the meaning of being. In terms of determining the number of clusters, researchers just need to create as needed. For instance, if they realize that a code does not share relationship with any of the members in the existing clusters, they create a new one to accommodate it.

Transforming emerging themes into meaningful themes

At this stage, a researcher is expected to subject the emerging themes to an intensive review, making sure they are appropriate interpretations of participants' disclosures about their experience. The questions researchers could think about when reviewing the themes include: Do the themes adequately represent the codes under them? Do participants' speech-acts support the themes, which are the products of interpretations of their attestations? And is there an avenue

Participant 5

1. **How old are you?** 65

2. **How long have you been in this profession?** 30 years

3. **What is your gender?** Female

4. **What is your ethnicity?** Asian

5. **How did you become interested in medicine?** I come from a long line of medical doctors, nurses, therapist, and it was just natural for me to want to do something with healthcare.

6. **Do you experience burnout/stress at work?** Not usually

7. **How do you experience burnout?** If and when, I did experience burnout it was in my earlier years when I first started out in my career. I was young, and new at the practice of medicine, and much was expected of me, and if I had trouble delivering, it would just cause so much stress for me. However, as I grew to be as seasoned physician, that stress became less and less, and now that I own my own private practice, those stressors don't really come up anymore. If anything, the stress is more so in ensuring my business is successful.

   — Being incapable to complete tasks
   — Things get better with experience

8. **What do you think are the causes of the burnout?** Causes of burnout for many physicians, are the expectations that many of our families, patients, and society place on us: ie. We are expected to know the answers for all medical problems, even when at times, there may not be a definitive answer.

   — Pressured to meet unrealistic expectations

9. **What do you do to reduce your burnout?** I practice positive thinking, I attend church, and volunteer at the local women's shelter in my neighborhood with my children.

   — Attending church
   — Practicing positive thinking
   — Engaging in volunteering

10. **How do you see the effects of burnout on your life?** It is minimal, when I focus on the things I can change, and less on the negative things.

    — Practicing positive thinking

11. **How do you experience burnout?** In my day to day work life, trying to accomplish, tasks that are expected of me at work.

    — Getting things done at work

12. **What do you see in your life that makes you conclude that you are experiencing burnout?** Feeling unsatisfied with the way some of my days end. They often feel overwhelming unless I find a way to take control of my work life.

    — Feeling unsatisfied with day's work

13. **What is it like to experience burnout?** It is difficult, especially if you don't have a good handle on your work-life balance.

    — Difficulty experiencing burnout

14. **What do you do to cope with burnout?** Focusing on ways to help others and thinking on the things of God that are peaceful, and hopeful.

    — Focusing on helping others
    — Practicing positive thinking

EXHIBIT 7.10   Coded Transcript From Participant "P5" Using Interpretation-Focused Coding Strategy

Note: This figure captures the coding done using QDA Miner Lite (Version 2.0.8; Provalis Research, 2020).

to merge some of themes? This critical review process could lead to adjustments and merging of some of the themes. Other themes may remain the same. At the end, a researcher should have meaningful themes ready for the next step, which is the drafting of a meaningful narrative.

Steps taken on the transformation of emerging themes (arriving at meaningful themes) (see table 7.14)

1. Reviewed the characteristics of the emerging themes by comparing them to the codes they were representing;
2. Compared the themes with their assigned relevant excerpts to examine the appropriateness of the interpretation;
3. Explored the possibility of merging some of the themes;
4. Adjusted the themes when needed.

TABLE 7.10 Initial Codes Generated Using Interpretation-Focused Coding Strategy (From an Interpretative Phenomenological Perspective)

Initial Code	Case Count (Number of Participants)	Code Count (Number of Relevant Excerpts)
'Feeling excessively fatigued'	4	5
Difficulty in experiencing burnout	4	4
Spending time with family	3	4
Being incapable of completing tasks	2	2
Engaging in exercising	2	2
Engaging in 'prayer and reflection'	2	3
Focusing on source of happiness	2	2
Having 'personal health' issues	2	3
Having relatively high workload	2	3
'Having a short fuse'	1	1
'Having less patience'	1	2
Attending church	1	1
Being ready dealing with burnout	1	1
Being young and inexperienced	1	1
Engaging in volunteering	1	1
Experiencing unwillingness to work	1	1
Feeling mentally and physically drained	1	1
Feeling unsatisfied with day's work	1	1
Focusing on helping others	1	1
Getting things done at work	1	1
Having 'long hours'	1	1
Having 'personal relationship' issues	1	1
Having a conversation about stressors	1	1
Having a demanding workload	1	1
Having a flexible schedule	1	1
Having control over working hours	1	1
Having long working hours	1	1
Having time with self	1	1
Lacking work–life balance	1	1
Learning as much as possible	1	1
Practicing positive thinking	1	3
Pressured to meet unrealistic expectations	1	1
Things get better with experience	1	1
Wishing for 'shorter workload'	1	1
Working harder than normal	1	1
Working under limited time	1	1
Work–life imbalance	1	1
Work–life imbalance resulting in fatigue	1	1

TABLE 7.11 Sorted Codes (About Primary Care Physicians' Experience of Burnout) Under Their Respective Clusters (From an Interpretative Phenomenological Perspective)

Cluster 1	Cluster 2	Cluster 3	Cluster 4	Cluster 5	Cluster 6	Cluster 7	Cluster 8
• 'Feeling excessively fatigued' • Difficulty experiencing burnout • Feeling mentally and physically drained • Having 'personal health' issues	• Engaging in 'prayer and reflection' • Practicing positive thinking • Engaging in exercising • Focusing on source of happiness • Having time with self • Attending church	• Being incapable of completing tasks • Being young and inexperienced • Pressured to meet unrealistic expectations • Getting things done at work	• Having relatively high workload • Having 'long hours' • Working under limited time • Wishing for "shorter workload" • Having a demanding workload • Having long working hours • Working harder than normal	• Engaging in volunteering • Focusing on helping others • Spending time with family	• Being ready dealing with burnout • Having control over working hours • Having a flexible schedule • Having a conversation about stressors • Learning as much as possible • Things get better with experience	• 'Having less patience' • 'Having a short fuse' • Feeling unsatisfied with day's work • Experiencing unwillingness to work • Having 'personal relationship' issues	• Having work-life imbalance resulting in fatigue • Having work-life imbalance • Lacking work-life balance

TABLE 7.12 Sorted Codes (About Primary Care Physicians' Experience of Burnout) Under Their Respective Labeled Clusters (From an Interpretative Phenomenological Perspective)

Cluster 1: Having symptoms of exhaustion	Cluster 2: Engaging in self-help activities	Cluster 3: Feeling ill-equipped to complete tasks	Cluster 4: Inability to handle demanding workload	Cluster 5: Spending time with family and helping others	Cluster 6: Utilizing burnout-resistant strategies	Cluster 7: Having a negative attitude toward work-related issues	Cluster 8: Inability to attain work-life balance
• 'Feeling excessively fatigued' • Difficulty experiencing burnout • Feeling mentally and physically drained • Having 'personal health' issues	• Engaging in 'prayer and reflection' • Practicing positive thinking • Engaging in exercising • Focusing on source of happiness • Having time with self • Attending church	• Being incapable of completing tasks • Being young and inexperienced • Pressured to meet unrealistic expectations • Getting things done at work	• Having relatively high workload • Having 'long hours' • Working under limited time • Wishing for 'shorter workload' • Having a demanding workload • Having long working hours • Working harder than normal	• Engaging in volunteering • Focusing on helping others • Spending time with family	• Being ready dealing with burnout • Having control over working hours • Having a flexible schedule • Having a conversation about stressors • Learning as much as possible • Things get better with experience	• 'Having less patience' • 'Having a short fuse' • Feeling unsatisfied with day's work • Experiencing unwillingness to work • Having 'personal relationship' issues	• Having work–life imbalance resulting in fatigue • Having work–life imbalance • Lacking work–life balance

Outcome (arriving at meaningful themes)

1. The theme *Inability to attain work–life balance* was merged into *Working under demanding workload*.
2. After the critical review of the emerging themes, seven of them were labeled as meaningful themes (see Table 7.14).

TABLE 7.13 Emerging Themes Reflecting Primary Care Physicians' Experience of Burnout (From an Interpretative Phenomenological Perspective)

Emerging Theme	Case Count (Number of Participants)	Code Count (Number of Relevant Excerpts)
1. Having symptoms of exhaustion	5	13
2. Engaging in self-help activities	4	12
3. Working under demanding workload	4	9
4. Spending time with family and helping others	4	6
5. Utilizing burnout-resistant strategies	4	6
6. Having a negative attitude toward work-related issues	3	6
7. Feeling ill-equipped to complete tasks	2	5
8. Inability to attain work–life balance	1	3

TABLE 7.14 Meaningful Themes Reflecting Primary Care Physicians' Experience of Burnout (From an Interpretative Phenomenological Perspective)

Meaningful Theme (Not Informed by The Framework Concepts)	Meaningful Theme (Informed by The Framework Concepts)	Case Count	Code Count
1. Having symptoms of exhaustion	1. Experiencing the adverse effects of inequity	5	13
2. Engaging in self-help activities	2. Engaging in recovery of investment loss	4	12
3. Working under demanding workload	3. Working under demanding workload	4	12
4. Spending time with family and helping others	4. Replenishing loss of investment	4	6
5. Utilizing burnout-resistant strategies	5. Utilizing mitigating measures to fight inequity	4	6
6. Having a negative attitude toward work-related issues	6. Having a negative attitude toward work-related issues	3	6
7. Feeling ill-equipped to complete tasks	7. Lacking resources to invest	2	5

Commentary 7.8: As shown in the outcome of the theme transformation process, there were not many changes, which was not surprising. Most of the time, it will require minor changes to the contents of the themes and a few mergers. The most important thing is to make sure the themes are fair reflections of the interpretation of participants' attestations. Here is where most of the early researchers and dissertating students (who are using interpretative phenomenological perspective) end. They arrive at the themes and present them to address the research question, with some presenting the connection between the themes. They complete their research projects without inquiring into the essence of participants' being.

In Table 7.14, the first column contains the original meaningful themes (i.e., themes that were not informed by the framework concepts), and the second column houses meaningful themes informed by the framework concepts. Chapter 6 has the description and illustration of the theoretical/conceptual framework developed under a study connected to interpretative phenomenology (see Figure 6.7). If you plan to use some of the framework concepts to inform the themes, this is an appropriate stage to do that. In this case, we used concepts related to equity theory to inspire the transformation of the original meaningful themes to revised versions as we maintained the meaning of the themes. At the end, we revised all with the exception of two themes: *Working under demanding workload* and *Having a negative attitude toward work-related issues*. This shows that researchers do not have to revise all the meaningful themes if the concepts available are not adequate to transform the themes without changing the original meaning. At this stage, there is a temptation to mold the themes and the relationships between them to fit the theoretical/conceptual framework. Researchers should always be mindful that they have bracketed the explanatory power of the framework/theory, and its concepts could only be used as interpretation tools. The next couple of steps will show how to uncover the meaning of being of a primary care physician experiencing burnout.

Creating a narrative of being

Think about the following situation: Primary care physicians provided their stories about their experience of burnout. We, as researchers, reviewed their attestations and extracted relevant portions of their speech-acts. These fragments of speech-acts (which were about their actions, intentions and reactions related to their experience of burnout) were interpreted, leading to the development of seven meaningful themes. These themes, which reflect the physicians' interactions with the phenomenon (i.e., burnout), hold the key to the discovery of their being. All these pieces of understanding of their experience can be brought together to form a meaningful narrative, making the primary care physician the main character (Ricoeur, 1979).

Steps taken (creating a narrative of being) (see Table 7.15)

1   Categorized the meaningful themes based on the three main elements of a plot (i.e., orientation, complicating action and resolution; see Richmond, 2002, pp. 3–4).

TABLE 7.15 Meaningful Themes and Their Corresponding Elements of a Plot

Original Meaningful Theme	Meaningful Theme (Informed by The Framework Concepts)	Orientation (Preceding Event)	Complication Action (Problem)	Resolution (Solution)
1. Having symptoms of exhaustion	1. Experiencing the adverse effects of inequity	✓		
2. Engaging in self-help activities	2. Engaging in recovery of investment loss			✓
3. Working under demanding workload	3. Working under demanding workload	✓		
4. Spending time with family and helping others	4. Replenishing loss of investment			✓
5. Utilizing burnout-resistant strategies	5. Utilizing mitigating measures to fight inequity			✓
6. Having a negative attitude toward work-related issues	6. Having a negative attitude toward work-related issues		✓	
7. Feeling ill-equipped to complete tasks	7. Lacking resources to invest		✓	

2   Wrote a narrative with a physician as the main character experiencing burnout.

3   Covered all the meaningful themes when drafting the narrative of being.

Outcome (creating a narrative of being)

Here is the narrative of being of a primary care physician experiencing burnout:

Option 1: Based on original meaningful themes

Dr. Johnson is a primary care physician working under a demanding work-load. She works for long hours and, most of the time, performs harder than some of her colleagues. Dr. Johnson's work is overwhelming to the extent that she sometimes feels ill-equipped to complete tasks, addressing countless questions from patients who have an expectation that she has answers to all medical-related questions. This unbearable work demand begins to take a toll on Dr. Johnson. She starts experiencing symptoms of exhaustion, such as feeling tired and mentally drained. Consequently, she begins to have a negative attitude toward work-related issues. Realizing the adverse effects of burnout and needing to do something about it, Dr. Johnson utilizes burnout-resistant strategies such as engaging in self-help activities, spending time with family, and helping others, such as engaging in volunteering.

Option 2: Based on meaningful themes informed by the framework concepts

Dr. Johnson is a primary care physician working under a demanding work-load. She works for long hours and, most of the time, performs harder than some of her colleagues. Dr. Johnson's work is overwhelming to the extent that she sometimes lacks the resources to invest in (or commit to) her work, such as addressing countless questions from patients who have an expectation that she has answers to all medical-related questions. This unbearable work demand begins to take a toll on Dr. Johnson. She starts experiencing the adverse effects of inequity such as feeling tired and mentally drained. Consequently, she begins to have a negative attitude toward work-related issues. Realizing the adverse effects of burnout and needing to do something about it, Dr. Johnson utilizes mitigating measures to fight inequity, such as engaging in self-help activities, spending time with family, and helping others, such as engaging in volunteering.

Below are definitions of some of the concepts used in the above narrative:

- **Equity:** It is a perceived balance between what a physician invests and what he/she got in return.
- **Inequity:** It is a perceived imbalance between what a physician invests and what he/she got in return.
- **Investment:** It is the commitment put into something or someone with the expectation of gaining comparable desired outcomes.

Commentary 7.9: Completing the narrative of being was a rewarding experience; seeing abstract themes being transformed to generate a mini story about a primary care physician was exciting. We purposefully gave a pseudonym to the character to bring "life" to the narrative. Knowing more about the meaning and characteristics of a narrative (especially the main element of plot) becomes handy at this stage. Richmond's (2002) article, "Learners' lives: A narrative analysis," could be a useful resource. Also, Bell's (2003) article, "A Narrative Approach to Research" would be helpful, too. The narrative shows that we added a few specific examples to provide supporting evidence to some of the themes. Those examples were from extracts from the data connected to the themes. We used these specific examples to make the story interesting and more realistic. However, researchers should try not to bring information outside what the data tell them. Researchers should also make sure that they have all the main elements of a plot and the story revolves around the main character.

We presented two options for the narrative of being: The first option was based on the original meaningful themes while the other was based on the new meaningful themes which were inspired by our framework concepts. We found that it is easier to first draft the narrative of being using the original meaningful themes before revising it to incorporate the transformed meaningful themes.

Uncovering the meaning of being

We have reached the final stage of the data analysis process of a phenomenological study informed by interpretative phenomenology. This is the stage at which we addressed the research question: *What does it mean to be a primary care physician experiencing burnout?* Heidegger's (2010) classic example of how people experience objects in the world would help in understanding what is expected of the researchers: trying to uncover the meaning of being. Heidegger (2010) asserted that,

> the less we just stare at the thing called hammer, the more we take hold of it and use it, the more original our relation to it becomes and the more undisguisedly it is encountered as what it is, as a useful thing.
>
> *(p. 69)*

This means that to discover the being of the hammer, we need to experience it by using it. Based on how we experience it, we can make evaluative assertions (i.e., references) about the hammer, leading to attaining the meaning of being of the hammer as a handy tool, which is useful in driving a nail into wood. Similarly, researchers experience participants through an intensive interaction with their speech–acts, helping them to make sense of their existence within the context of experiencing burnout. After our experience, we came up with our characterizations (i.e., evaluative assertions) of a primary care physician who is experiencing burnout. These assertions were then transformed to bring to light the meaning of their being.

Steps taken (uncovering the meaning of being) (see Figure 7.4 & Figure 7.5)

1   Reviewed the narrative of being we created;
2   Took note of the situations the character faces and her responses;
3   Assigned labels (evaluative assertion or references) to the portions of the narrative depicting who she is within the context of experiencing burnout.

Outcome (uncovering the meaning of being)

•   There were four evaluative assertions created to depict the meaning of being of a primary care physician experiencing burnout. They were:

   •   *Hardworking physician;*
   •   *Under-supported physician;*
   •   *Disappointed physician;*
   •   *Proactive physician.*

•   Here is a statement depicting the meaning of a primary care physician's being

A primary care physician is often hardworking and feels under-supported. In this case, she is disappointed about certain undesirable outcomes, considering the effort she has invested in meeting the needs of her patients. However, she is proactive in mitigating the adverse effects of burnout she is experiencing.

Commentary 7.10: In case researchers plan to present the findings, we recommend that they first share the meaningful themes (or the revised meaningful themes if they used the framework concepts to help transform the original themes) generated in terms of their meaning and what they represent (Adu, 2019a). In addition, the presentation should include the narrative of being based on the revised meaningful themes, evaluative assertions and statement depicting the meaning of being. Another key piece of information to present is how the researcher arrived at the findings. This will help promote the credibility of the results (Adu, 2019a).

Make sure any meaning of being you come up with is supported by the narrative of being. Therefore, we recommend that you connect the meanings you

A Narrative of Being

Dr. Johnson works as a primary care physician working under a demanding workload. She works for long hours and most of the time, performs harder than some of her colleagues. Dr. Johnson's work is overwhelming to the extent that she sometimes feels ill-equipped to complete tasks – addressing countless questions from patients who have an expectation that she has answers to all medical related questions. This unbearable work demand begins to take a toll on Dr. Johnson. She starts experiencing symptoms of exhaustion such as feeling tired and mentally drained. Consequently, she begins to have a negative attitude towards work-related issues. Realizing the adverse effects of burnout and needing to do something about it, Dr. Johnson utilizes burnout-resistant strategies such as engaging in self-help activities, spending time with family and helping others such as engaging in volunteering.

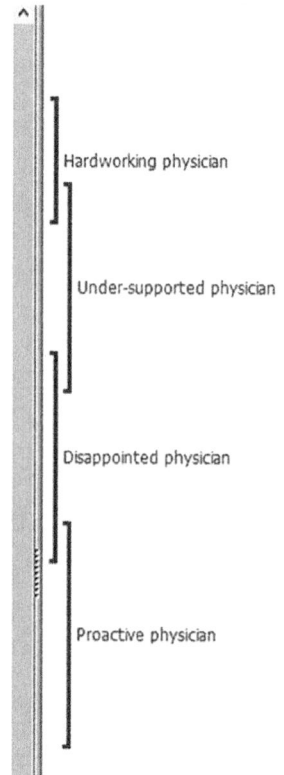

Hardworking physician

Under-supported physician

Disappointed physician

Proactive physician

FIGURE 7.4 Evaluative Assertions Generated After Review of the Narrative of Being

Source: (Based on Original Meaningful Themes)

A Narrative of Being

Dr. Johnson works as a primary care physician working under a demanding workload. She works for long hours and most of the time, performs harder than some of her colleagues. Dr. Johnson's work is overwhelming to the extent that she sometimes feels ill-equipped to complete tasks – addressing countless questions from patients who have an expectation that she has answers to all medical related questions. This unbearable work demand begins to take a toll on Dr. Johnson. She starts experiencing symptoms of exhaustion such as feeling tired and mentally drained. Consequently, she begins to have a negative attitude towards work-related issues. Realizing the adverse effects of burnout and needing to do something about it, Dr. Johnson utilizes burnout-resistant strategies such as engaging in self-help activities, spending time with family and helping others such as engaging in volunteering.

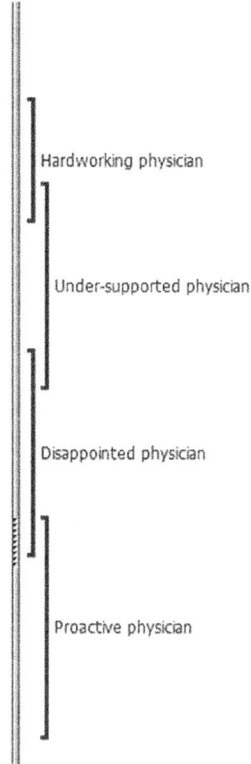

Hardworking physician

Under-supported physician

Disappointed physician

Proactive physician

FIGURE 7.5 Evaluative Assertions Generated After Review of the Narrative of Being

Source: (Based on Meaningful Themes Informed by the Framework Concepts)

arrived at to the portions of the narrative statement that support your evaluative assertions.

Summary

Data analysis under a phenomenological study is different from the generic way of analyzing qualitative data. If a researcher uses transcendental phenomenology perspective, their interest is to analyze the experience to arrive at the essence of the experience. However, with an interpretative phenomenology-informed study, the researcher wants to examine participants' experiences to help get to the meaning of being. In this chapter, we have demonstrated how to extensively analyze qualitative data, following sound steps that are supported by the foundational literature of phenomenology. We have also demonstrated the subtle ways of applying some of the concepts of the theoretical/conceptual framework the researcher developed.

As shown in Table 7.16, the outcome of the analysis informed by transcendental phenomenology is different from that of the one informed by interpretative

TABLE 7.16 Data Analysis Process and Outcome Under Their Respective Two Main Perspectives of Phenomenology

	Data Analysis Informed by Transcendental Phenomenology	*Data Analysis Informed by Interpretative Phenomenology*
Research question	What does it mean for primary care physicians to experience burnout?	What does it mean to be a primary care physician experiencing burnout?
Stage 1	Practicing epoché and phenomenological reduction	Practicing epoché and reduction
Stage 2	Using description-focused coding strategy to generate codes	Using interpretation-focused coding strategy to generate codes
Stage 3	Using individual-based sorting strategy to create emerging themes	Using individual-based sorting strategy to create emerging themes
Stage 4	Applying imaginative variation to arrive at essential themes	Transforming emerging themes into meaningful themes
Stage 5	Uncovering the essence of the experience	Creating a narrative of being & uncovering the meaning of being
Outcome	*Essence of the experience:* • *Burnout often manifests among primary care physicians in the midst of experiencing dwindling cognitive resources and carrying out cognitive tasks with limited cognitive resources. The experience of burnout is also coupled with having a negative attitude toward work. The experience could be addressed by being proactive in solving declining resources and engaging in restoration of the resources.*	*Meaning of being:* • *A primary care physician is often hardworking and feels under-supported. In this case, she is disappointed about certain undesirable outcomes, considering the effort she has invested in meeting the needs of her patients. However, she is proactive in mitigating the adverse effects of burnout she is experiencing.*

(existential) phenomenology. The focus of the former is about the meaning of experience – making the *experience* as the point of reference in the outcome statement. However, the focus of the latter is about the meaning of being, with the *being* becoming the focal point. We hope this chapter helps in analyzing qualitative data in a phenomenological study, contributing to the field of study.

References

Adu, P. (2017). Using grounded theory approach: From start to finish [PowerPoint slides]. *SlideShare.* www.slideshare.net/kontorphilip/using-grounded-theory-approach-from-start-to-finish

Adu, P. (2019a). *A step-by-step guide to qualitative data coding.* Routledge.

Adu, P. (2019b). Coding qualitative data: A practical guide to completing qualitative data analysis [PowerPoint slides]. *SlideShare*. www2.slideshare.net/kontorphilip/coding-qualitative-data-a-practical-guide-to-completing-qualitative-data-analysis

Bell, A. (2003). A narrative approach to research. *Canadian Journal of Environmental Education, 8*, 95–110.

Casagrande, J. B., & Hale, K. L. (1967). Semantic relationship in Papago folk-definitions. In D. Hymes & W. E. Bittle (Eds.), *Studies in Southwestern ethnolinguistics: Meaning and history in the languages of the American Southwest* (pp. 166–193). Mouton & Co.

Charmaz, K. (2014). *Constructing grounded theory*. Sage Publications.

Churchill, S. D. (2014). Phenomenology. In T. Teo (Ed.), *Encyclopedia of critical psychology*. Springer. https://doi.org/10.1007/978-1-4614-5583-7_219

Dennett, D. C. (1991). *Consciousness explained*. Back Bay Books. Little Brown Company. ISBN-10: 0316180661

Giorgi, A. (2006). Concerning variations in the application of the phenomenological method. *The Humanistic Psychologist, 34*(4), 305–319. https://doi.org/10.1207/s15473333thp3404_2

Giorgi, A. (2010). Phenomenology and the practice of science. *Journal of the Society for Existential Analysis, 21*(1), 3–23.

Heidegger, M. (2010). *Being and time*. University of New York Press. ISBN-10: 1438432763

Husserl, E. (2001). *The shorter logical investigations*. Routledge. ISBN: 9780415241922

Husserl, E. (2017). *Ideas: General introduction to pure phenomenology*. Unwin Brothers Ltd. ISBN-10: 0415519039

Provalis Research. (2020). *QDA Miner Lite*. Version 2.0.8 [Computer software]. https://provalisresearch.com/products/qualitative-data-analysis-software/freeware/

QSR International Pty Ltd. (2019). *NVivo 12*. Version 12.6.959 [Computer software]. www.qsrinternational.com/nvivo/nvivo-products

Richmond, H. J. (2002). Learners' lives: A narrative analysis. *The Qualitative Report, 7*(3), 1–14. http://nsuworks.nova.edu/tqr/vol7/iss3/4

Ricoeur, P. (1979). The human experience of time and narrative. *Research in Phenomenology, 9*(1), 17–34.

Ricoeur, P. (1994). *Oneself as another*. The University of Chicago Press. ISBN: 0-226-71329-6

8

A GUIDE FOR DESIGNING PHENOMENOLOGICAL RESEARCH

Objectives

Readers will be able to:

1   Choose an appropriate phenomenological perspective for their phenomenological study;
2   Frame and justify their subject matter;
3   Determine the number of participants for their phenomenological study.

In the previous chapters, we traced the emergence of phenomenology from Husserl and Heidegger's investigation into the meaning of thought and the meaning of being into a theoretical conceptualization of experience and down to applied schools of phenomenology. This is indeed a lot to process, and, with this chapter, we will try to present the phenomenological research design in the form of a decision tree. The assumption is that we, at this stage, have gone through the procedure of selecting a topic, demonstrating the existence of a researchable problem and identified a research gap that invites to a phenomenological investigation of the problem. Subsequently, the researcher is confronted with a range of choices in designing the research:

1   Clarifying the subject matter;
2   Justifying the subject matter;
3   Phenomenologically conceptualizing and framing the subject matter of experiences;
4   Choosing analytical and reflective procedures;
5   Determining the number of participants.

One of the most serious challenges is to ensure that all these components are aligned. It is from the alignment of our conceptualization of subject matter with methodology that we can argue that our research outcomes are credible. In other words, scholars must justify that the data they have gathered reflect the subject matter of the experience, and they submit these data to an analytical and reflective procedure that is aligned with their phenomenological understandings of the experience, as argued in Chapter 3.

Clarifying the subject matter

The first step is to clarify the subject matter of research. Applied phenomenological researchers often consider perception as their starting point. It is important to remember that Merleau-Ponty (1978) particularly pointed out that perception is not an opinion or a point of view. According to him, "perception is not a science of the world; it is not even an act of deliberate taking up a position; it is the background from which all acts stand out" (p. xi). Likely, novice researchers mean "understanding" rather than "perception" because what follows is typically a thematic analysis of how their subjects interpret a given experience. The subject matter within transcendental and psychological phenomenology is subjectivity, while that of existential phenomenology is the being (existence) of beings. Therefore, the subject matter of applied phenomenological research is always experience (see Figure 8.1).

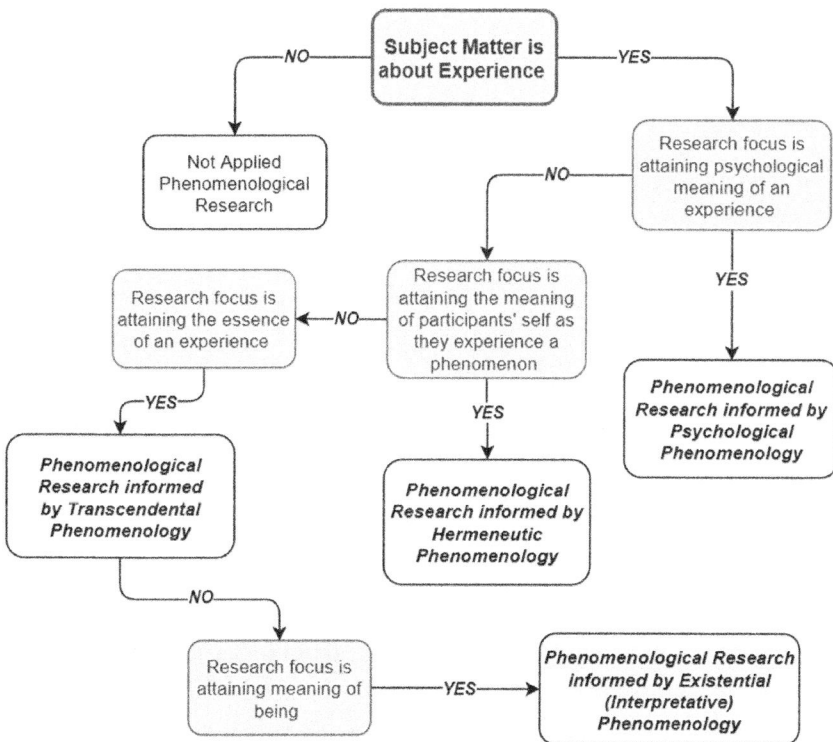

FIGURE 8.1   Decision Tree Related to Types of Applied Phenomenological Research

Varela and Shear (1999) broadly defined the experience as first-person "cognitive and mental events" (p. 1), of which the subject is conscious. Hereunder:

1   The experience occurs in the first-person realm, which defines our existence.
2   The experience refers to an actual occurrence, encounters or doings and dealings of which the subject is aware.
3   The experience is a "privileged entry point."
4   The experience is for exploration of subjectivity and meanings.

Justifying the subject matter of experience

The next step is to justify why a study of first-person conscious or lived experiences is relevant in elucidating the research problem. First of all, researchers focus on conscious experiences because they have a phenomenal dimension in the sense of how the world looks from the first-person perspective or what it is like to experience something or be somebody with certain experiences. The phenomenal aspect of experiences is what researchers normally consider under subjectivity (which is the perspective of a meaning given to an experience). Because phenomenology assumes that only the subject can objectify, researchers also consider that what they sense as objective reality is largely constituted by subjective meaning-making. Therefore, examining the subjective first-person perspective is the researcher's access to understanding the universal meaning of a phenomenon.

From a phenomenological epistemological perspective, researchers use first-person accounts to understand the universal meaning and dimensionality of a phenomenon. From a phenomenological ontological perspective, researchers turn away from subjectivity. Instead of trying to generalize regarding various phenomena, they try to understand just one phenomenon (i.e., the phenomenon of being). However, the phenomenon of being is not understood in an individual sense but in the sense of the general ways of being that are revealed from interpreting lived experiences.

From this elaboration, it is clear that research approaches that produce outcomes that can be generalized to a broader population are not in a methodological position to generalize toward a phenomenon of being because neither the phenomenon nor the being are actual people, but truths. Thus, being able to generalize an experience toward a population says nothing about the universal truth of that experience, and that is what phenomenology aims to accomplish. No study is perfect, and the ambition of truth over generalizability is fraught with pitfalls. The most obvious of these are the lack of understanding of the basic phenomenological concepts and methods and, subsequently, a haphazard alignment of research components. These, in turn, are the real limitations of phenomenological studies and threats to the credibility of the outcomes and not a statement that phenomenology is limited as the findings cannot be generalized to the broader population. The latter is never the purpose to begin with.

Phenomenologically conceptualizing and framing the subject matter of experiences

Experience is, however, not a construct that can be taken for granted. Intuitively, scholars understand what an experience is, but as Merleau-Ponty also pointed out, once they begin to conceptualize what they mean by an experience, they realize that it is far from given what an experience really entails. To this end, the foundational literature presents a range of ideas that can help emerging scholars frame their research phenomenologically. In this book, we have presented four different conceptualizations. Choosing which one to frame the subject matter presents researchers with the first significant decision in the process of designing their studies (Table 8.1).

In addition, the researcher can expand the conceptualization of the experience by including theoretical perspectives that align with the phenomenological domains of experiences and their associated concepts. The purpose is, of course, not to explain the experience in terms of cause and effect, but in the reduction, ordinary psychological and social theories can serve as a descriptive and terminological repository. In this way, researchers can acquire a conceptualization of the experience that speaks to a specific scholarly domain, such as psychology, sociology, education or health care. The key point is to justify the choice and demonstrate alignment of ideas and procedures throughout the design.

Developing the research question

The ultimate conceptualization decision will be the *research question* that needs to signal alignment with the phenomenological experience domain under investigation as well as any supporting theoretical concepts chosen by the researchers. For example, *"what is it like for a nurse to experience burnout?"* This question signals alignment of psychological subjectivity (psychological phenomenology) with the notion of "what is it like" and, at the same time, addresses concepts that are not available in the phenomenological literature, such as burnout. Of course, burnout covers a range of concrete psychological and actual experiences, but the

TABLE 8.1 Types of Phenomenology and Their Respective Experience Domain and Concept

Phenomenology	Experience Domain	Experience Concept
Psychological phenomenology	Psychological subjectivity	Apperception
Existential phenomenology	Dasein	Interpretation-mediated understanding
Hermeneutic phenomenology	Narrative self	Emplotment
Transcendental phenomenology	Transcendental subjectivity	Givenness intentionality

incorporation of supporting theoretical lenses can assist researchers with opera-tionalizing in the form of a range of topical subquestions. Similarly, a question such as *"what does it mean to be a culturally competent leader?"* signals alignment with existential and hermeneutic phenomenology as well as cultural compe-tency. Thus, theories pertaining to the latter construct can assist researchers with operationalizing their research by pointing to specific behavioral traits that can be subject to empirical investigations. Irrespective of how scholars end up for-mulating their research question, the key point is that it should clearly address the first-person perspective on experiences because these are the data we need in order to deliver on the goal of elucidating what is true about the phenomenon or the being under investigation.

Deciding on what kind of experience data to gather

The next consideration researchers have to make is what kind of data appropri-ately represent the experience domain and the conceptualization of experience. Transcendental subjectivity is a realm that appears to be outside the scope of ordinary empirical research because it involves the correlation between noesis and noema. Ashworth (2017) therefore argued that it is far from straightforward to describe what goes on inside intentionality due to the researcher's difficulty in remaining within the reduction. Thus, in our elaborations in Chapter 2, we concluded that, for the purpose of empirical research, scholars cannot make a distinction between noesis and the noema due to the fact that they can only rec-ognize "thinking acts" via what is being thought about. Consequently, empirical research pertaining to intentionality inadvertently becomes a form of psycho-logical phenomenology, as no distinct noesis data can be collected.

Apperceptions can, however, be deduced from disclosures, and the data schol-ars would be interested in pertain first and foremost to experiences as they are recalled and, subsequently, how the subjects make sense of these experiences and what it was like to have these experiences. The researchers would try to gather data that pertain to how the subjects felt and their reactions to the experience, basically, data that can assist in illuminating the inner subjective experience.

Existential phenomenology and hermeneutic phenomenology, in equal mea-sure, rely on verbal disclosures, but the theoretical presumptions are quite dif-ferent from phenomenological psychology. Thus, both Heidegger (1988, p. 69) and Ricoeur (2019, pp. 72–73) considered the role psychological subjectivity plays in elucidating the meaning of being or the meaning of selfhood to be only marginal. Dasein should therefore not be misconstrued as another term for *ego*. Dasein is public; it is happening; it is "Daseining" around in the world (Dreyfus, 1995, p. 163). As Merleau-Ponty (1978) posited, "truth does not inhabit only the inner man or more accurately, there is no inner man, man is in the world and only in the world does he know himself" (p. xi). In other words, the being is not a subject and the world is not its object. Dasein is part of the world, and the world is part of Dasein. The being of Dasein is therefore to be interpreted from what

Dasein is doing in the world. Consequently, the data scholars would be looking at have to do with actions, doings, copings and taking care of *for-the-sake-of* and *in-order-to* (Dreyfus, 1995, p. 245). In other words, these data deal with how the subjects understand their lived experiences. Ricoeur (1994) was well aligned with Heidegger's notion of being in the world but understood the data more literally as a story, where the narrative self discloses its identity through the stories it tells about its dealings with other people. Consequently, the data scholars would be looking for are speech-acts that signify the narrative self's role in dealings and copings, together with and in relation to other people (i.e., its emplotment).

To illustrate the above consideration, consider the existential/hermeneutic research question: *What does it mean to be a kindergarten teacher?* From our theoretical understanding of the being of Dasein in terms of lived experiences, this overarching research question could be operationalized with subquestions such as *what are the lived experiences of kindergarten teachers? What are the essential (meaningful) themes of these lived experiences* (see Chapter 7)? These subquestions allow scholars to begin to describe the actual experience as it was and is happening, and the subsequent methodological treatment of the data will allow scholars to idealize these experiences into meanings that may hold true for being a kindergarten teacher.

In contrast, a research question that states *what are principals' perceptions of teachers' lived experiences of teaching kindergarten?* is problematic. First, scholars are not really able to access other people's perceptions, so what is meant here could be "understandings of." Second, the question breaks the first-first person perspective in the sense that A's experience of B's experiences does not constitute a true first-first person experience. Therefore, investigating how principals conceive of teachers' lived experiences cannot, from the perspective of phenomenology, elucidate what it means to be a kindergarten teacher.

Formulating the interview questions

Bevan (2014) proposed that the data should be gathered through interviews that are structured in three ways that provide context, insight into the phenomenon and meaning. Inspired by this structure, we propose three categories of interview questions:

- *Clarification of the temporal and spatial horizons of the participants' experiences:* This is asking about how the participant came to experience what they experienced. For example, if the researcher aims to investigate how a person copes with illness, then it is relevant to ask the subjects how they became ill, which reveals something about how they make sense of their current situation.
- *Explication of the participants' encounter with the phenomenon.* This entails asking questions about the subjects' direct experiences with something actual (real), for example, by asking subjects to describe a typical situation where

they have experience with the central phenomenon under investigation. Here, the researchers could ask questions that elicit the subjects' feelings and emotions associated with the experiences (i.e., what it was like). The researchers could also, through questioning, emphasize what the subjects did, the actions they took to cope with the experience or the roles they and other people involved in the experiences played.

- *Interpretative questions pertaining to meanings:* This is aimed at giving participants the chance to clarify their experiences in terms of how they make sense of it, for example, what sense the experience made to the subjects, what they learned from the experience and how they understand the situation, their roles and the role of others. Bevan (2014) proposed that one way to clarify the meaning of the experience in the interview situation is to ask hypothetical follow-up questions in the sense of presenting the subjects with a different scenario or actors from what actually occurred. Bevan (2014) likened this to Husserl's notion of imaginative variation. The approach could better be compared to *thematic apperception* tests/interviews, where subjects are confronted with ambiguous imaginary situations in order to decontextualize the exploration of subjects, beliefs, biases or preferences.

Bevan's (2014) interview approach could be further guided by including Ashworth's (2016) notion of lifeworld fractions. This includes notions of: "*self, sociality, embodiment, temporality, spatiality, project, discourse and moodness*" (p. 23; for further details, see Chapter 4). Table 8.2 demonstrates how these fractions may inform the researchers' articulation of domain-appropriate interview questions from the exploration of context to the elucidaiton of meaning.

In the following section, we have tried to articulate examples of questions that follow the three-step model of context, direct experiences and meanings, while simultaneously incorporating fractions of the lifeworld in a manner that points toward the elucidation of psychological subjectivity, Dasein's interpretation-mediated understanding or the identity of the narrative self. In this manner,

TABLE 8.2 Kinds of Interview Questions Under Their Respective Domain

Experience Domain	*Contextual Questions (Spatiality & Temporality)*	*Direct Experience Questions*	*Meaning-Making Questions*
Psychological subjectivity *(Psychological phenomenology)*	About embodiment		About sense-making (apperception)
Dasein *(Existential phenomenology)*	About project and moodness		About understanding
Narrative self *(Hermeneutic phenomenology)*	About discourse & sociality		About emplotment of self

Experience Domain	Contextual Questions (Spatiality & Temporality)	Direct Experience Questions	Meaning-Making Questions
Psychological subjectivity (*Psychological phenomenology*)	**Spatiality:** • Where did this take place? • Where were you at the time of . . .? • Describe the place where this happened? **Temporality:** • What lead up to this event?	**About embodiment:** • How did this make you feel? • How did you react when? • How do you see yourself?	**About apperceptions:** • Would you have reacted differently if the person were younger? • Had you known the person was gay would you have acted differently? • Would you have acted differently if it were a woman? • What would you have done if it were you who were in charge?
Dasein (*Existential phenomenology*)	• How did you come to this decision? • How did you end up in this situation?	**About project:** • What did you do? • What actions did you take? • What was the purpose of . . .? • What outcome did you hope to achieve? **About moodness:** • What were the norms at the time? • What were the rules? • What was the shared view? • What were the generally held beliefs at the time?	**About understandings:** • What was your interpretation of the situation? • What did you learn about yourself from this experience? • How did this change your life? • What does this mean for your future? • Did anything change because of this?
Narrative self (*Hermeneutic phenomenology*)		**About discourse:** • Who were speaking? • Who said what? • What did you say? **About sociality:** • What is your relationship with this person like? • How are your professional relations with . . .? • How would you describe your cooperation with this person?	**About emplotment:** • What were your intentions? • What motivated you to? • What were the intentions of the others? • How did you overcome? • Who challenged you? • Who acted against you? • How do you think other people see you now?

we can see how the choice of interview questions has its own epistemological orientation, which further highlights the importance of developing a thoughtful interview protocol that can acquire the data appropriately for how the experience was framed (see Table 8.3).

Choosing analytical and reflective procedures

Varela and Shear (1999) identified two minimum criteria for what constitutes a scientific phenomenological method:

1   A "clear procedure for accessing some phenomena domain."
2   "A clear means of an expression and validation within a community of observers who have familiarity with the procedures."

(p. 6)

Within phenomenology, the commonly agreed-on procedure is epoché and reduction. This procedure contains its own kind of epistemology. In other words, the epoché and reduction procedure presumes that the research outcome is meaning. The question, however, is which one of the variations of epoché and reduction we have described in Chapter 3 should the researcher choose?

Contingent on how the researchers conceptualize the experience, conducted the interviews and thereby the character of the collected data, they should choose the phenomenological analytical and reflective procedure that is best aligned. The schematic in the following table is an attempt at illustrating the alignment between domain, data and procedures (see Table 8.4). This is, however, not meant as a rigid delimitation because the subjects do not conform to our conceptualizations and will present a fluid picture of their experiences. It is nevertheless worthwhile to align the research components in order to convey credibility of both the procedures and the outcomes. Essentially, a thoughtful phenomenological conceptualization enables researchers to justify every decision they make regarding their research design. This, in turn, adds credibility to the notion that the outcome speaks to the universality of the phenomenon under investigation, and it provides other scholars with an opportunity to assess the research.

Interpretative phenomenological analysis (IPA) poses somewhat of a problem because this school does not profess to any particular kind of procedure. It is here worth remembering that IPA essentially is ideographic and therefore the meanings that this approach attempts to uncover are not idealized meanings for the purpose of elucidating universal truths about the phenomenon. The meanings IPA focuses on are the subjects' personal meanings. Therefore, IPA relies more on a thick description of a few subjects' concrete experiences than any of the idealizing procedures we considered in Chapter 3. Thus, IPA provides more flexibility in terms of how the research is conceptualized, but typically suffers somewhat in terms of credibility within the phenomenological tradition, as it can be difficult to assess the analytical and reflective procedures in IPA research.

TABLE 8.4 Type of Data, Epoché and Reduction Procedure and Outcome Under Their Respective Experience Domain

Domain	Data	Epoché and Reduction Procedures	Outcome
Psychological subjectivity *(Psychological phenomenology)*	*About:* Spatiality Temporality Embodiment Apperceptions	1. Epoché 2. Psychological reduction 3. Deconstruction 4. Transformation 5. Decontextualization 6. Abstraction	Psychological essence: Meaning of phenomenal experience
Dasein *(Existential phenomenology)*	*About:* Spatiality Temporality Project Moodness Interpretations Understandings	1. Reduction (being) 2. Construction 3. Destruction	Meaning of being as possibilities
Narrative self *(Hermeneutic phenomenology)*	*About:* Spatiality Temporality Discourse Sociality Plot	1. Distanciation 2. Interpretation: Faith and suspicion 3. Appropriation	Selfhood: Sameness Otherness Character

Consideration of the research gap

Researchers have to ask themselves *how does finding the meaning of an experience both answer the stated research questions in a credible manner and at the same time address the research gap they have identified in the literature?* As researchers, we are not trying to solve problems, but to understand existing problems in greater details and from new and different perspectives. We are, however, not conducting our research in a scholarly vacuum and for the effort to be justifiable, we must carefully consider if finding the meaning of an experience or the essence addresses a research need or a gap. Evidence of research gaps can be found in the discussion sections of research articles, where scholars, that came before us, identify the need for future studies. We should therefore not engage in phenomenological research just because we are fascinated by Husserl's ideas, but because the specific outcomes (the essence) that phenomenology produces meet a stated need.

Determining the number of participants

It is general knowledge that researchers need fewer participants for a qualitative study compared to a quantitative study. However, how many participants are needed to conduct qualitative research (specifically a phenomenological study)? Depending on who a researcher consults or the literature they read, they will get varied recommendations for an appropriate sample size for a phenomenological study, ranging from as low as three participants and as high as 25 participants (see Baker & Edwards, 2012; Creswell, 2013; Guest et al., 2006). Because the number of participants is not the only factor contributing to the gathering of rich qualitative data, the question a researcher needs to ask is *what is needed to reach the equilibrium of data quality?'*

Qualitative data quality

Qualitative data quality is about how appropriate qualitative data should be, considering the kind of data, sources of data and sample size proposed for the study. In other words, data quality is achieved when a researcher has the right kind of data from an accurate source coupled with a good number of participants. During the data collection stage, if everything goes as planned (in terms of accessing the right participants, having the recommended sample size and collecting the right kind of data), the equilibrium of data quality has been achieved. Specifically, all things being equal with respect to having the right source and kind of data, a researcher needs at least five participants with a study informed by hermeneutic or interpretative (existential) phenomenology and at least 10 participants for psychological or transcendental phenomenology. However, because the world is imperfect, filled with uncertainties and every phenomenon of study is unique, taking this suggested sample size at face value could adversely affect the credibility of the findings.

As shown in the illustration below, a researcher is more likely to access participants with similar experiences of the phenomenon of study if they plan to focus on a sample size of at least five. This recommendation applies to a study utilizing a hermeneutic or interpretative perspective. A researcher with this perspective is not concerned with how experience varies across contexts but is interested in interpreting and understanding participants' experience in terms of what they did and the meaning of what they did. So, at the end of data analysis, the researcher will come up with a uniform meaning of their experience. With this type of inquiry, researchers do not need to look at participants' varied experiences to arrive at the findings with ideographic features. Therefore, having a sample size of 5–10 is appropriate under phenomenological study inspired by either hermeneutic or interpretative phenomenology.

Imagine a researcher asks 12 volunteers to stand at any preferred part of a house to observe the exterior potion of the house and share their experience. Some observe from the front of the house, while others stand at the back and sides of the house to experience it. Assume the researcher selected only two out of the 12 volunteers to talk about their experience. There is a high probability that the researcher will get limited information about their experience and will not be able to generate an overall experience that reflects the varied experiences of the house. To adhere to the practice of imaginative variation, the researcher needs to sample volunteers representing experiences of each part of the house

(Giorgi, 2006). Similarly, under a study with a psychological or transcendental perspective, accessing participants with varied experiences is the key to reaching the universal truth. This is about selecting a *context*, such as types of units in a hospital, with the goal of accessing participants across those units. It could also be about selecting a *demographic feature* such as income levels and recruiting people across the levels. When analyzing data, researchers are looking for a shared experience across difference perspectives on how the phenomenon was experienced. Therefore, without exhausting the existing variances of participants' experiences when sampling them, the outcome of the analysis could be inaccurate. Also, the greater the sample size, the greater the likelihood that participants will have varied ranges of experiences (see Figure 8.2). Hence, having a sample size of 10–15 is appropriate under a phenomenological study inspired by either psychological or transcendental phenomenology.

Equilibrium of data quality

As mentioned earlier, there are three main components that form the equilibrium of data quality: data source, kind of data and sampling size. An adjustment

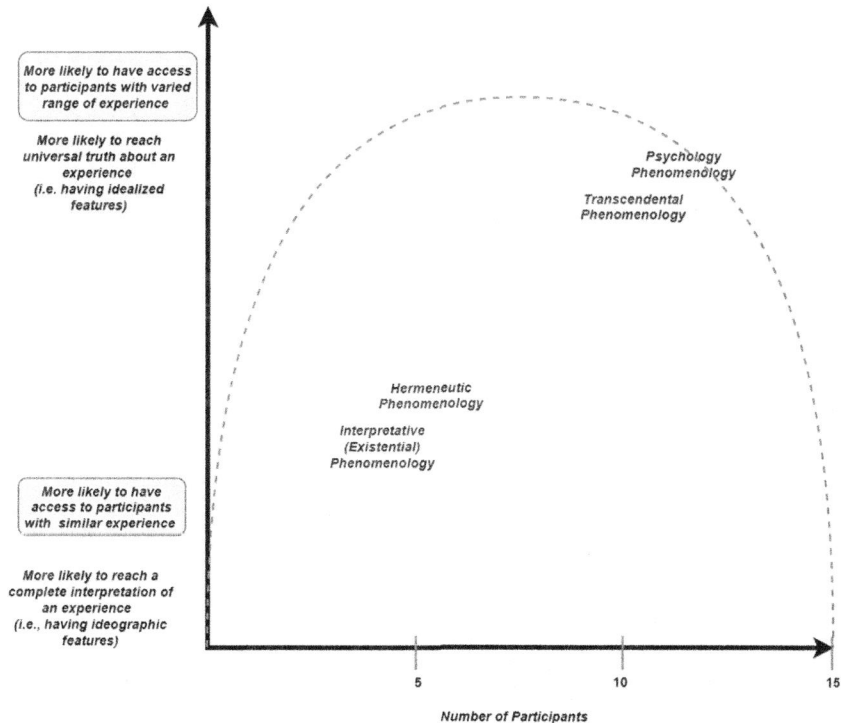

FIGURE 8.2 Sample Size Range and the Level of Variations or Similarities of Experience

TABLE 8.5 Equilibrium of Data Quality-Related Challenges and Their Optimization Strategies

Problem	Optimization Strategy (What Could Be Done to Restore the Equilibrium of Data Quality)	
	Hermeneutic and Interpretative Phenomenology	Psychological and Transcendental Phenomenology
About sample size: **Having a sample size below what is recommended**	• Doing an extensive interview with each participant—making sure all areas about their experience are covered • Encouraging detailed responses from participants using a strategy such as probing questions during interviews • Conducting follow-up interview when necessary	• Giving participants the chance to describe the experience across multiple situations or incidence—capturing varied experience from each participant • Doing an extensive interview with each participant—making sure all areas about their experience are covered • Conducting follow-up interview when necessary
About data source: **Having participants with homogenous demographic background or situational context**	• No substantial impact on the equilibrium of data quality	• Giving participants the chance to describe the experience across multiple situations or incidence—capturing varied experience from each participant
About data source: **Having participants with heterogenous demographic background or situational context**	• Increasing sample size more than initially recommended	• No substantial impact on the equilibrium of data quality because having participants with heterogenous demographic background or situational context would help to capture their varied experience
About kind of data: **Facing a situation where participants are reluctant to fully share their experience**	• Increasing sample size more than initially recommended with the hope of gathering limited pieces of information from each participant and bringing them together to have a substantial amount of data	• Increasing sample size more than initially recommended with the hope of gathering limited pieces of information from each participant and bringing them together to have a substantial amount of data

of any of these components could affect the balance of the quality of data. The common problems that could adversely influence the equilibrium are:

- Having a sample size below what is recommended;
- Having participants with homogenous demographic background or situational context;
- Having participants with heterogenous demographic background or situational context;
- Facing a situation where participants are reluctant to fully share their experience.

With these kinds of problems, an optimization strategy is used to help restore the equilibrium (see Table 8.5). A researcher could create a table similar to Table 8.5 when planning a phenomenological study, conducting equilibrium optimization analysis to help decide on the appropriate number of the participants. This activity would help the researcher make a strong argument in support of the sample size decision. In a nutshell, sample size is just one of the factors contributing to the equilibrium of data quality. So, it is important to critically review the role of all of the factors to help maintain the data quality balance.

Summary

We emphasized that the subject matter of a phenomenological study should be about experience. Also, participants who had a first-hand experience of a phenomenon of study should be the source of data. In addition, before deciding on the source of data, researchers could use the decision tree to help confirm the phenomenological perspective they plan to use. Making this decision is the beginning of ensuring that there is a consistency across every part of the design of a phenomenological study, such as research questions, kind of data and interview questions. We ended this chapter with a discussion of how to determine the number of participants for the study. We argued for the need to conduct equilibrium optimization analysis to make sure the researcher has the right number of participants with the appropriate source and kind of data for the study. By doing so, researchers will conduct a rigorous phenomenological study and attain credible findings.

References

Ashworth, P. D. (2016). The lifeworld-enriching qualitative evidence. *Qualitative Research in Psychology*, *13*(1), 20–32. https://doi.org/10.1080/14780887.2015.1076917

Ashworth, P. D. (2017). Interiority, exteriority and the realm of intentionality. *Journal of Phenomenological Psychology*, *48*(1), 39–62. https://doi.org/10.1163/15691624-12341321

Baker, S. E., & Edwards, R. (2012). *How many qualitative interviews is enough?* National Center for Research Methods.

Bevan, M. T. (2014). A method of phenomenological interviewing. *Qualitative Health Research*, *24*(1), 136–144. https://doi.org/10.1177/1049732313519710

Creswell, J. W. (2013). *Qualitative inquiry and research design: Choosing among five approaches* (3rd ed.). Sage Publications.

Dreyfus, H. L. (1995). *Being-in-the-world: A complimentary on Heidegger's being and time, division 1.* The MIT Press. ISBN: 0-262-54056-8

Giorgi, A. (2006). Concerning variations in the application of the phenomenological method. *The Humanistic Psychologist, 34*(4), 305–319. https://doi.org/10.1207/s15473 333thp3404_2

Guest, G., Bunce, A., & Johnson, L. (2006). How many interviews are enough? An experiment with data saturation and variability. *Field Methods, 18*(1), 59–82. https:// doi.org/10.1177/1525822X05279903

Heidegger, M. (1988). *The basic problems of phenomenology.* Indiana University Press. ISBN-10: 0253176875

Merleau-Ponty, M. (1978). *Phenomenology of perception.* Routledge & Kegan Paul. ISBN-10: 0710036132

Ricoeur, P. (1994). *Oneself as another.* The University of Chicago Press. ISBN: 0-226-71329-6

Ricoeur, P. (2019). *Hermeneutics and the human sciences.* Cambridge University Press. ISBN-10: 0521280028

Varela, F. J., & Shear, J. (1999). First-person methodologies: What, why, how? *Journal of Consciousness Studies, 6*(2–3), 1–14.

INDEX

Note: Page numbers in *italics* indicate a figure and page numbers in **bold** indicate a table on the corresponding page. Page numbers followed by "e" indicate an exhibit.

Printed in Great Britain
by Amazon